Computer Architecture

Dr.T.S. Sivakumaran

S.K.B. Sangeetha

S.K.B. Rathika

Published by

Computer Architecture

ISBN 978-93-86638-53-3

Authors

Dr.T.S. Sivakumaran

S.K.B. Sangeetha

S.K.B. Rathika

Bonfring

309, 2nd Floor, 5th Street Extension, Gandhipuram,

Coimbatore-641 012.

Tamilnadu, India.

E-mail: info@bonfring.org

Website: www.bonfring.org

Phone: 0422 4213231

About the Authors

Dr.T.S. Sivakumaran was born in Panruti, India, on December 18, 1969. He has obtained B.E (Electrical and Electronics) and M.Tech (Power Electronics) in 1998 and 2002 respectively from Annamalai University and VIT University Vellore and then Ph.D in Power Electronics from Annamalai University, Chidambaram in 2009. He also has knowledge on computer architecture and designs. He is currently Principal/Professor in Sasurie Academy of Engineering, Coimbatore, India. He has 14 and 56 publications in national and International journals. His research interests are in modeling and control of DC-DC converters and multiple connected power electronic converters, control of resonant converters, embedded control for multi level inverters and matrix converters etc. He is a life member of Instrument Society of India and Indian Society for Technical Education.

S.K.B. Sangeetha is currently working as an Senior assistant professor in Rajalakshmi Engineering College, Chennai. She is pursuing her PhD from Anna University, Chennai. She accomplished her Master's Degree from Dr.Mahalingam College of Engineering and Technology, Coimbatore and the Bachelor's Degree from Christian College of Engineering and Technology, Dindigul, both graduated from anna university.

She has 10 years of Teaching and Research experience which has helped her to gain immense knowledge in myriad fields of Computer Science and Engineering. She is a life member of Indian Society for Technical Education, The Indian Institute of Engineers. Apart from being an educator, She also encompasses herself in many co-curricular activities and take up responsibilities only to complete them with complete appreciation. She has written three books for engineering curriculam.

She has organized and attended many seminars, faculty development programs, workshops and conferences of both National and International level. She has published around 41 research papers in several international and national forums which include various ISI, Scopus, IEEE indexed international conferences as well. She is also being an editor and reviewer for some international journals as well.

S.K.B. Rathika completed her master degree in Computer Science and Engineering. Currently she holds a position of Assistant Professor in the Department of Computer Science & Engineering, SASURIE Academy of Engineering, Coimbatore. She received her B.E degree in Computer Science and Engineering from Anna University, Chennai in 2010 and the M.E degree in Computer Science and Engineering from Anna University, Chennai in 2012.She has three years of teaching experience. She has also published 16 International and National conferences. Her area of interest is computer networks, mobile computing.

<table>
<tr><td>Unit</td><td align="center">Contents</td><td>Page No</td></tr>
</table>

Unit I

Overview & Instructions

Eight ideas – Components of a computer system – Technology – Performance – Power wall – Uni-processors to multiprocessors; Instructions – operations and operands – representing instructions – Logical operations – control operations – Addressing and addressing modes.

1.1. Introduction

In the recent past, the following applications were "computer science fiction."

·Computers in automobiles: Until microprocessors improved dramatically in price and performance in the early 1980s, computer control of cars was ludicrous. Today, computers reduce pollution, improve fuel efficiency via engine controls, and increase safety through blind spot warnings, lane departure warnings, moving object detection, and air bag inflation to protect occupants in a crash.

·Cell phones: Who would have dreamed that advances in computer systems would lead to more than half of the planet having mobile phones, allowing person-to-person communication to almost anyone anywhere in the world?

·Human genome project: The cost of computer equipment to map and analyze human DNA sequences was hundreds of millions of dollars. It's unlikely that anyone would have considered this project had the computer costs been 10 to 100 times higher, as they would have been 15 to 25 years earlier. Moreover, costs continue to drop; you will soon be able to acquire your own genome, allowing medical care to be tailored to you.

·World Wide Web: Not in existence at the time of the first edition of this book, the web has transformed our society. For many, the web has replaced libraries and newspapers.

·Search engines: As the content of the web grew in size and in value, finding relevant information became increasingly important. Today, many people rely on search engines for such a large part of their lives that it would be a hardship to go without them.

Classes of Computing Applications and Their Characteristics personal computer (PC) A computer designed for use by an individual, usually incorporating a graphics display, a keyboard, and a mouse.

Server a computer used for running larger programs for multiple users, often simultaneously, and typically accessed only via a network.

Supercomputer a class of computers with the highest performance and cost; they are configured as servers and typically cost tens to hundreds of millions of dollars.

Terabyte (TB) Originally 1,099,511,627,776 (240) bytes, although communications and secondary storage systems developers started using the term to mean 1,000,000,000,000 (1012) bytes. To reduce confusion, we now use the term tebibyte (tib) for 240 bytes, defining *terabyte* (TB) to mean 1012 bytes.

Embedded computer A computer inside another device used for running one predetermined application or collection of software.

Personal mobile devices (pmds) are small wireless devices to connect to the Internet; they rely on batteries for power, and soft ware is installed by downloading apps. Conventional examples are smart phones and tablets.

Cloud Computing refers to large collections of servers that provide services over the Internet; some providers rent dynamically varying numbers of servers as a utility.

Software as a Service (saas) delivers soft ware and data as a service over the Internet, usually via a thin program such as a browser that runs on local client devices, instead of binary code that must be installed, and runs wholly on that device. Examples include web search and social networking.

Decimal term	Abbreviation	Value	Binary term	Abbreviation	Value	% Larger
kilobyte	KB	10^3	kibibyte	KiB	2^{10}	2%
megabyte	MB	10^6	mebibyte	MiB	2^{20}	5%
gigabyte	GB	10^9	gibibyte	GiB	2^{30}	7%
terabyte	TB	10^{12}	tebibyte	TiB	2^{40}	10%
petabyte	PB	10^{15}	pebibyte	PiB	2^{50}	13%
exabyte	EB	10^{18}	exbibyte	EiB	2^{60}	15%
zettabyte	ZB	10^{21}	zebibyte	ZiB	2^{70}	18%
yottabyte	YB	10^{24}	yobibyte	YiB	2^{80}	21%

1.2.　Eight Great Ideas in Computer Architecture

1.　Design for Moore's Law

The one constant for computer designers is rapid change, which is driven largely by **Moore's Law.** It states that integrated circuit resources double every 18–24 months. Moore's Law resulted from a 1965 prediction of such growth in IC capacity made by Gordon Moore, one of the founders of Intel. As computer designs can take years, the resources available per chip can easily double or quadruple between the start and finish of the project. Like a skeet shooter, computer architects must anticipate where the technology will be when the design finishes rather than design for where it starts. Use an "up and to the right" Moore's Law graph to represent designing for rapid change.

2. Use Abstraction to Simplify Design

Both computer architects and programmers had to invent techniques to make themselves more productive, for otherwise design time would lengthen as dramatically as resources grew by Moore's Law. A major productivity technique for hardware and soft ware is to use **abstractions** to represent the design at different levels of representation; lower-level details are hidden to offer a simpler model at higher levels. Use the abstract painting icon to represent this second great idea.

3. Make the Common Case Fast

Making the **common case fast** will tend to enhance performance better than optimizing the rare case. Ironically, the common case is often simpler than the rare case and hence is often easier to enhance. This common sense advice implies that you know what the common case is, which is only possible with careful experimentation and measurement. Use a sports car as the icon for making the common case fast, as the most common trip has one or two passengers, and it's surely easier to make a fast sports car than a fast minivan!

4. Performance Via Parallelism

Since the dawn of computing, computer architects have offered designs that get more performance by performing operations in parallel. We'll see many examples of parallelism in this book. Use multiple jet engines of a plane as our icon for **parallel performance.**

5. Performance Via Pipelining

A particular pattern of parallelism is so prevalent in computer architecture that it merits its own name: **pipelining.** For example, before fire engines, a "bucket brigade" would respond to a fire, which many cowboy movies show in response to a dastardly act by the villain. The townsfolk form a human chain to carry a water source to fire, as they could much more quickly move buckets up the chain instead of individuals running back and forth. Pipeline icon is a sequence of pipes, with each section representing one stage of the pipeline.

6. *Performance Via Prediction*

Following the saying that it can be better to ask for forgiveness than to ask for permission, the final great idea is **prediction**. In some cases it can be faster on average to guess and start working rather than wait until you know for sure, assuming that the mechanism to recover from a mis prediction is not too expensive and your prediction is relatively accurate. Use the fortune-teller's crystal ball as our prediction icon.

7. *Hierarchy of Memories*

Programmers want memory to be fast, large, and cheap, as memory speed often shapes performance, capacity limits the size of problems that can be solved, and the cost of memory today is often the majority of computer cost. Architects have found that they can address these conflicting demands with a **hierarchy of memories**, with the fastest, smallest, and most expensive memory per bit at the top of the hierarchy and the slowest, largest, and cheapest per bit at the bottom. Caches give the programmer the illusion that main memory is nearly as fast as the top of the hierarchy and nearly as big and cheap as the bottom of the hierarchy. Use a layered triangle icon to represent the memory hierarchy. The shape indicates speed, cost, and size: the closer to the top, the faster and more expensive per bit the memory; the wider the base of the layer, the bigger the memory.

8. *Dependability Via Redundancy*

Computers not only need to be fast; they need to be dependable. Since any physical device can fail, we make systems **dependable** by including redundant components that can take over when a failure occurs *and* to help detect failures. Use the tractor-trailer as our icon, since the dual tires on each side of its rear axels allow the truck to continue driving even when one tire fails. (Presumably, the truck driver heads immediately to a repair facility so the fl at tire can be fixed, thereby restoring redundancy!)

Below Your Program

A typical application, such as a word processor or a large database system, may consist of millions of lines of code and rely on sophisticated software libraries that implement complex functions in support of the application. As we will see, the hardware in a computer can only execute extremely simple low-level instructions. To go from a complex application to the simple instructions involves several layers of soft ware that interpret or translate high-level operations into simple computer instructions, an example of the great idea of **abstraction**.

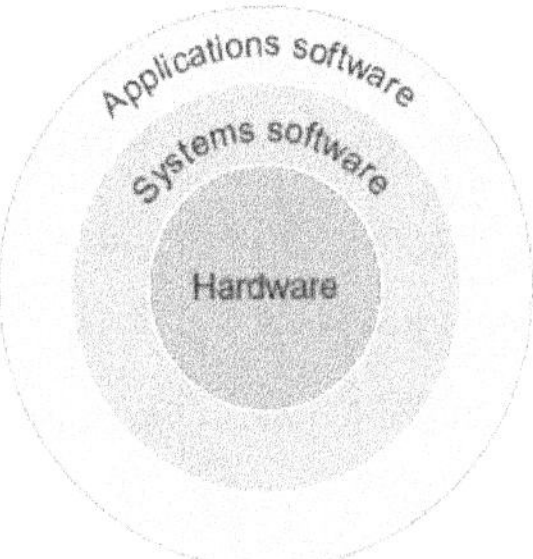

A simplified view of hardware and software as hierarchical layers, shown as concentric circles with hardware in the center and applications software outermost.

In complex applications, there are often multiple layers of application software as well. For example, a database system may run on top of the systems software hosting an application, which in turn runs on top of the database.

Systems software that provides services that are commonly useful, including operating systems, compilers, loaders, and assemblers.

Operating system Supervising program that manages the resources of a computer for the benefit of the programs that run on that computer. Among the most important functions are:

- Handling basic input and output operations.
- Allocating storage and memory.
- Providing for protected sharing of the computer among multiple applications Using it simultaneously.

Examples of operating systems in use today are Linux, ios, and Windows.

Compilers perform another vital function: the translation of a program written In a high-level language, such as C, C++, Java, or Visual Basic into instructions That the hardware can execute.

From a High-Level Language to the Language of Hardware.

Binary digit Also called a bit. One of the two numbers in base 2 (0 or 1) that are the components of information.

Instruction a command that computer hardware understands and obeys.

Assembler a program that translates a symbolic version of instructions into the binary version.

For example, the programmer would write

Add A,B

And the assembler would translate this notation into

1000110010100000

This instruction tells the computer to add the two numbers A and B.

Assembly language a symbolic representation of machine instructions.

Machine language a binary representation of machine instructions.

High-level programming language a portable language such as C, C++, Java, or Visual Basic that is composed of words and algebraic notation that can be translated by a compiler into assembly language.

C program compiled into assembly language and then assembled into binary machine language. Although the translation from high-level language to binary machine language is shown in two steps, some compilers cut out the middleman and produce binary machine language directly.

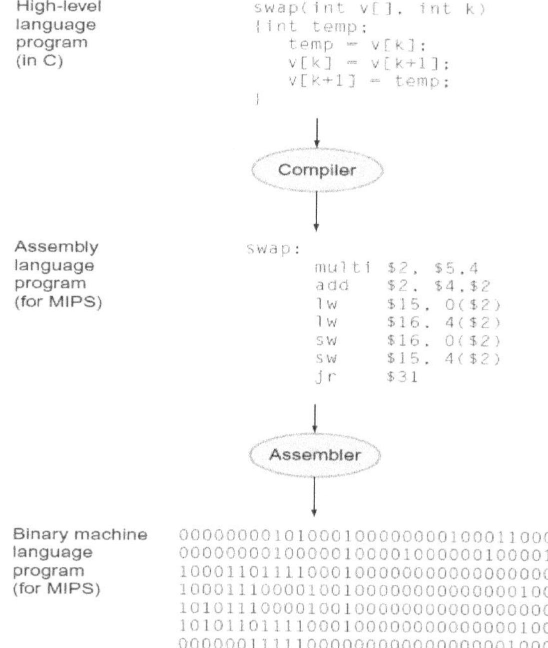

1.3. Components of a Computer System

The five classic components of a computer are input, output, memory, data path, and control, with the last two sometimes combined and called the processor.

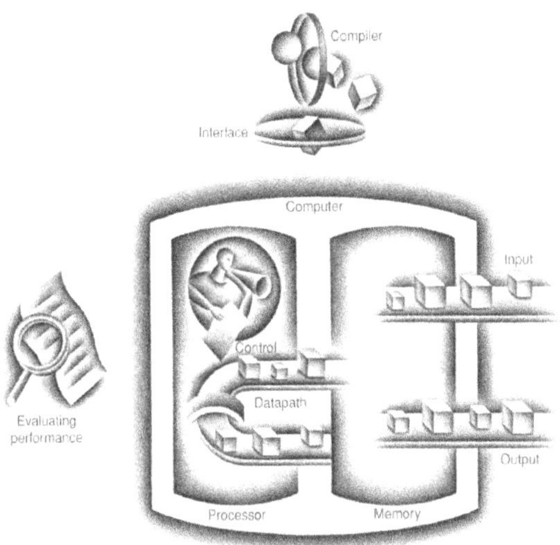

The organization of a computer, showing the five classic components. The processor gets instructions and data from memory. Input writes data to memory, and output reads data from memory. Control sends the signals that determine the operations of the data path, memory, input, and output.

Input Device

Input device a mechanism through which the computer is fed information, such as a keyboard.

Touch Screen

While PCs also use LCD displays, the tablets and smartphones of the PostPC era have replaced the keyboard and mouse with touch sensitive displays, which has the wonderful user interface advantage of users pointing directly what they are interested in rather than indirectly with a mouse. While there are a variety of ways to implement a touch screen, many tablets today use capacitive sensing. Since people are electrical conductors, if an insulator like glass is covered with a transparent conductor, touching distorts the electrostatic field of the screen, which results in a change in capacitance. This technology can allow multiple touches simultaneously, which allows gestures that can lead to attractive user interfaces.

Output Device

Output device a mechanism that conveys the result of a computation to a user, such as a display, or to another computer.

The most fascinating I/O device is probably the graphics display. Most personal mobile devices use **liquid crystal displays (LCDs)** to get a thin, low-power display.

Graphics Display

The LCD is not the source of light; instead, it controls the transmission of light.A typical LCD includes rod-shaped molecules in a liquid that form a twisting helix that bends light entering the display, from either a light source behind the display or less oft en from reflected light. The rods straighten out when a current is applied and no longer bend the light. Since the liquid crystal material is between two screens polarized at 90 degrees, the light cannot pass through unless it is bent. Today, most LCD displays use an **active matrix** that has a tiny transistor switch at each pixel to precisely control current and make sharper images. A red-green-blue mask associated with each dot on the display determines the intensity of the three color components in the final image; in a color active matrix LCD, there are three transistor switches at each point.

The image is composed of a matrix of picture elements, or **pixels**, which can be represented as a matrix of bits, called a bit *map*. Depending on the size of the screen and the resolution, the display matrix in a typical tablet ranges in size from 1024 _ 768 to 2048 _ 1536. A color display might use 8 bits for each of the three colors (red, blue, and green), for 24 bits per pixel, permitting millions of different colors to be displayed.

The computer hardware support for graphics consists mainly of a *raster refresh buffer*, or *frame buffer*, to store the bit map. The image to be represented onscreen is stored in the frame buffer, and the bit pattern per pixel is read out to the graphics display at the refresh rate

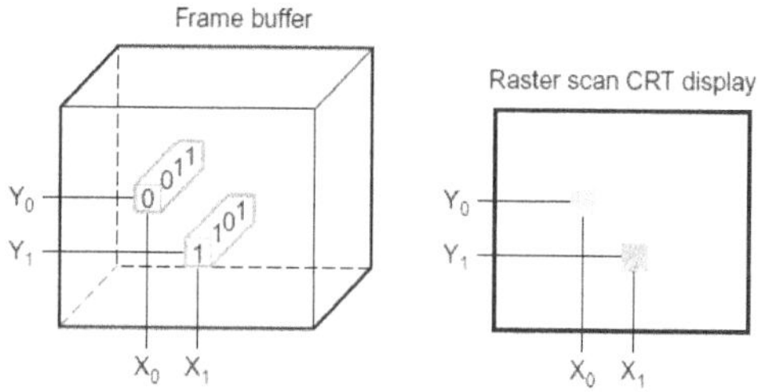

Figure shows a frame buffer with a simplified design of just 4 bits per pixel. **Each coordinate in the frame buffer on the left determines the shade of the corresponding coordinate for the raster scan CRT display on the right.**

Pixel (X0, Y0) contains the bit pattern 0011, which is a lighter shade on the screen than the bit pattern 1101 in pixel (X1, Y1).The goal of the bit map is to faithfully represent what is on the screen. The challenges in graphics systems arise because the human eye is very good at detecting even subtle changes on the screen.

The list of I/O devices includes a capacitive multi touch LCD display, front facing camera, rear facing camera, microphone, headphone jack, speakers, accelerometer, gyroscope, Wi-Fi network, and Bluetooth network. The datapath, control, and memory are a tiny portion of the components.

Arithmetic and Logic Unit

Datapath the component of the processor that performs arithmetic operations.

Instruction set architecture also called **architecture**. An abstract interface between the hardware and the lowest-level soft ware that encompasses all the information necessary to write a machine language program that will run correctly, including instructions, registers, memory access, I/O, and so on.

Application binary interface (ABI) The user portion of the instruction set plus the operating system interfaces used by application programmers. It defines a standard for binary portability across computers.

Implémentation Hardware that obeys the architecture abstraction.

Control Unit

Control the component of the processor that commands the datapath, memory, and I/O devices according to the instructions of the program.

Memory Unit

Memory the storage area in which programs are kept when they are running and that contains the data needed by the running programs. The memory is built from DRAM chips. *DRAM* stands for **dynamic random access memory. Dynamic random access memory (DRAM)** Memory built as an integrated circuit; it provides random access to any location. Access times are 50 nanoseconds and cost per gigabyte in 2012 was $5 to $10. Multiple drams are used together to contain the instructions and data of a program. In contrast to sequential access memories, such as magnetic tapes, the *RAM* portion of the term DRAM means that memory accesses take basically the same amount of time no matter what portion of the memory is read.**cache memory** A small, fast memory that acts as a buffer for a slower, larger memory. **static random access memory (SRAM)** Also memory built as an integrated circuit, but faster and less dense than DRAM.

A Safe Place for Data

Volatile memory Storage, such as DRAM, that retains data only if it is receiving power.

Nonvolatile memory a form of memory that retains data even in the absence of a power source and that is used to store programs between runs. A DVD disk is nonvolatile.

Main memory also called **primary memory**. Memory used to hold programs while they are running; typically consists of DRAM in today's computers.

Secondary memory

Nonvolatile memory used to store programs and data between runs; typically consists of flash memory in pmds and magnetic disks in servers.

Magnetic disk also called **hard disk**. A form of nonvolatile secondary memory composed of rotating platters coated with a magnetic recording material. Because they are rotating mechanical devices, access times are about 5 to 20 milliseconds and cost per gigabyte in 2012 was $0.05 to $0.10.

Flash memory a nonvolatile semiconductor memory. It is cheaper and slower than DRAM but more expensive per bit and faster than magnetic disks. Access times are about 5 to 50 microseconds and cost per gigabyte in 2012 was $0.75 to $1.00.

Communicating with Other Computers

Networks have become so popular that they are the backbone of current computer systems; a new personal mobile device or server without a network interface would be ridiculed. Networked computers have several major advantages:

- *Communication*: Information is exchanged between computers at high speeds.
- *Resource sharing*: Rather than each computer having its own I/O devices, computers on the network can share I/O devices.
- *Nonlocal access*: By connecting computers over long distances, users need not be near the computer they are using.

Local area network (LAN) a network designed to carry data within a geographically confined area, typically within a single building.

Wide area network (WAN) a network extended over hundreds of kilometers that can span a continent.

1.4. Technology

Technologies for Building Processors and Memory

- Processors and memory have improved at an incredible rate, because computer designers have long embraced the latest in electronic technology to try to win the race to design a better computer.

Relative performance per unit cost of technologies used in computers over time.

Year	Technology used in computers	Relative performance/unit cost
1951	Vacuum tube	1
1965	Transistor	35
1975	Integrated circuit	900
1995	Very large-scale integrated circuit	2,400,000
2013	Ultra large-scale integrated circuit	250,000,000,000

- A transistor is simply an on/off switch controlled by electricity. The integrated circuit (IC) combined dozens to hundreds of transistors into a single chip. When Gordon Moore predicted the continuous doubling of resources, he was predicting the growth rate of the number of transistors per chip. To describe the tremendous increase in the number of transistors from hundreds to millions, the adjective very large scale is added to the term, creating the abbreviation VLSI, for very large-scale integrated circuit.
- The manufacture of a chip begins with silicon, a substance found in sand. Because silicon does not conduct electricity well, it is called a semiconductor. With a special chemical process, it is possible to add materials to silicon that allow tiny areas to transform into one of three devices:
    - Excellent conductors of electricity (using either microscopic copper or aluminum wire).
    - Excellent insulators from electricity (like plastic sheathing or glass).
    - Areas that can conduct or insulate under special conditions (as a switch) .
- Transistors fall in the last category. A VLSI circuit, then, is just billions of combinations of conductors, insulators, and switches manufactured in a single small package.

- The process starts with a silicon crystal ingot, which looks like a giant sausage. Today, ingots are 8–12 inches in diameter and about 12–24 inches long. An ingot is finely sliced into wafers no more than 0.1 inches thick. These wafers then go through a series of processing steps, during which patterns of chemicals are placed on each wafer, creating the transistors, conductors, and insulators discussed earlier.

- Today's integrated circuits contain only one layer of transistors but may have from two to eight levels of metal conductor, separated by layers of insulators.

Silicon crystal ingot,A rod composed of a silicon crystal that is between 8 and 12 inches in diameter and about 12 to 24 inches long.

Wafer, a slice from a silicon ingot no more than 0.1 inches thick, used to create chips.

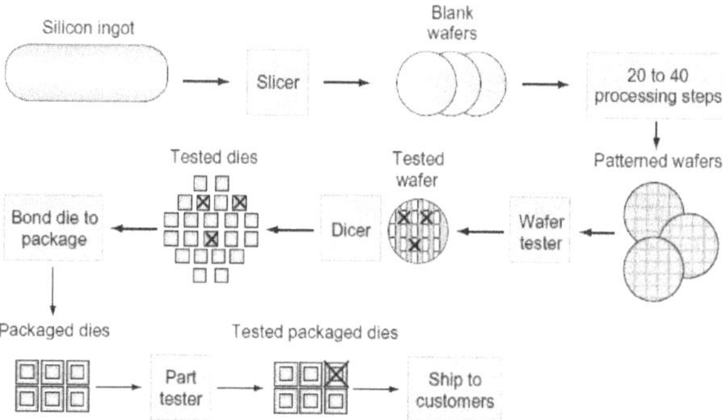

The chip manufacturing process. After being sliced from the silicon ingot, blank wafers are put through 20 to 40 steps to create patterned wafers. These patterned wafers are then tested with a wafer tester, and a map of the good parts is made. Then, the wafers are diced into dies. In this figure, one wafer produced 20 dies, of which 17 passed testing. (X means the die is bad.)

- The yield of good dies in this case was 17/20, or 85%. These good dies are then bonded into packages and tested one more time before shipping the packaged parts to customers. One bad packaged part was found in this final test.

- A single microscopic flaw in the wafer itself or in one of the dozens of patterning steps can result in that area of the wafer failing. These defects, as they are called, make it virtually impossible to manufacture a perfect wafer. Defect, a microscopic flaw in a wafer or in patterning steps that can result in the failure of the die containing that defect.

- The simplest way to cope with imperfection is to place many independent components on a single wafer. The patterned wafer is then chopped up, or diced, into these components, called dies and more informally known as chips.

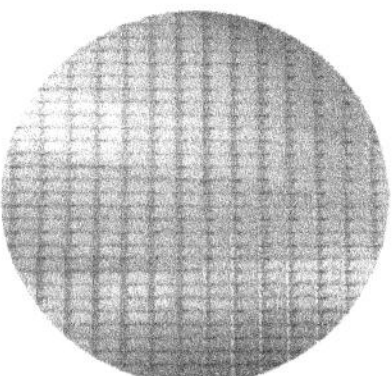

A 12-inch (300 mm) wafer of Intel Core i7 (Courtesy Intel). The number of dies on this 300 mm (12 inch) wafer at 100% yield is 280, each 20.7 by 10.5 mm. The several dozen partially rounded chips at the boundaries of the wafer are useless; they are included because it's easier to create the masks used to pattern the silicon. This die uses a 32-nanometer technology, which means that the smallest features are approximately 32 nm in size, although they are typically somewhat smaller than the actual feature size, which refers to the size of the transistors as "drawn" versus the final manufactured size. Die, the individual rectangular sections that are cut from a wafer, more informally known as chips.

Yield , the percentage of good dies from the total number of dies on the wafer.

- The cost of an integrated circuit rises quickly as the die size increases, due both to the lower yield and the smaller number of dies that fit on a wafer. To reduce the cost, using the next generation process shrinks a large die as it uses smaller sizes for both transistors and wires. This improves the yield and the die count per wafer. A 32-nanometer (nm) process was typical in 2012, which means essentially that the smallest feature size on the die is 32 nm.

Once you've found good dies, they are connected to the input/output pins of a package, using a process called bonding. These packaged parts are tested a final time, since mistakes can occur in packaging, and then they are shipped to customers.

The cost of an integrated circuit can be expressed in three simple equations:

$$\text{Cost per die} = \frac{\text{Cost per wafer}}{\text{Dies per wafer} \times \text{yield}}$$

$$\text{Dies per wafer} \approx \frac{\text{Wafer area}}{\text{Die area}}$$

$$\text{Yield} = \frac{1}{(1 + (\text{Defects per area} \times \text{Die area}/2))^2}$$

1.5. Performance

Response time also called execution time, The total time required for the computer to complete a task, including disk accesses, memory accesses, I/O activities, operating system overhead, CPU execution time, and so on.

Throughput also called bandwidth, another measure of performance, it is the number of tasks completed per unit time.

Do the following changes to a computer system increase throughput, decrease response time, or both?

1. Replacing the processor in a computer with a faster version
2. Adding additional processors to a system that uses multiple processors for separate tasks for example, searching the web decreasing response time almost always improves throughput. Hence, in case 1, both response time and throughput are improved. In case 2, no one task gets work done faster, so only throughput increases.

If, however, the demand for processing in the second case was almost as large as the throughput, the system might force requests to queue up. In this case, increasing the throughput could also improve response time, since it would reduce the waiting time in the queue. Thus, in many real computer systems, changing either execution time or throughput often affects the other.

Performance and execution time for a computer X:

$$\text{Performance}_X = \frac{1}{\text{Execution time}_X}$$

This means that for two computers X and Y, if the performance of X is greater than the performance of Y, we have

$$\text{Performance}_X > \text{Performance}_Y$$
$$\frac{1}{\text{Execution time}_X} > \frac{1}{\text{Execution time}_Y}$$
$$\text{Execution time}_Y > \text{Execution time}_X$$

That is, the execution time on Y is longer than that on X, if X is faster than Y.

In discussing a computer design, we often want to relate the performance of two different computers quantitatively. We will use the phrase "X is n times faster than

Y"—or equivalently "X is n times as fast as Y"—to mean

$$\frac{\text{Performance}_X}{\text{Performance}_Y} = n$$

If X is n times as fast as Y, then the execution time on Y is n times as long as it is on X:

$$\frac{\text{Performance}_X}{\text{Performance}_Y} = \frac{\text{Execution time}_Y}{\text{Execution time}_X} = n$$

Relative Performance

If computer a runs a program in 10 seconds and computer B runs the same program in 15 seconds, how much faster is A than B? We know that A is n times as fast as B if,

$$\frac{\text{Performance}_A}{\text{Performance}_B} = \frac{\text{Execution time}_B}{\text{Execution time}_A} = n$$

Thus the performance ratio is,

$$\frac{15}{10} = 1.5$$

And A is therefore 1.5 times as fast as B.

In the above example, we could also say that computer B is 1.5 times slower than computer A.

Since,

$$\frac{\text{Performance}_A}{\text{Performance}_B} = 1.5$$

Means that,

$$\frac{\text{Performance}_A}{1.5} = \text{Performance}_B$$

Measuring Performance

Time is the measure of computer performance: the computer that performs the same amount of work in the least time is the fastest. Program execution time is measured in seconds per program. However, time can be defined in different ways, depending on what we count. The most straightforward definition of time is called wall clock time, response time, or elapsed time. These terms mean the total time to complete a task, including disk accesses, memory accesses, input/output (I/O) activities, operating system overhead everything.

CPU execution time Also called CPU time, the actual time the CPU spends computing for a specific task.

User CPU time, The CPU time spent in a program itself.

System CPU time, The CPU time spent in the operating system performing tasks on behalf of the program.

Almost all computers are constructed using a clock that determines when events take place in the hardware. These discrete time intervals are called clock cycles (or ticks, clock ticks, clock periods, clocks, cycles). Designers refer to the length of a clock period both as the time for a complete clock cycle (e.g., 250 picoseconds, or 250 ps) and as the clock rate (e.g., 4 gigahertz, or 4 GHz), which is the inverse of the clock period.

Clock cycle also called tick, clock tick, clock period, clock, or cycle, The time for one clock period, usually of the processor clock, which runs at a constant rate.

Clock period, the length of each clock cycle.

CPU Performance and Its Factors

A simple formula relates the most basic metrics (clock cycles and clock cycle time) to CPU time:

$$\text{CPU execution time for a program} = \text{CPU clock cycles for a program} \times \text{Clock cycle time}$$

Alternatively, because clock rate and clock cycle time are inverses,

$$\text{CPU execution time for a program} = \frac{\text{CPU clock cycles for a program}}{\text{Clock rate}}$$

This formula makes it clear that the hardware designer can improve performance by reducing the number of clock cycles required for a program or the length of the clock cycle.

Improving Performance

Our favorite program runs in 10 seconds on computer A, which has a 2 GHz clock. We are trying to help a computer designer build a computer, B, which will run this program in 6 seconds. The designer has determined that a substantial increase in the clock rate is possible, but this increase will affect the rest of the CPU design, causing computer B to require 1.2 times as many clock cycles as computer A for this program. What clock rate should we tell the designer to target?

Let's first find the number of clock cycles required for the program on A:

$$\text{CPU time}_A = \frac{\text{CPU clock cycles}_A}{\text{Clock rate}_A}$$

$$10 \text{ seconds} = \frac{\text{CPU clock cycles}_A}{2 \times 10^9 \; \frac{\text{cycles}}{\text{second}}}$$

$$\text{CPU clock cycles}_A = 10 \text{ seconds} \times 2 \times 10^9 \; \frac{\text{cycles}}{\text{second}} = 20 \times 10^9 \text{ cycles}$$

CPU time for B can be found using this equation:

$$\text{CPU time}_B = \frac{1.2 \times \text{CPU clock cycles}_A}{\text{Clock rate}_B}$$

$$6 \text{ seconds} = \frac{1.2 \times 20 \times 10^9 \text{ cycles}}{\text{Clock rate}_B}$$

$$\text{Clock rate}_B = \frac{1.2 \times 20 \times 10^9 \text{ cycles}}{6 \text{ seconds}} = \frac{0.2 \times 20 \times 10^9 \text{ cycles}}{\text{second}} = \frac{4 \times 10^9 \text{ cycles}}{\text{second}} = 4 \text{ GHz}$$

To run the program in 6 seconds, B must have twice the clock rate of A.

Instruction Performance

The performance equations above did not include any reference to the number of instructions needed for the program. However, since the compiler clearly generated instructions to execute, and the computer had to execute the instructions to run the program, the execution time must depend on the number of instructions in a program. One way to think about execution time is that it equals the number of instructions executed multiplied by the average time per instruction. Therefore, the number of clock cycles required for a program can be written as clock cycles per instruction (CPI), Average number of clock cycles per instruction for a program or program fragment.

Using the Performance Equation

Suppose we have two implementations of the same instruction set architecture.

Computer A has a clock cycle time of 250 ps and a CPI of 2.0 for some program, and computer B has a clock cycle time of 500 ps and a CPI of 1.2 for the same program. Which computer is faster for this program and by how much?

We know that each computer executes the same number of instructions for the program; let's call this number I. First, find the number of processor clock cycles for each computer:

$$\text{CPU clock cycles}_A = I \times 2.0$$
$$\text{CPU clock cycles}_B = I \times 1.2$$

Now we can compute the CPU time for each computer:

$$\text{CPU time}_A = \text{CPU clock cycles}_A \times \text{Clock cycle time}$$
$$= I \times 2.0 \times 250 \text{ ps} = 500 \times I \text{ ps}$$

Likewise for B:

$$\text{CPU time}_B = I \times 1.2 \times 500 \text{ ps} = 600 \times I \text{ ps}$$

Clearly, computer A is faster. The amount faster is given by the ratio of the execution times:

$$\frac{\text{CPU performance}_A}{\text{CPU performance}_B} = \frac{\text{Execution time}_B}{\text{Execution time}_A} = \frac{600 \times I \text{ ps}}{500 \times I \text{ ps}} = 1.2$$

We can conclude that computer A is 1.2 times as fast as computer B for this Program.

The Classic CPU Performance Equation

We can now write this basic performance equation in terms of instruction count (the number of instructions executed by the program), CPI, and clock cycle time:

$$\text{CPU time} = \text{Instruction count} \times \text{CPI} \times \text{Clock cycle time}$$

or, since the clock rate is the inverse of clock cycle time:

$$\text{CPU time} = \frac{\text{Instruction count} \times \text{CPI}}{\text{Clock rate}}$$

Instructions count The number of instructions executed by the program.

Comparing Code Segments

A compiler designer is trying to decide between two code sequences for a particular computer. The hardware designers have supplied the following facts:

	CPI for each instruction class		
	A	B	C
CPI	1	2	3

For a particular high-level language statement, the compiler writer is considering two code sequences that require the following instruction counts:

Code sequence	Instruction counts for each instruction class		
	A	B	C
1	2	1	2
2	4	1	1

Which code sequence executes the most instructions? Which will be faster?

What is the CPI for each sequence?

Sequence 1 executes 2 + 1 + 2 = 5 instructions. Sequence 2 executes 4+ 1 +1 =6 instructions. Therefore, sequence 1 executes fewer instructions.

We can use the equation for CPU clock cycles based on instruction count and CPI to find the total number of clock cycles for each sequence:

$$\text{CPU clock cycles} = \sum_{i=1}^{n}(CPI_i \times C_i)$$

This yields,

CPU clock cycles1= (2 *1)+ (1* 2)+ (2* 3)= 2+ 2+ 6= 10 cycles

CPU clock cycles2= (4* 1)+ (1* 2)+ (1* 3)= 4+ 2+ 3= 9 cycles

So code sequence 2 is faster, even though it executes one extra instruction. Since code sequence 2 takes fewer overall clock cycles but has more instructions, it must have a lower CPI. The CPI values can be computed by

$$CPI = \frac{\text{CPU clock cycles}}{\text{Instruction count}}$$

$$CPI_1 = \frac{\text{CPU clock cycles}_1}{\text{Instruction count}_1} = \frac{10}{5} = 2.0$$

$$CPI_2 = \frac{\text{CPU clock cycles}_2}{\text{Instruction count}_2} = \frac{9}{6} = 1.5$$

The basic components of performance and how each is measured.

Components of performance	Units of measure
CPU execution time for a program	Seconds for the program
Instruction count	Instructions executed for the program
Clock cycles per instruction (CPI)	Average number of clock cycles per instruction
Clock cycle time	Seconds per clock cycle

When comparing two computers, you must look at all three components, which combine to form execution time. If some of the factors are identical, like the clock rate in the above example, performance can be determined by comparing all the non identical factors. Since CPI varies by instruction mix, both instruction count and CPI must be compared, even if clock rates are identical. **Instruction mix**, A measure of the dynamic frequency of instructions across one or many programs. The performance of a program depends on the algorithm, the language, the compiler, the architecture, and the actual hardware.

Hardware or software component	Affects what?	How?
Algorithm	Instruction count, possibly CPI	The algorithm determines the number of source program instructions executed and hence the number of processor instructions executed. The algorithm may also affect the CPI, by favoring slower or faster instructions. For example, if the algorithm uses more divides, it will tend to have a higher CPI.
Programming language	Instruction count, CPI	The programming language certainly affects the instruction count, since statements in the language are translated to processor instructions, which determine instruction count. The language may also affect the CPI because of its features; for example, a language with heavy support for data abstraction (e.g., Java) will require indirect calls, which will use higher CPI instructions.
Compiler	Instruction count, CPI	The efficiency of the compiler affects both the instruction count and average cycles per instruction, since the compiler determines the translation of the source language instructions into computer instructions. The compiler's role can be very complex and affect the CPI in complex ways.
Instruction set architecture	Instruction count, clock rate, CPI	The instruction set architecture affects all three aspects of CPU performance, since it affects the instructions needed for a function, the cost in cycles of each instruction, and the overall clock rate of the processor.

1.6. Power Wall

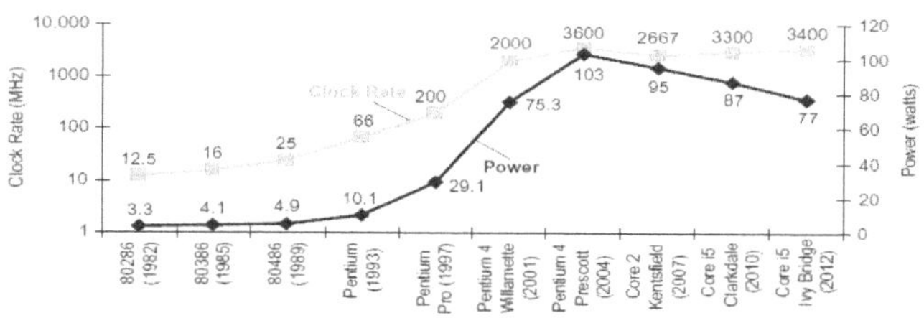

Clock rate and Power for Intel x86 microprocessors over eight generations and 25 years. The Pentium 4 made a dramatic jump in clock rate and power but less so in performance. The Prescott thermal problems led to the abandonment of the Pentium 4 line. The Core 2 line reverts to a simpler pipeline with lower clock rates and multiple processors per chip. The Core i5 pipelines follow in its footsteps.

- Although power provides a limit to what we can cool, in the PostPC Era the really critical resource is energy. Battery life can trump performance in the personal mobile device, and the architects of warehouse scale computers try to reduce the costs of powering and cooling 100,000 servers as the costs are high at this scale. Just as measuring time in seconds is a safer measure of program performance than a rate like MIPS , the energy metric joules is a better measure than a power rate like watts, which is just joules/second.

- The dominant technology for integrated circuits is called CMOS (complementary metal oxide semiconductor). For CMOS, the primary source of energy consumption is so-called dynamic energy that is, energy that is consumed when transistors switch states from 0 to 1 and vice versa. The dynamic energy depends on the capacitive loading of each transistor and the voltage applied:

$$Energy \propto Capacitive\ load \times Voltage^2$$

This equation is the energy of a pulse during the logic transition of $0 \rightarrow 1 \rightarrow 0$ or $1 \rightarrow 0 \rightarrow 1$. The energy of a single transition is then,

$$Energy \propto 1/2 \times Capacitive\ load \times Voltage^2$$

The power required per transistor is just the product of energy of a transition and the frequency of transitions:

$$Power \propto 1/2 \times Capacitive\ load \times Voltage^2 \times Frequency\ switched$$

Frequency switched is a function of the clock rate. The capacitive load per transistor is a function of both the number of transistors connected to an output (called the fanout) and the technology, which determines the capacitance of both wires and transistors.

Example

Suppose we developed a new, simpler processor that has 85% of the capacitive load of the more complex older processor. Further, assume that it has adjustable voltage so that it can reduce voltage 15% compared to processor B, which results in a 15% shrink in frequency. What is the impact on dynamic power?

$$\frac{Power_{new}}{Power_{old}} = \frac{(Capacitive\ load \times 0.85) \times (Voltage \times 0.85)^2 \times (Frequency\ switched \times 0.85)}{Capacitive\ load \times Voltage^2 \times Frequency\ switched}$$

Thus the power ratio is,

$$0.85^4 = 0.52$$

Hence, the new processor uses about half the power of the old processor.

- The problem today is that further lowering of the voltage appears to make the transistors too leaky, like water faucets that cannot be completely shut off. Even today about 40% of the power consumption in server chips is due to leakage. If transistors started leaking more, the whole process could become unwieldy.

- To try to address the power problem, designers have already attached large devices to increase cooling, and they turn off parts of the chip that are not used in a given clock cycle. Although there are many more expensive ways to cool chips and thereby raise their power to, say, 300 watts, these techniques are generally too expensive for personal computers and even servers, not to mention personal mobile devices.

- Since computer designers slammed into a power wall, they needed a new way forward. They chose a different path from the way they designed microprocessors for their first 30 years.

- Although dynamic energy is the primary source of energy consumption in CMOS, static energy consumption occurs because of leakage current that flows even when a transistor is off. In servers, leakage is typically responsible for 40% of the energy consumption. Thus, increasing the number of transistors increases power dissipation, even if the transistors are always off. A variety of design techniques and technology innovations are being deployed to control leakage, but it's hard to lower voltage further.

- Power is a challenge for integrated circuits for two reasons. First, power must be brought in and distributed around the chip; modern microprocessors use hundreds of pins just for power and ground! Similarly, multiple levels of chip interconnect are used solely for power and ground distribution to portions of the chip. Second, power is dissipated as heat and must be removed. Server chips can burn more than 100 watts, and cooling the chip and the surrounding system is a major expense in Warehouse Scale Computers.

1.7. Uniprocessors to Multiprocessors

- The power limit has forced a dramatic change in the design of microprocessors.

- Rather than continuing to decrease the response time of a single program running on the single processor, as of 2006 all desktop and server companies are shipping microprocessors with multiple processors per chip, where the benefit is oft en more on throughput than on response time. To reduce confusion between the words processor and microprocessor, companies refer to processors as "cores," and such microprocessors are generically called multicore microprocessors. Hence, a "quadcore" microprocessor is a chip that contains four processors or four cores.

- Parallelism has always been critical to performance in computing, but it was oft en hidden. This is one example of instruction-level parallelism, where the parallel nature of the hardware is abstracted away so the programmer and compiler can think of the hardware as executing instructions sequentially.

1.8. Instructions

- **Instruction set**, The vocabulary of commands understood by a given architecture.
- The chosen instruction set comes from MIPS Technologies, and is an elegant example of the instruction sets designed since the 1980s. To demonstrate how easy it is to pick up other instruction sets, we will take a quick look at three other popular instruction sets.
    1. ARMv7 is similar to MIPS. More than 9 billion chips with ARM processors were manufactured in 2011, making it the most popular instruction set in the world.
    2. The second example is the Intel x86, which powers both the PC and the cloud of the PostPC Era.
    3. The third example is ARMv8, which extends the address size of the ARMv7 from 32 bits to 64 bits. Ironically, as we shall see, this 2013 instruction set is closer to MIPS than it is to ARMv7.
- **Stored-program concept**, The idea that instructions and data of many types can be stored in memory as numbers, leading to the stored program computer.

1.9. Operations

- Every computer must be able to perform arithmetic. The MIPS assembly language notation add a, b, c instructs a computer to add the two variables b and c and to put their sum in a.
- This notation is rigid in that each MIPS arithmetic instruction performs only one operation and must always have exactly three variables. For example, suppose we want to place the sum of four variables b, c, d, and e into variable a.

The following sequence of instructions adds the four variables:

```
add a, b, c   # The sum of b and c is placed in a
add a, a, d   # The sum of b, c, and d is now in a
add a, a, e   # The sum of b, c, d, and e is now in a
```

Thus, it takes three instructions to sum the four variables.

- The words to the right of the sharp symbol (#) on each line above are comments for the human reader, so the computer ignores them.

MIPS operands

Name	Example	Comments
32 registers	$s0-$s7, $t0-$t9, $zero, $a0-$a3, $v0-$v1, $gp, $fp, $sp, $ra, $at	Fast locations for data. In MIPS, data must be in registers to perform arithmetic, register $zero always equals 0, and register $at is reserved by the assembler to handle large constants.
2^{30} memory words	Memory[0], Memory[4], . . . , Memory[4294967292]	Accessed only by data transfer instructions. MIPS uses byte addresses, so sequential word addresses differ by 4. Memory holds data structures, arrays, and spilled registers.

MIPS assembly language

Category	Instruction	Example	Meaning	Comments
Arithmetic	add	add $s1,$s2,$s3	$s1 = $s2 + $s3	Three register operands
	subtract	sub $s1,$s2,$s3	$s1 = $s2 − $s3	Three register operands
	add immediate	addi $s1,$s2,20	$s1 = $s2 + 20	Used to add constants
Data transfer	load word	lw $s1,20($s2)	$s1 = Memory[$s2 + 20]	Word from memory to register
	store word	sw $s1,20($s2)	Memory[$s2 + 20] = $s1	Word from register to memory
	load half	lh $s1,20($s2)	$s1 = Memory[$s2 + 20]	Halfword memory to register
	load half unsigned	lhu $s1,20($s2)	$s1 = Memory[$s2 + 20]	Halfword memory to register
	store half	sh $s1,20($s2)	Memory[$s2 + 20] = $s1	Halfword register to memory
	load byte	lb $s1,20($s2)	$s1 = Memory[$s2 + 20]	Byte from memory to register
	load byte unsigned	lbu $s1,20($s2)	$s1 = Memory[$s2 + 20]	Byte from memory to register
	store byte	sb $s1,20($s2)	Memory[$s2 + 20] = $s1	Byte from register to memory
	load linked word	ll $s1,20($s2)	$s1 = Memory[$s2 + 20]	Load word as 1st half of atomic swap
	store condition. word	sc $s1,20($s2)	Memory[$s2+20]=$s1;$s1=0 or 1	Store word as 2nd half of atomic swap
	load upper immed.	lui $s1,20	$s1 = 20 * 2^{16}	Loads constant in upper 16 bits
Logical	and	and $s1,$s2,$s3	$s1 = $s2 & $s3	Three reg. operands; bit-by-bit AND
	or	or $s1,$s2,$s3	$s1 = $s2 | $s3	Three reg. operands; bit-by-bit OR
	nor	nor $s1,$s2,$s3	$s1 = ~($s2 | $s3)	Three reg. operands; bit-by-bit NOR
	and immediate	andi $s1,$s2,20	$s1 = $s2 & 20	Bit-by-bit AND reg with constant
	or immediate	ori $s1,$s2,20	$s1 = $s2 | 20	Bit-by-bit OR reg with constant
	shift left logical	sll $s1,$s2,10	$s1 = $s2 << 10	Shift left by constant
	shift right logical	srl $s1,$s2,10	$s1 = $s2 >> 10	Shift right by constant
Conditional branch	branch on equal	beq $s1,$s2,25	if ($s1 == $s2) go to PC + 4 + 100	Equal test; PC-relative branch
	branch on not equal	bne $s1,$s2,25	if ($s1!= $s2) go to PC + 4 + 100	Not equal test; PC-relative
	set on less than	slt $s1,$s2,$s3	if ($s2 < $s3) $s1 = 1; else $s1 = 0	Compare less than; for beq, bne
	set on less than unsigned	sltu $s1,$s2,$s3	if ($s2 < $s3) $s1 = 1; else $s1 = 0	Compare less than unsigned
	set less than immediate	slti $s1,$s2,20	if ($s2 < 20) $s1 = 1; else $s1 = 0	Compare less than constant
	set less than immediate unsigned	sltiu $s1,$s2,20	if ($s2 < 20) $s1 = 1; else $s1 = 0	Compare less than constant unsigned
Unconditional jump	jump	j 2500	go to 10000	Jump to target address
	jump register	jr $ra	go to $ra	For switch, procedure return
	jump and link	jal 2500	$ra = PC + 4; go to 10000	For procedure call

- Hardware for a variable number of operands is more complicated than hardware for a fixed number. This situation illustrates the first of three underlying principles of hardware design:

Design Principle 1: Simplicity favors regularity.

Compiling Two C Assignment Statements into MIPS

This segment of a C program contains the five variables a, b, c, d, and e. Since Java evolved from C, this example and the next few work for either high-level programming language:

$$a = b + c;$$
$$d = a - e;$$

The translation from C to MIPS assembly language instructions is performed by the compiler. Show the MIPS code produced by a compiler.

A MIPS instruction operates on two source operands and places the result in one destination operand. Hence, the two simple statements above compile directly into these two MIPS assembly language instructions:

$$add\ a,\ b,\ c$$
$$sub\ d,\ a,\ e$$

Compiling a Complex C Assignment into MIPS

A somewhat complex statement contains the five variables f, g, h, i, and j:

$$f = (g + h) - (i + j);$$

What might a C compiler produce?

The compiler must break this statement into several assembly instructions, since only one operation is performed per MIPS instruction. The first MIPS instruction calculates the sum of g and h. We must place the result somewhere, so the compiler creates a temporary variable, called t0:

$$add\ t0,g,h\ \#\ temporary\ variable\ t0\ contains\ g + h$$

Although the next operation is subtract, we need to calculate the sum of i and j before we can subtract. Thus, the second instruction places the sum of i and j in another temporary variable created by the compiler, called t1:

$$add\ t1,i,j\quad \#\ temporary\ variable\ t1\ contains\ i + j$$

Finally, the subtract instruction subtracts the second sum from the first and places the difference in the variable f, completing the compiled code:

$$\text{sub f,t0,t1} \quad \text{\# f gets t0 – t1, which is (g + h) – (i + j)}$$

1.10. Operands

Word, The natural unit of access in a computer, usually a group of 32 bits; corresponds to the size of a register in the MIPS architecture.

One major difference between the variables of a programming language and registers is the limited number of registers, typically 32 on current computers, like MIPS. Thus, continuing in our top-down, stepwise evolution of the symbolic representation of the MIPS language, we have added the restriction that the three operands of MIPS arithmetic instructions must each be chosen from one of the 32.

32-bit registers.

The reason for the limit of 32 registers may be found in the second of our three underlying design principles of hardware technology:

Design Principle 2: Smaller is faster.

A very large number of registers may increase the clock cycle time simply because it takes electronic signals longer when they must travel farther.

Although we could simply write instructions using numbers for registers, from 0 to 31, the MIPS convention is to use two-character names following a dollar sign to represent a register

For now, we will use $s0, $s1, . . . for registers that correspond to variables in C and Java programs and $t0, $t1, . . . for temporary registers needed to compile the program into MIPS instructions.

Compiling a C Assignment Using Registers

It is the compiler's job to associate program variables with registers. Take, for instance, the assignment statement from our earlier example:

$$f = (g + h) – (i + j);$$

The variables f, g, h, i, and j are assigned to the registers $s0, $s1, $s2, $s3, and $s4, respectively. What is the compiled MIPS code?

The compiled program is very similar to the prior example, except we replace the variables with the register names mentioned above plus two temporary registers, $t0 and $t1, which correspond to the temporary variables above:

$$\text{add \$t0,\$s1,\$s2} \quad \text{\# register \$t0 contains g + h}$$

add $t1,$s3,$s4 # register $t1 contains i + j

sub $s0,$t0,$t1 # f gets $t0 – $t1, which is (g + h)–(i + j)

Memory Operands

Programming languages have simple variables that contain single data elements, as in these examples, but they also have more complex data structures—arrays and structures. These complex data structures can contain many more data elements than there are registers in a computer.

The processor can keep only a small amount of data in registers, but computer memory contains billions of data elements. Hence, data structures (arrays and structures) are kept in memory.

Data transfer instruction, A command that moves data between memory and registers.

Address a value used to delineate the location of a specific data element within a memory array.

Memory is just a large, single-dimensional array, with the address acting as the index to that array, starting at 0. For example, the address of the third data element is 2, and the value of Memory [2] is 10.

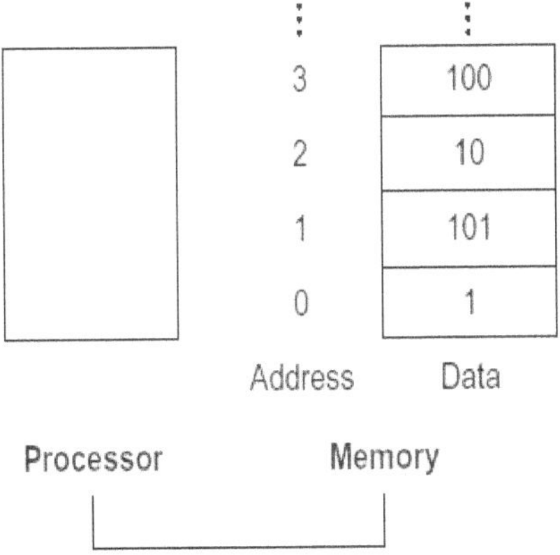

The data transfer instruction that copies data from memory to a register is traditionally called load. The format of the load instruction is the name of the operation followed by the register to be loaded, then a constant and register used to access memory. The sum of the constant portion of the instruction and the contents of the second register forms the memory address. The actual MIPS name for this instruction is lw, standing for load word.

Compiling an Assignment When an Operand Is in Memory

Let's assume that A is an array of 100 words and that the compiler has associated the variables g and h with the registers $s1 and $s2 as before.

Let's also assume that the starting address, or base address, of the array is in $s3. Compile this C assignment statement:

$$g = h + A[8];$$

Although there is a single operation in this assignment statement, one of the operands is in memory, so we must first transfer A[8] to a register. The address of this array element is the sum of the base of the array A, found in register $s3, plus the number to select element 8. The data should be placed in a temporary register for use in the next instruction. The first compiled instruction is lw $t0,8($s3) # Temporary reg $t0 gets A[8] (We'll be making a slight adjustment to this instruction, but we'll use this simplified version for now.) The following instruction can operate on the value in $t0 (which equals A[8]) since it is in a register. The instruction must add h (contained in $s2) to A[8] (contained in $t0) and put the sum in the register corresponding to g (associated with $s1):

$$\text{add } \$s1,\$s2,\$t0 \ \# \ g = h + A[8]$$

The constant in a data transfer instruction (8) is called the offset, and the register added to form the address ($s3) is called the base register.

Alignment restriction: A requirement that data be aligned in memory on natural boundaries.

Computers divide into those that use the address of the left most or "big end" byte as the word address versus those that use the rightmost or "little end" byte.

For example, in a big-endian machine, the directive .byte 0, 1, 2, 3 would result in a memory word containing

Byte #			
0	1	2	3

While in a little-endian machine, the word would contain

Byte #			
3	2	1	0

Byte addressing also affects the array index. To get the proper byte address in the code above, the offset to be added to the base register $s3 must be 48, or 32, so that the load address will select A[8] and not A[8/4].

Compiling Using Load and Store

Assume variable h is associated with register $s2 and the base address of the array A is in $s3.

- What is the MIPS assembly code for the C assignment statement below?

$$A[12] = h + A[8];$$

- Although there is a single operation in the C statement, now two of the operands are in memory, so we need even more MIPS instructions. The first two instructions are the same as in the prior example, except this time we use the proper offset for byte addressing in the load word instruction to select A[8], and the add instruction places the sum in $t0:

```
lw $t0,32($s3)   # Temporary reg $t0 gets A[8]
add $t0,$s2,$t0 # Temporary reg $t0 gets h + A[8]
```

The final instruction stores the sum into A[12], using 48 (4 12) as the offset and register $s3 as the base register.

```
sw $t0,48($s3) # Stores h + A[8] back into A[12]
```

Load word and store word are the instructions that copy words between memory and registers in the MIPS architecture.

Other brands of computers use other instructions along with load and store to transfer data.

- Consequently, the compiler tries to keep the most frequently used variables in registers and places the rest in memory, using loads and stores to move variables between registers and memory. The process of putting less commonly used variables (or those needed later) into memory is called spilling registers.

- Thus, registers take less time to access and have higher throughput than memory, making data in registers both faster to access and simpler to use. Accessing registers also uses less energy than accessing memory. To achieve highest performance and conserve energy, an instruction set architecture must have a sufficient number of registers, and compilers must use registers efficiently.

Constant or Immediate Operands

- Many times a program will use a constant in an operation-for example, incrementing an index to point to the next element of an array.

For example, to add the constant 4 to register $s3, we could use the code

lw $t0, AddrConstant4($s1)   # $t0 = constant 4

add $s3,$s3,$t0 # $s3 = $s3 + $t0 ($t0 == 4)

Assuming that $s1 + AddrConstant4 is the memory address of the constant 4.

- An alternative that avoids the load instruction is to offer versions of the arithmetic instructions in which one operand is a constant. This quick add instruction with one constant operand is called add immediate or addi. To add 4 to register $s3, we just write

addi $s3,$s3,4 # $s3 = $s3 + 4

- Constant operands occur frequently, and by including constants inside arithmetic instructions, operations are much faster and use less energy than if constants were loaded from memory

1.11. Representing Instructions

Representing Instructions in the Computer

Since registers are referred to in instructions, there must be a convention to map register names into numbers. In MIPS assembly language, registers $s0 to $s7 map onto registers 16 to 23, and registers $t0 to $t7 map onto registers 8 to 15. Hence, $s0 means register 16, $s1 means register 17, $s2 means register 18, . . . , $t0 means register 8, $t1 means register 9, and so on.

Translating a MIPS Assembly Instruction into a Machine Instruction.

add $t0,$s1,$s2

First as a combination of decimal numbers and then of binary numbers.

The decimal representation is,

0	17	18	8	0	32

Each of these segments of an instruction is called a field. The first and last fields (containing 0 and 32 in this case) in combination tell the MIPS computer that this instruction performs addition. The second field gives the number of the register that is the first source operand of the addition operation (17 $s1), and the third field gives the other source operand for the addition (18 $s2). The fourth field contains the number of the register that is to receive the sum (8 $t0). The fifth field is unused in this instruction, so it is set to 0. Thus, this instruction adds register $s1 to register $s2 and places the sum in register $t0.

This instruction can also be represented as fields of binary numbers as opposed to decimal:

000000	10001	10010	01000	00000	100000
6 bits	5 bits	5 bits	5 bits	5 bits	6 bits

Instruction format: A form of representation of an instruction composed of fields of binary numbers.

Machine language: Binary representation used for communication within a computer system.

Hexadecimal	Binary	Hexadecimal	Binary	Hexadecimal	Binary	Hexadecimal	Binary
0_{hex}	0000_{two}	4_{hex}	0100_{two}	8_{hex}	1000_{two}	c_{hex}	1100_{two}
1_{hex}	0001_{two}	5_{hex}	0101_{two}	9_{hex}	1001_{two}	d_{hex}	1101_{two}
2_{hex}	0010_{two}	6_{hex}	0110_{two}	a_{hex}	1010_{two}	e_{hex}	1110_{two}
3_{hex}	0011_{two}	7_{hex}	0111_{two}	b_{hex}	1011_{two}	f_{hex}	1111_{two}

Binary to Hexadecimal and Back

Convert the following hexadecimal and binary numbers into the other base:

$$eca8 \quad 6420_{hex}$$

$$0001 \quad 0011 \; 0101 \quad 0111 \; 1001 \quad 1011 \quad 1101 \quad 1111_{two}$$

$$eca8 \quad 6420_{hex}$$

$$1110 \; 1100 \; 1010 \; 1000 \; 0110 \; 0100 \; 0010 \; 0000_{two}$$

And then the other direction:

$$0001 \; 0011 \; 0101 \quad 0111 \; 1001 \; 1011 \; 1101 \; 1111_{two}$$

$$1357 \quad 9bdf_{hex}$$

MIPS Fields

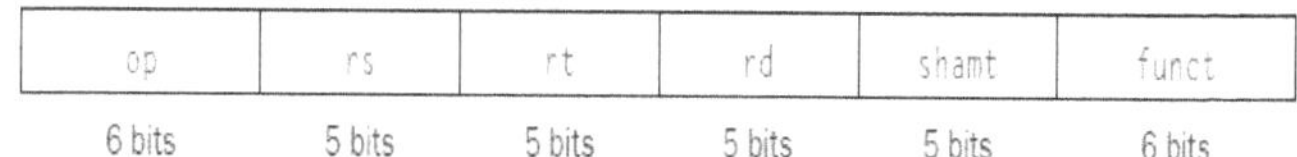

Here is the meaning of each name of the fields in MIPS instructions:

- op: Basic operation of the instruction, traditionally called the opcode.
- rs: The first register source operand.
- rt: The second register source operand.
- rd: The register destination operand. It gets the result of the operation.
- shamt: Shift amount. (Section 2.6 explains shift instructions and this term; it will not be used until then, and hence the field contains zero in this section.)
- funct: Function. This field, often called the function code, selects the specific variant of the operation in the op field.

Design Principle 3: Good Design Demands Good Compromises

The compromise chosen by the MIPS designers is to keep all instructions the same length, thereby requiring different kinds of instruction formats for different kinds of instructions. For example, the format above is called R-type (for register) or R-format.

A second type of instruction format is called I-type (for immediate) or I-format and is used by the immediate and data transfer instructions. The fields of I-format are

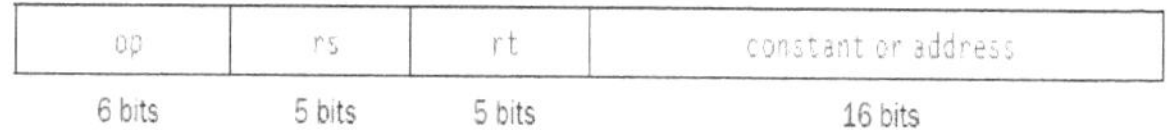

Instruction	Format	op	rs	rt	rd	shamt	funct	address
add	R	0	reg	reg	reg	0	32_{ten}	n.a.
sub (subtract)	R	0	reg	reg	reg	0	34_{ten}	n.a.
add immediate	I	8_{ten}	reg	reg	n.a.	n.a.	n.a.	constant
lw (load word)	I	35_{ten}	reg	reg	n.a.	n.a.	n.a.	address
sw (store word)	I	43_{ten}	reg	reg	n.a.	n.a.	n.a.	address

Translating MIPS Assembly Language into Machine Language

We can now take an example all the way from what the programmer writes to what the computer executes. If $t1 has the base of the array A and $s2 corresponds to h, the assignment statement

$$A[300] = h + A[300];$$

Is compiled into:

```
lw $t0,1200($t1) # Temporary reg $t0 gets A[300]
add $t0,$s2,$t0  # Temporary reg $t0 gets h + A[300]
sw $t0,1200($t1) # Stores h + A[300] back into A[300]
```

What is the MIPS machine language code for these three instructions?

For convenience, let's first represent the machine language instructions using decimal numbers.

Op	rs	rt	rd	address/shamt	funct
35	9	8		1200	
0	18	8	8	0	32
43	9	8		1200	

The lw instruction is identified by 35 in the first field (op). The base register 9 ($t1) is specified in the second field (rs), and the destination register 8 ($t0) is specified in the third field (rt). The off set to select A[300] (1200 = 300 *4) is found in the final field (address).

The add instruction that follows is specified with 0 in the first field (op) and 32 in the last field (funct). The three register operands (18, 8, and 8) are found in the second, third, and fourth fields and correspond to $s2, $t0, and $t0.

The sw instruction is identified with 43 in the first field. The rest of this final instruction is identical to the lw instruction.

Since $1200_{ten} = 0000\ 0100\ 1011\ 0000_{two}$, the binary equivalent to the decimal form is:

Note the similarity of the binary representations of the first and last instructions. The only difference is in the third bit from the left, which is highlighted here.

Name	Format	Example						Comments
add	R	0	18	19	17	0	32	add $s1,$s2,$s3
sub	R	0	18	19	17	0	34	sub $s1,$s2,$s3
addi	I	8	18	17	100			addi $s1,$s2,100
lw	I	35	18	17	100			lw $s1,100($s2)
sw	I	43	18	17	100			sw $s1,100($s2)
Field size		6 bits	5 bits	5 bits	5 bits	5 bits	6 bits	All MIPS instructions are 32 bits long
R-format	R	op	rs	rt	rd	shamt	funct	Arithmetic instruction format
I-format	I	op	rs	rt	address			Data transfer format

1.12. Logical Operations

The first class of such operations is called *shift s*. They move all the bits in a word to the left or right, filling the emptied bits with 0s. For example, if register $s0 contained

$$0000\ 0000\ 0000\ 0000\ 0000\ 0000\ 0000\ 1001_{two} = 9_{ten}$$

And the instruction to shift left by 4 was executed, the new value would be:

$$0000\ 0000\ 0000\ 0000\ 0000\ 0000\ 1001\ 0000_{two} = 144_{ten}$$

The dual of a shift left is a shift right. The actual name of the two MIPS shift instructions are called *shift left logical* (sll) and *shift right logical* (srl). The following instruction performs the operation above, assuming that the original value was in register $s0 and the result should go in register $t2:

sll $t2,$s0,4 # reg $t2 = reg $s0 << 4 bits

Used in shift instructions,

It stands for *shift amount*. Hence, the machine language version of the instruction above is,

op	rs	rt	rd	shamt	funct
0	0	16	10	4	0

The encoding of sll is 0 in both the op and funct fields, rd contains 10 (register $t2), rt contains 16 (register $s0), and shamt contains 4. The rs field is unused and thus is set to 0.

Shifting left by *i* bits gives the same result as multiplying by 2*i*, just as shifting a decimal number by *i* digits is equivalent to multiplying by 10*i*. For example, the above sll shift s by 4, which gives the same result as multiplying by 24 or 16. The first bit pattern above represents 9, and 9 *16 = 144, the value of the second bit pattern.

AND A logical bitby-bit operation with two operands that calculates a 1 only if there is a 1 in *both* operands.

AND is a bit by- bit operation that leaves a 1 in the result only if both bits of the operands are 1. For example, if register $t2 contains

$$0000\ 0000\ 0000\ 0000\ 0000\ 1101\ 1100\ 0000_{two}$$

And register $t1 contains

$$0000\ 0000\ 0000\ 0000\ 0011\ 1100\ 0000\ 0000_{two}$$

Then, after executing the MIPS instruction.

And

$$\$t0,\$t1,\$t2 \#\ reg\ \$t0 = reg\ \$t1\ \&\ reg\ \$t2$$

The value of register $t0 would be

$$0000\ 0000\ 0000\ 0000\ 0000\ 1100\ 0000\ 0000_{two}$$

As you can see, AND can apply a bit pattern to a set of bits to force 0s where there is a 0 in the bit pattern. Such a bit pattern in conjunction with AND is traditionally called a *mask*, since the mask "conceals" some bits.

OR A logical bit-by-bit operation with two operands that calculates a 1 if there is a 1 in *either* operand. It is a bit-by-bit operation that places a 1 in the result if *either* operand bit is a 1. To elaborate, if the registers $t1 and $t2 are unchanged from the preceding example, the result of the MIPS instruction or

$$\$t0,\ \$t1,\$t2 \#\ reg\ \$t0 = reg\ \$t1\ |\ reg\ \$t2$$

is this value in register $t0:

$$0000\ 0000\ 0000\ 0000\ 0011\ 1101\ 1100\ 0000_{two}$$

NOT A logical bit-by-bit operation with one operand that inverts the bits; that is, it replaces every 1 with a 0, and every 0 with a 1. **NOT** takes one operand and places a 1 in the result if one operand bit is a 0, and vice versa.

NOR A logical bit-by-bit operation with two operands that calculates the NOT of the OR of the two operands. That is, it calculates a 1 only if there is a 0 in *both* operands.

If one operand is zero, then it is equivalent to NOT: A NOR 0 =NOT (A OR 0) = NOT (A).

If the register $t1 is unchanged from the preceding example and register $t3 has the value 0, the result of the MIPS instruction.

$$nor\ \$t0,\$t1,\$t3\ \#\ reg\ \$t0 = \sim (reg\ \$t1\ |\ reg\ \$t3)$$

is this value in register $t0:

$$1111\ 1111\ 1111\ 1111\ 1100\ 0011\ 1111\ 1111_{two}$$

1.13. Control Operations

Decision making is commonly represented in programming languages using the *if* statement, sometimes combined with *go to* statements and labels. MIPS assembly language includes two decision-making instructions, similar to an *if* statement with a *go to*. The first instruction is beq register1, register2, L1.

This instruction means go to the statement labeled L1 if the value in register1 equals the value in register2. The mnemonic beq stands for *branch if equal.*

The second instruction is bne register1, register2, L1

It means go to the statement labeled L1 if the value in register1 does *not* equal the value in register2. The mnemonic bne stands for *branch if not equal.* These two instructions are traditionally called **conditional branches**.

Conditional branch An instruction that requires the comparison of two values and that allows for a subsequent transfer of control to a new address in the program based on the outcome of the comparison.

Compiling if-Then-Else into Conditional Branches

In the following code segment, f, g, h, i, and j are variables. If the five variables f through j correspond to the five registers $s0 through $s4, what is the compiled MIPS code for this C *if* statement?

$$\text{if (i == j) f = g + h; else f = g - h;}$$

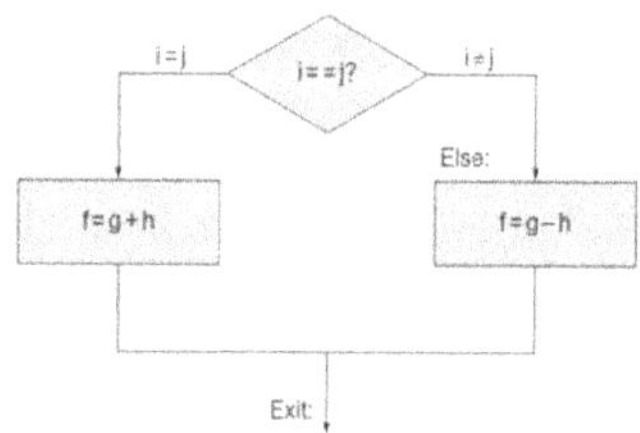

The first expression compares for equality, so it would seem that we would want the branch if registers are equal instruction (beq). In general, the code will be more efficient if we test for the opposite condition to branch over the code that performs the subsequent *then* part of the *if* (the label Else is defined below) and so we use the branch if registers are *not* equal instruction (bne):

bne $s3,$s4,Else   # go to Else if i ≠ j

The next assignment statement performs a single operation, and if all the operands are allocated to registers, it is just one instruction:

add $s0,$s1,$s2 # f = g + h (skipped if i ≠ j)

We now need to go to the end of the *if* statement. This example introduces another kind of branch, oft en called an *unconditional branch*. This instruction says that the processor always follows the branch. To distinguish between conditional and unconditional branches, the MIPS name for this type of instruction is *jump*, abbreviated as j (the label Exit is defined below).

j Exit   # go to Exit

The assignment statement in the *else* portion of the *if* statement can again be compiled into a single instruction. We just need to append the label Else to this instruction. We also show the label Exit that is aft er this instruction, showing the end of the *if-then-else* compiled code:

Else: sub $s0,$s1,$s2 # f = g – h (skipped if i = j)

Exit:

Loops

Decisions are important both for choosing between two alternatives—found in *if* statements—and for iterating a computation—found in loops. The same assembly instructions are the building blocks for both cases.

Compiling a while Loop in C

Here is a traditional loop in C:

while (save[i] == k)
    i += 1;

Assume that i and k correspond to registers $s3 and $s5 and the base of the array save is in $s6. What is the MIPS assembly code corresponding to this C segment?

The first step is to load save[i] into a temporary register. Before we can load save[i] into a temporary register, we need to have its address. Before we can add i to the base of array save to form the address, we must multiply the index i by 4 due to the byte addressing problem. Fortunately, we can use shift left logical, since shifting left by 2 bits multiplies by 2^2 or 4. We need to add the label Loop to it so that we can branch back to that instruction at the end of the loop:

Loop: sll $t1,$s3,2 # Temp reg $t1 = i * 4

To get the address of save[i], we need to add $t1 and the base of save in $s6:

add $t1,$t1,$s6   # $t1 = address of save[i]

Now we can use that address to load save[i] into a temporary register:

lw $t0,0($t1) # Temp reg $t0 = save[i]

The next instruction performs the loop test, exiting if save[i] ≠ k:

bne $t0,$s5, Exit # go to Exit if save[i] ≠ k

The next instruction adds 1 to i:

addi $s3,$s3,1 # i = i + 1

The end of the loop branches back to the *while* test at the top of the loop. We just add the Exit label after it, and we're done:

j Loop # go to Loop

Exit:

basic block A sequence of instructions without branches (except possibly at the end) and without branch targets or branch labels (except possibly at the beginning). The test for equality or inequality is probably the most popular test, but sometimes it is useful to see if a variable is less than another variable. For example, a *for* loop may want to test to see if the index variable is less than 0. Such comparisons are accomplished in MIPS assembly language with an instruction that compares two registers and sets a third register to 1 if the first is less than the second; otherwise, it is set to 0. The MIPS instruction is called *set on less than,* or slt.

For example,

slt $t0, $s3, $s4   # $t0 = 1 if $s3 < $s4

Means that register $t0 is set to 1 if the value in register $s3 is less than the value in register $s4; otherwise, register $t0 is set to 0.

Constant operands are popular in comparisons, so there is an immediate version of the set on less than instruction. To test if register $s2 is less than the constant 10, we can just write

slti $t0,$s2,10 # $t0 = 1 if $s2 < 10

Signed Versus Unsigned Comparison

Suppose register $s0 has the binary number

1111 1111 1111 1111 1111 1111 1111 1111$_{two}$

and that register $s1 has the binary number

0000 0000 0000 0000 0000 0000 0000 0001$_{two}$

What are the values of registers $t0 and $t1 aft er these two instructions?

slt $t0, $s0, $s1# signed comparison

sltu $t1, $s0, $s1 # unsigned comparison

The value in register $s0 represents -1_{ten} if it is an integer and $4,294,967,295_{ten}$

if it is an unsigned integer. The value in register $s1 represents 1_{ten} in either case. Then register $t0 has the value 1, since $-1_{ten} < 1_{ten}$, and register $t1 has the value 0, since $4,294,967,295_{ten} > 1_{ten}$.

Treating signed numbers as if they were unsigned gives us a low cost way of checking if $0 <= x < y$, which matches the index out-of-bounds check for arrays. The key is that negative integers in two's complement notation look like large numbers in unsigned notation; that is, the most significant bit is a sign bit in the former notation but a large part of the number in the latter. Thus, an unsigned comparison of $x < y$ also checks if x is negative as well as if x is less than y.

Bounds Check Shortcut

Use this shortcut to reduce an index-out-of-bounds check: jump to IndexOutOfBounds if $s1 $\geq$ $t2 or if $s1 is negative.

The checking code just uses u to do both checks:

sltu $t0,$s1,$t2 # $t0=0 if $s1>=length or $s1<0

beq $t0,$zero,IndexOutOfBounds   #if bad, goto Error

Case/Switch Statement

Most programming languages have a *case* or *switch* statement that allows the programmer to select one of many alternatives depending on a single value. The simplest way to implement *switch* is via a sequence of conditional tests, turning the *switch* statement into a chain of *if-then-else* statements.

Sometimes the alternatives may be more efficiently encoded as a table of addresses of alternative instruction sequences, called a **jump address table** or **jump table**, and the program needs only to index into the table and then jump to the appropriate sequence. The jump table is then just an array of words containing addresses that correspond to labels in the code. The program loads the appropriate entry from the jump table into a register. It then needs to jump using the address in the register. To support such situations, computers like MIPS include a *jump register* instruction (jr), meaning an unconditional jump to the address specified in a register. Then it jumps to the proper address using this instruction.

1.14. Addressing and Addressing Modes

Addressing mode One of several addressing regimes delimited by their varied use of operands and/or addresses. The MIPS addressing modes are the following:

1. *Immediate addressing,* where the operand is a constant within the instruction itself
2. *Register addressing,* where the operand is a register
3. *Base* or *displacement addressing,* where the operand is at the memory location whose address is the sum of a register and a constant in the instruction
4. *PC-relative addressing,* where the branch address is the sum of the PC and a constant in the instruction
5. *Pseudodirect addressing,* where the jump address is the 26 bits of the instruction concatenated with the upper bits of the PC.

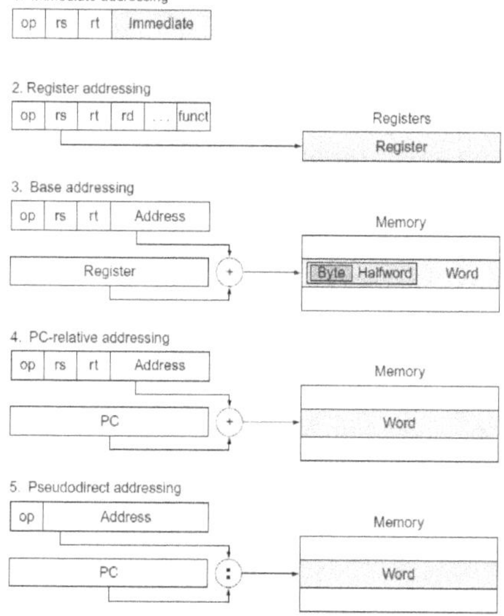

The operands are shaded in color. The operand of mode 3 is in memory, whereas the operand for mode 2 is a register. Note that versions of load and store access bytes, halfwords, or words. For mode 1, the operand is 16 bits of the instruction itself. Modes 4 and 5 address instructions in memory, with mode 4 adding a 16-bit address shifted left 2 bits to the PC and mode 5 concatenating a 26-bit address shifted left 2 bits with the 4 upper bits of the PC. Note that a single operation can use more than one addressing mode. Add, for example, uses both immediate (addi). and register (add) addressing.

UNIT II

ARITHMETIC OPERATIONS

ALU - Addition and subtraction – Multiplication – Division – Floating Point operations – Sub word parallelism.

2.1.   ALU

Addition is just what you would expect in computers. Digits are added bit by bit from right to left, with carries passed to the next digit to the left, just as you would do by hand. Subtraction uses addition: the appropriate operand is simply negated before being added.

Binary Addition and Subtraction

Let's try adding 6ten to 7ten in binary and then subtracting 6ten from 7ten in binary.

$$
\begin{array}{rll}
 & 0000\ 0000\ 0000\ 0000\ 0000\ 0000\ 0000\ 0111_{two} & = 7_{ten} \\
+ & 0000\ 0000\ 0000\ 0000\ 0000\ 0000\ 0000\ 0110_{two} & = 6_{ten} \\
\hline
= & 0000\ 0000\ 0000\ 0000\ 0000\ 0000\ 0000\ 1101_{two} & = 13_{ten}
\end{array}
$$

Subtracting 6ten from 7ten can be done directly:

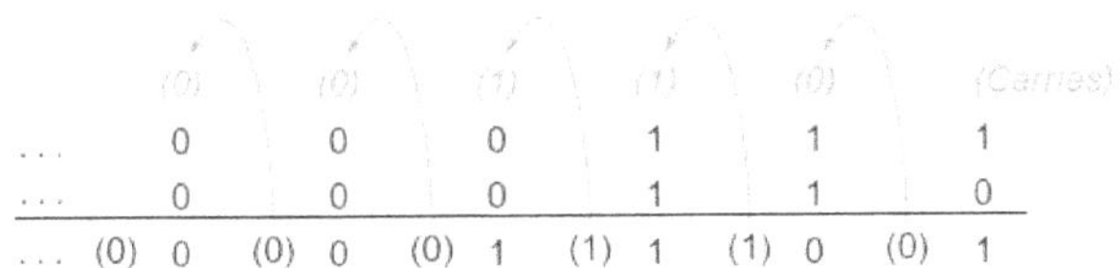

The rightmost bit adds 1 to 0, resulting in the sum of this bit being 1 and the carry out from this bit being 0. Hence, the operation for the second digit to the right is 0 +1 +1. This generates a 0 for this sum bit and a carry out of 1. The third digit is the sum of 1 +1 +1, resulting in a carry out of 1 and a sum bit of 1. The fourth bit is 1+0+ 0, yielding a 1 sum and no carry.

$$
\begin{array}{rll}
 & 0000\ 0000\ 0000\ 0000\ 0000\ 0000\ 0000\ 0111_{two} & = 7_{ten} \\
- & 0000\ 0000\ 0000\ 0000\ 0000\ 0000\ 0000\ 0110_{two} & = 6_{ten} \\
\hline
= & 0000\ 0000\ 0000\ 0000\ 0000\ 0000\ 0000\ 0001_{two} & = 1_{ten}
\end{array}
$$

Or via addition using the two's complement representation of -6:

$$
\begin{array}{rll}
 & 0000\ 0000\ 0000\ 0000\ 0000\ 0000\ 0000\ 0111_{two} & = 7_{ten} \\
+ & 1111\ 1111\ 1111\ 1111\ 1111\ 1111\ 1111\ 1010_{two} & = -6_{ten} \\
\hline
= & 0000\ 0000\ 0000\ 0000\ 0000\ 0000\ 0000\ 0001_{two} & = 1_{ten}
\end{array}
$$

When adding operands with different signs, overflow cannot occur. The reason is the sum must be no larger than one of the operands.

For example, -10 + 4= -6. Since the operands fit in 32 bits and the sum is no larger than an operand, the sum must fit in 32 bits as well. Therefore, no overflow can occur when adding positive and negative operands.

There are similar restrictions to the occurrence of overflow during subtract, but it's just the opposite principle: when the signs of the operands are the *same*, overflow cannot occur. To see this, remember that $c - a = c + (-a)$ because we subtract by negating the second operand and then add. Therefore, when we subtract operands of the same sign we end up by *adding* operands of *different* signs. From the prior paragraph, we know that overflow cannot occur in this case either.

Overflow occurs in subtraction when we subtract a negative number from a positive number and get a negative result, or when we subtract a positive number from a negative number and get a positive result. Such a ridiculous result means a borrow occurred from the sign bit.

Overflow Conditions for Addition and Subtraction

Operation	Operand A	Operand B	Result indicating overflow
$A + B$	≥ 0	≥ 0	< 0
$A + B$	< 0	< 0	≥ 0
$A - B$	≥ 0	< 0	< 0
$A - B$	< 0	≥ 0	≥ 0

The MIPS solution is to have two kinds of arithmetic instructions to recognize the two choices:

- Add (add), add immediate (addi), and subtract (sub) cause exceptions on overflow.
- Add unsigned (addu), add immediate unsigned (addiu), and subtract unsigned (subu) do *not* cause exceptions on overflow.

Because C ignores overflows, the MIPS C compilers will always generate the unsigned versions of the arithmetic instructions addu, addiu, and subu, no matter what the type of the variables. The MIPS Fortran compilers, however, pick the appropriate arithmetic instructions, depending on the type of the operands.

Arithmetic Logic Unit (ALU) Hardware that performs addition, subtraction, and usually logical operations such as AND and OR. **Exception** Also called **interrupt** on many computers. An unscheduled event that disrupts program execution; used to detect overflow. **Interrupt** An exception that comes from outside of the processor. MIPS includes a register called the *exception program counter* (EPC) to contain the address of the instruction that caused the exception. The instruction *move from system control* (mfc0) is used to copy EPC into a general-purpose register so that MIPS soft ware has the option of returning to the off ending instruction via a jump register instruction.

2.2.   Multiplication

First, let's review the multiplication of decimal numbers in longhand to remind ourselves of the steps of multiplication and the names of the operands. For reasons that will become clear shortly, we limit this decimal example to using only the digits 0 and 1. Multiplying 1000ten by 1001ten:

$$
\begin{array}{lr}
\text{Multiplicand} & 1000_{ten} \\
\text{Multiplier} \quad \times & 1001_{ten} \\
\hline
& 1000 \\
& 0000 \\
& 0000 \\
& 1000 \\
\hline
\text{Product} & 1001000_{ten}
\end{array}
$$

The first operand is called the *multiplicand* and the second the *multiplier*.

The final result is called the *product.* As you may recall, the algorithm learned in grammar school is to take the digits of the multiplier one at a time from right to left , multiplying the multiplicand by the single digit of the multiplier, and shifting the intermediate product one digit to the left of the earlier intermediate products.

The first observation is that the number of digits in the product is considerably larger than the number in either the multiplicand or the multiplier. In fact, if we ignore the sign bits, the length of the multiplication of an n-bit multiplicand and an m-bit multiplier is a product that is $n + m$ bits long. That is, $n + m$ bits are required to represent all possible products. Hence, like add, multiply must cope with overflow because we frequently want a 32-bit product as the result of multiplying two 32-bit numbers.

In this example, we restricted the decimal digits to 0 and 1. With only two choices, each step of the multiplication is simple:

1. Just place a copy of the multiplicand (1 * multiplicand) in the proper place if the multiplier digit is a 1.
2. Place 0 (0 *multiplicand) in the proper place if the digit is 0.

Although the decimal example above happens to use only 0 and 1, multiplication of binary numbers must always use 0 and 1, and thus always offers only these two choices.

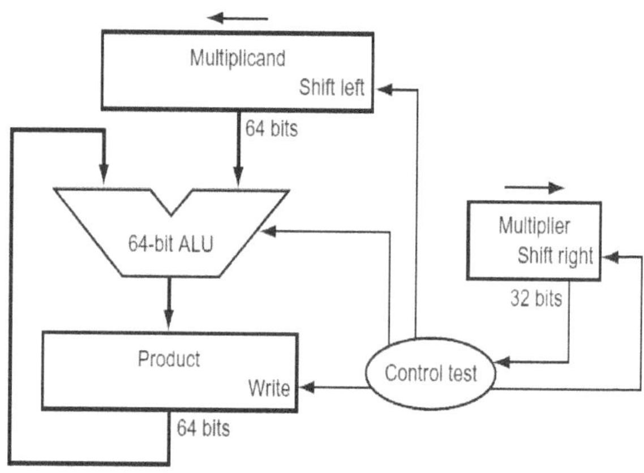

First Version of the Multiplication Hardware

The Multiplicand register, ALU, and Product register are all 64 bits wide, with only the Multiplier register containing 32 bits.

The 32-bit multiplicand starts in the right half of the Multiplicand register and is shifted left 1 bit on each step. The multiplier is shifted in the opposite direction at each step. The algorithm starts with the product initialized to 0. Control decides when to shift the Multiplicand and Multiplier registers and when to write new values into the Product register.

Sequential Version of the Multiplication Algorithm and Hardware

Let's assume that the multiplier is in the 32-bit Multiplier register and that the 64-bit Product register is initialized to 0. From the paper-and-pencil example above, it's clear that we will need to move the multiplicand left one digit each step, as it may be added to the intermediate products. Over 32 steps, a 32-bit multiplicand would move 32 bits to the left. Hence, we need a 64-bit Multiplicand register, initialized with the 32-bit multiplicand in the right half and zero in the left half. This register is then shifted left 1 bit each step to align the multiplicand with the sum being accumulated in the 64-bit Product register.

The least significant bit of the multiplier (Multiplier0) determines whether the multiplicand is added to the Product register. The left shift in step 2 has the effect of moving the intermediate operands to the left, just as when multiplying with paper and pencil. The shift right in step 3 gives us the next bit of the multiplier to examine in the following iteration.

These three steps are repeated 32 times to obtain the product. If each step took a clock cycle, this algorithm would require almost 100 clock cycles to multiply two 32-bit numbers. The relative importance of arithmetic operations like multiply varies with the program, but addition and subtraction may be anywhere from 5 to 100 times more popular than multiply. Accordingly, in many applications, multiply can take multiple clock cycles without significantly affecting performance.

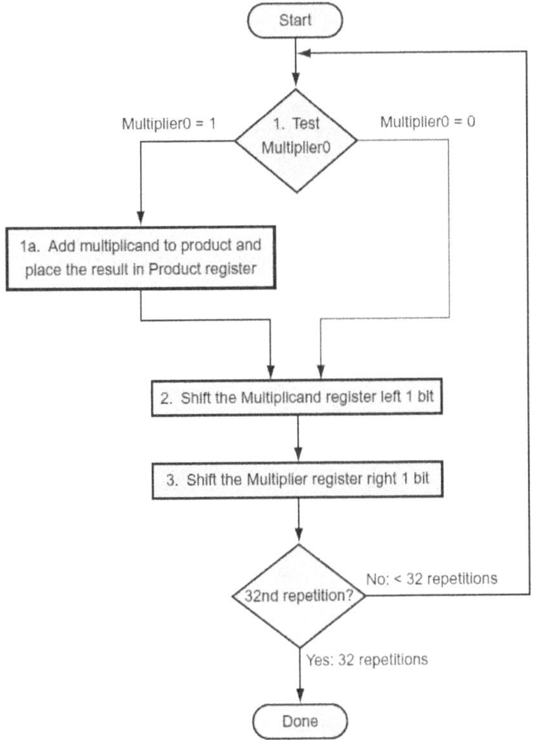

If the least significant bit of the multiplier is 1, add the multiplicand to the product. If not, go to the next step. Shift the multiplicand left and the multiplier right in the next two steps. These three steps are repeated 32 times.

This algorithm and hardware are easily refined to take 1 clock cycle per step.

The speed-up comes from performing the operations in parallel: the multiplier and multiplicand are shifted while the multiplicand is added to the product if the multiplier bit is a 1. The hardware just has to ensure that it tests the right bit of the multiplier and gets the pre shifted version of the multiplicand. The hardware is usually further optimized to halve the width of the adder and registers by noticing where there are unused portions of registers and adders.

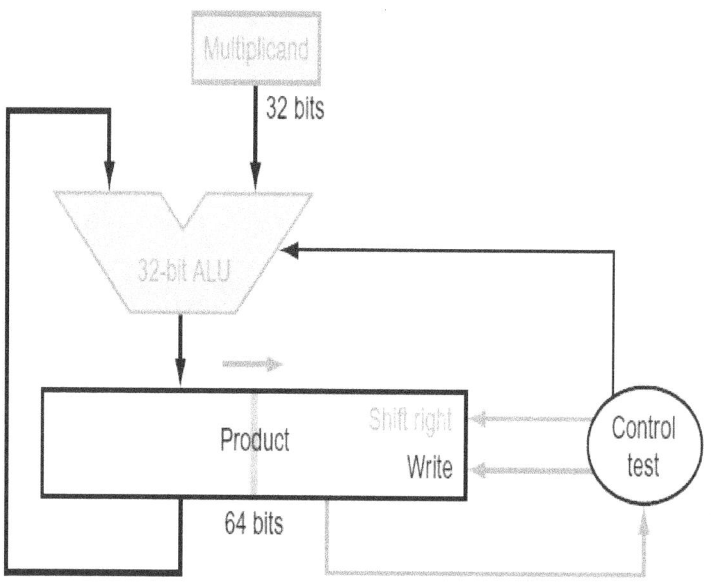

Refined Version of the Multiplication Hardware

The Multiplicand register, ALU, and Multiplier register are all 32 bits wide, with only the Product register left at 64 bits. Now the product is shifted right.

The separate Multiplier register also disappeared. The multiplier is placed instead in the right half of the Product register.

Replacing arithmetic by shift s can also occur when multiplying by constants. Some compilers replace multiplies by short constants with a series of shift s and adds.

Because one bit to the left represents a number twice as large in base 2, shifting the bits left has the same effect as multiplying by a power of 2.

A Multiply Algorithm

Using 4-bit numbers to save space, multiply 2ten *3ten, or 0010two *0011two.

Iteration	Step	Multiplier	Multiplicand	Product
0	Initial values	0011	0000 0010	0000 0000
1	1a: 1 $\Rightarrow$ Prod = Prod + Mcand	0011	0000 0010	0000 0010
	2: Shift left Multiplicand	0011	0000 0100	0000 0010
	3: Shift right Multiplier	0001	0000 0100	0000 0010
2	1a: 1 $\Rightarrow$ Prod = Prod + Mcand	0001	0000 0100	0000 0110
	2: Shift left Multiplicand	0001	0000 1000	0000 0110
	3: Shift right Multiplier	0000	0000 1000	0000 0110
3	1: 0 $\Rightarrow$ No operation	0000	0000 1000	0000 0110
	2: Shift left Multiplicand	0000	0001 0000	0000 0110
	3: Shift right Multiplier	0000	0001 0000	0000 0110
4	1: 0 $\Rightarrow$ No operation	0000	0001 0000	0000 0110
	2: Shift left Multiplicand	0000	0010 0000	0000 0110
	3: Shift right Multiplier	0000	0010 0000	0000 0110

Signed Multiplication

The easiest way to understand how to deal with signed numbers is to first convert the multiplier and multiplicand to positive numbers and then remember the original signs. The algorithms should then be run for 31 iterations, leaving the signs out of the calculation.

It turns out that the last algorithm will work for signed numbers, provided that we remember that we are dealing with numbers that have infinite digits, and we are only representing them with 32 bits.

Hence, the shifting steps would need to extend the sign of the product for signed numbers. When the algorithm completes, the lower word would have the 32-bit product.

Faster Multiplication

Moore's Law has provided so much more in resources that hardware designers can now build much faster multiplication hardware. Whether the multiplicand is to be added or not is known at the beginning of the multiplication by looking at each of the 32 multiplier bits. Faster multiplications are possible by essentially providing one 32-bit adder for each bit of the multiplier: one input is the multiplicand ANDed with a multiplier bit, and the other is the output of a prior adder.

A straightforward approach would be to connect the outputs of adders on the right to the inputs of adders on the left, making a stack of adders 32 high.

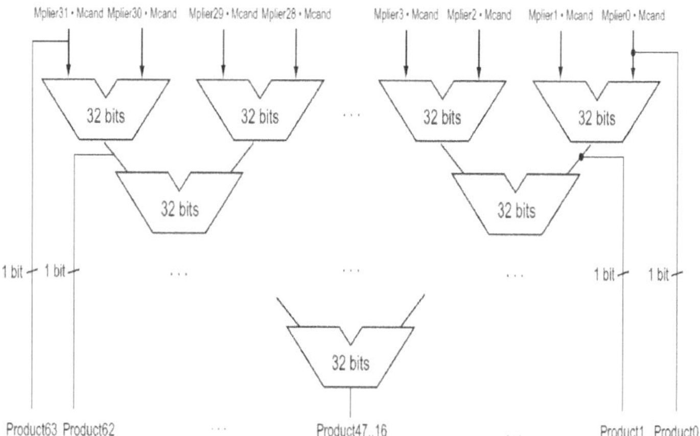

Fast multiplication hardware. Rather than use a single 32-bit adder 31 times, this hardware "unrolls the loop" to use 31 adders and then organizes them to minimize delay.

Multiply in MIPS

MIPS provides a separate pair of 32-bit registers to contain the 64-bit product, called *Hi* and *Lo*. To produce a properly signed or unsigned product, MIPS has two instructions: multiply (mult) and multiply unsigned (multu). To fetch the integer 32-bit product, the programmer uses *move from lo* (mflo). The MIPS assembler generates a pseudo instruction for multiply that specifies three general-purpose registers, generating mflo and mfhi instructions to place the product into registers.

Both MIPS multiply instructions ignore overflow, so it is up to the soft ware to check to see if the product is too big to fi t in 32 bits. There is no overflow if Hi is 0 for multu or the replicated sign of Lo for mult. The instruction *move from hi* (mfhi) can be used to transfer Hi to a general-purpose register to test for overflow.

2.3. Division

The reciprocal operation of multiply is divide, an operation that is even less frequent and even more quirky. It even offers the opportunity to perform a mathematically invalid operation: dividing by 0.

Let's start with an example of long division using decimal numbers to recall the names of the operands and the grammar school division algorithm. For reasons similar to those in the previous section, we limit the decimal digits to just 0 or 1.

The example is dividing 1,001,010ten by 1000ten:

$$
\begin{array}{r}
1001_{ten} \qquad \text{Quotient} \\
\text{Divisor } 1000_{ten} \overline{)\ 1001010_{ten}} \qquad \text{Dividend} \\
-1000 \qquad\qquad \\
\overline{10} \qquad\qquad\quad \\
101 \qquad\qquad\quad \\
1010 \qquad\qquad\quad \\
-1000 \qquad\qquad \\
\overline{10_{ten}} \qquad \text{Remainder}
\end{array}
$$

Dividend A number being divided.

Divisor A number that the dividend is divided by.

Quotient The primary result of a division; a number that when multiplied by the divisor and added to the remainder produces the dividend.

Remainder The secondary result of a division; a number that when added to the product of the quotient and the divisor produces the dividend.

Divide's two operands, called the **dividend** and **divisor**, and the result, called.

Quotient, are accompanied by a second result, called the **remainder**. Here is another way to express the relationship between the components:

Dividend =Quotient *Divisor + Remainder

Where the remainder is smaller than the divisor. Infrequently, programs use the divide instruction just to get the remainder, ignoring the quotient.

Let's assume that both the dividend and the divisor are positive and hence the quotient and the remainder are nonnegative. The division operands and both results are 32-bit values, and we will ignore the sign for now.

A Division Algorithm and Hardware

We start with the 32-bit Quotient register set to 0. Each iteration of the algorithm needs to move the divisor to the right one digit, so we start with the divisor placed in the left half of the 64-bit Divisor register and shift it right 1 bit each step to align it with the dividend. The Remainder register is initialized with the dividend.

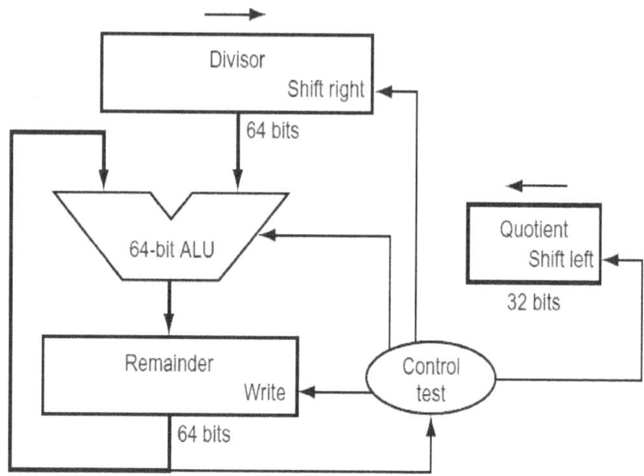

First Version of the Division Hardware

The Divisor register, ALU, and Remainder register are all 64 bits wide, with only the Quotient register being 32 bits. The 32-bit divisor starts in the left half of the Divisor register and is shifted right 1 bit each iteration.

The remainder is initialized with the dividend. Control decides when to shift the Divisor and Quotient registers and when to write the new value into the Remainder register.

If the result is positive, the divisor was smaller or equal to the dividend, so we generate a 1 in the quotient (step 2a). If the result is negative, the next step is to restore the original value by adding the divisor back to the remainder and generate a 0 in the quotient (step 2b). The divisor is shifted right and then we iterate again. The remainder and quotient will be found in their namesake registers aft er the iterations are complete.

A Divide Algorithm

Using a 4-bit version of the algorithm to save pages, let's try dividing 7_{ten} by 2_{ten}, or 0000 0111_{two} by 0010_{two}.

Notice that the test in step 2 of whether the remainder is positive or negative simply tests whether the sign bit of the Remainder register is a 0 or 1. The surprising requirement of this algorithm is that it takes $n + 1$ steps to get the proper quotient and remainder.

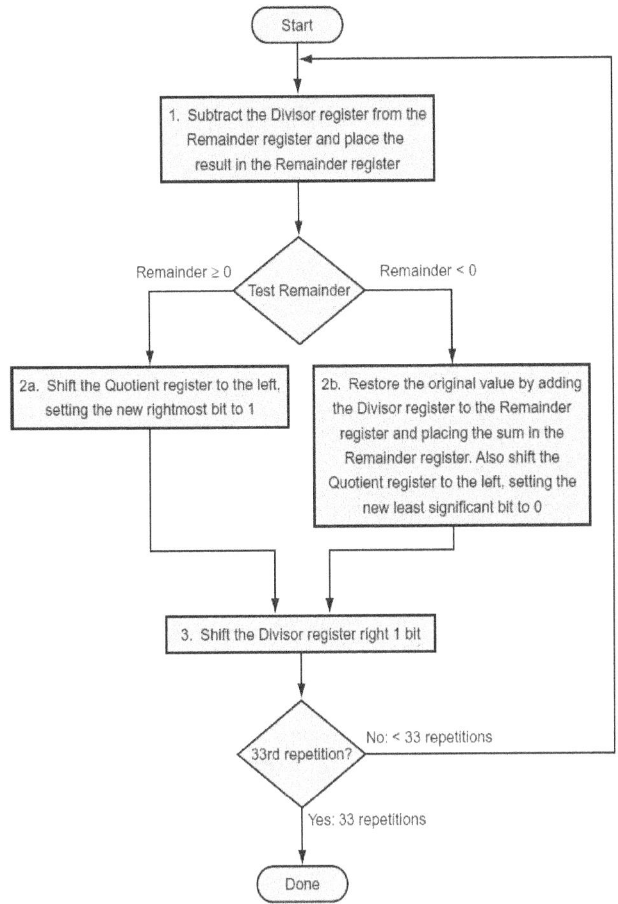

If the remainder is positive, the divisor did go into the dividend, so step 2a generates a 1 in the quotient. A negative remainder after step 1 means that the divisor did not go into the dividend, so step 2b generates a 0 in the quotient and adds the divisor to the remainder, thereby reversing the subtraction of step 1. The final shift, in step 3, aligns the divisor properly, relative to the dividend for the next iteration. These steps are repeated 33 times.

This algorithm and hardware can be refined to be faster and cheaper. The speedup comes from shifting the operands and the quotient simultaneously with the subtraction. This refinement halves the width of the adder and registers by noticing where there are unused portions of registers and adders.

Iteration	Step	Quotient	Divisor	Remainder
0	Initial values	0000	0010 0000	0000 0111
1	1: Rem = Rem – Div	0000	0010 0000	1110 0111
	2b: Rem < 0 $\Rightarrow$ +Div, sll Q, Q0 = 0	0000	0010 0000	0000 0111
	3: Shift Div right	0000	0001 0000	0000 0111
2	1: Rem = Rem – Div	0000	0001 0000	1111 0111
	2b: Rem < 0 $\Rightarrow$ +Div, sll Q, Q0 = 0	0000	0001 0000	0000 0111
	3: Shift Div right	0000	0000 1000	0000 0111
3	1: Rem = Rem – Div	0000	0000 1000	1111 1111
	2b: Rem < 0 $\Rightarrow$ +Div, sll Q, Q0 = 0	0000	0000 1000	0000 0111
	3: Shift Div right	0000	0000 0100	0000 0111
4	1: Rem = Rem – Div	0000	0000 0100	0000 0011
	2a: Rem $\geq$ 0 $\Rightarrow$ sll Q, Q0 = 1	0001	0000 0100	0000 0011
	3: Shift Div right	0001	0000 0010	0000 0011
5	1: Rem = Rem – Div	0001	0000 0010	0000 0001
	2a: Rem $\geq$ 0 $\Rightarrow$ sll Q, Q0 = 1	0011	0000 0010	0000 0001
	3: Shift Div right	0011	0000 0001	0000 0001

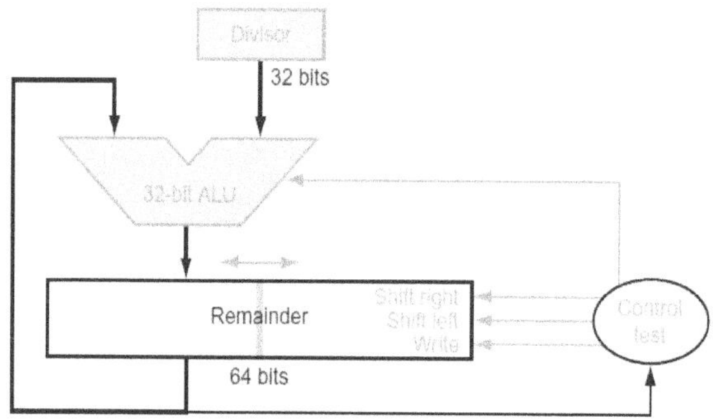

An Improved Version of the Division Hardware

The Divisor register, ALU, and

Quotient register are all 32 bits wide, with only the Remainder register left at 64 bits. This version also combines the Quotient register with the right half of the Remainder register.

Signed Division

The simplest solution is to remember the signs of the divisor and dividend and then negate the quotient if the signs disagree.

The one complication of signed division is that we must also set the sign of the remainder. Remember that the following equation must always hold:

$$Dividend = Quotient * Divisor + Remainder$$

To understand how to set the sign of the remainder, let's look at the example of dividing all the combinations of ±7ten by ±2ten. The first case is easy:

$$+7 \div +2: \text{Quotient} = +3, +\text{Remainder} = +1$$

Checking the results:

$$+7 = 3 \times 2 + (+1) = 6 + 1$$

If we change the sign of the dividend, the quotient must change as well:

$$+7 = 3 \times 2: \text{Quotient} = -3$$

Rewriting our basic formula to calculate the remainder:

$$\text{Remainder} = (\text{Dividend} - \text{Quotient} \times \text{Divisor}) = -7 - (-3x + 2)$$

$$= -7 - (-6) = -1$$

So,

$$-7 \div +2: \text{Quotient} = -3, \text{Remainder} = -1$$

Checking the results again:

$$-7 = -3 \times 2 + (-1) = -6 - 1$$

The reason the answer isn't a quotient of -4 and a remainder of -1, which would also fit this formula, is that the absolute value of the quotient would then change depending on the sign of the dividend and the divisor! Clearly, if

$$-(x \div y) \neq (-x) \div y$$

programming would be an even greater challenge. This anomalous behavior is avoided by following the rule that the dividend and remainder must have the same signs, no matter what the signs of the divisor and quotient. We calculate the other combinations by following the same rule:

$$+7 \div -2: \text{Quotient} = -3, \text{Remainder} = +1$$

$$-7 \div -2: \text{Quotient} = +3, \text{Remainder} = -1$$

Faster Division

Moore's Law applies to division hardware as well as multiplication, so we would like to be able to speed up division by throwing hardware at it. We used many adders to speed up multiply, but we cannot do the same trick for divide. The reason is that we need to know the sign of the difference before we can perform the next step of the algorithm, whereas with multiply we could calculate the 32 partial products immediately. There are techniques to produce more than one bit of the quotient per step.

The *SRT division* technique tries to **predict** several quotient bits per step, using a table lookup based on the upper bits of the dividend and remainder. It relies on subsequent steps to correct wrong predictions. A typical value today is 4 bits. The key is guessing the value to subtract. With binary division, there is only a single choice. These algorithms use 6 bits from the remainder and 4 bits from the divisor to index a table that determines the guess for each step.

Divide in MIPS

Category	Instruction	Example		Meaning	Comments
Arithmetic	add	add	$s1,$s2,$s3	$s1 = $s2 + $s3	Three operands; overflow detected
	subtract	sub	$s1,$s2,$s3	$s1 = $s2 − $s3	Three operands; overflow detected
	add immediate	addi	$s1,$s2,100	$s1 = $s2 + 100	+ constant; overflow detected
	add unsigned	addu	$s1,$s2,$s3	$s1 = $s2 + $s3	Three operands; overflow undetected
	subtract unsigned	subu	$s1,$s2,$s3	$s1 = $s2 − $s3	Three operands; overflow undetected
	add immediate unsigned	addiu	$s1,$s2,100	$s1 = $s2 + 100	+ constant; overflow undetected
	move from coprocessor register	mfc0	$s1,$epc	$s1 = $epc	Copy Exception PC + special regs
	multiply	mult	$s2,$s3	Hi, Lo = $s2 × $s3	64-bit signed product in Hi, Lo
	multiply unsigned	multu	$s2,$s3	Hi, Lo = $s2 × $s3	64-bit unsigned product in Hi, Lo
	divide	div	$s2,$s3	Lo = $s2 / $s3, Hi = $s2 mod $s3	Lo = quotient, Hi = remainder
	divide unsigned	divu	$s2,$s3	Lo = $s2 / $s3, Hi = $s2 mod $s3	Unsigned quotient and remainder
	move from Hi	mfhi	$s1	$s1 = Hi	Used to get copy of Hi
	move from Lo	mflo	$s1	$s1 = Lo	Used to get copy of Lo
Data transfer	load word	lw	$s1,20($s2)	$s1 = Memory[$s2 + 20]	Word from memory to register
	store word	sw	$s1,20($s2)	Memory[$s2 + 20] = $s1	Word from register to memory
	load half unsigned	lhu	$s1,20($s2)	$s1 = Memory[$s2 + 20]	Halfword memory to register
	store half	sh	$s1,20($s2)	Memory[$s2 + 20] = $s1	Halfword register to memory
	load byte unsigned	lbu	$s1,20($s2)	$s1 = Memory[$s2 + 20]	Byte from memory to register
	store byte	sb	$s1,20($s2)	Memory[$s2 + 20] = $s1	Byte from register to memory
	load linked word	ll	$s1,20($s2)	$s1 = Memory[$s2 + 20]	Load word as 1st half of atomic swap
	store conditional word	sc	$s1,20($s2)	Memory[$s2+20]=$s1 ; $s1=0 or 1	Store word as 2nd half atomic swap
	load upper immediate	lui	$s1,100	$s1 = 100 * 2^{16}	Loads constant in upper 16 bits
Logical	AND	AND	$s1,$s2,$s3	$s1 = $s2 & $s3	Three reg. operands; bit-by-bit AND
	OR	OR	$s1,$s2,$s3	$s1 = $s2 | $s3	Three reg. operands; bit-by-bit OR
	NOR	NOR	$s1,$s2,$s3	$s1 = ~ ($s2 |$s3)	Three reg. operands; bit-by-bit NOR
	AND immediate	ANDi	$s1,$s2,100	$s1 = $s2 & 100	Bit-by-bit AND with constant
	OR immediate	ORi	$s1,$s2,100	$s1 = $s2 | 100	Bit-by-bit OR with constant
	shift left logical	sll	$s1,$s2,10	$s1 = $s2 << 10	Shift left by constant
	shift right logical	srl	$s1,$s2,10	$s1 = $s2 >> 10	Shift right by constant
Conditional branch	branch on equal	beq	$s1,$s2,25	if ($s1 == $s2) go to PC + 4 + 100	Equal test; PC-relative branch
	branch on not equal	bne	$s1,$s2,25	if ($s1 != $s2) go to PC + 4 + 100	Not equal test; PC-relative
	set on less than	slt	$s1,$s2,$s3	if ($s2 < $s3) $s1 = 1; else $s1 = 0	Compare less than; two's complement
	set less than immediate	slti	$s1,$s2,100	if ($s2 < 100) $s1 = 1; else $s1 =0	Compare < constant; two's complement
	set less than unsigned	sltu	$s1,$s2,$s3	if ($s2 < $s3) $s1 = 1; else $s1 =0	Compare less than; natural numbers
	set less than immediate unsigned	sltiu	$s1,$s2,100	if ($s2 < 100) $s1 = 1; else $s1 = 0	Compare < constant; natural numbers
Unconditional jump	jump	j	2500	go to 10000	Jump to target address
	jump register	jr	$ra	go to $ra	For switch, procedure return
	jump and link	jal	2500	$ra = PC + 4; go to 10000	For procedure call

The only requirement is a 64-bit register that can shift left or right and a 32-bit ALU that adds or subtracts. Hence, MIPS uses the 32-bit Hi and 32-bit Lo registers for both multiply and divide. As we might expect from the algorithm above, Hi contains the remainder, and Lo contains the quotient aft er the divide instruction completes.

To handle both signed integers and unsigned integers, MIPS has two instructions: *divide* (div) and *divide unsigned* (divu). The MIPS assembler allows divide instructions to specify three registers, generating the mflo or mfhi instructions to place the desired result into a general-purpose register.

MIPS Core Architecture

MIPS divide instructions ignore overflow, so soft ware must determine whether the quotient is too large. In addition to overflow, division can also result in an improper calculation: division by 0. Some computers distinguish these two anomalous events.

MIPS soft ware must check the divisor to discover division by 0 as well as overflow.

2.4. Floating Point Operations

Scientific notation A notation that renders numbers with a single digit to the left of the decimal point.

Normalized A number in floating-point notation that has no leading 0s.

Here are some examples of reals:

$$3.14159265...\text{ ten (pi)}$$
$$2.71828...\text{ ten } (e)$$
$$0.000000001_{ten} \text{ or } 1.0_{ten} \times 10^{-9} \text{ (seconds in a nanosecond)}$$
$$3{,}155{,}760{,}000_{ten} \text{ or } 3.15576_{ten} \times 10^{9} \text{ (seconds in a typical century)}$$

Notice that in the last case, the number didn't represent a small fraction, but it was bigger than we could represent with a 32-bit signed integer. The alternative notation for the last two numbers is called **scientific notation**, which has a single digit to the left of the decimal point. A number in scientific notation that has no leading 0s is called a **normalized** number, which is the usual way to write it. For example, $1.0_{ten} \times 10^{-9}$ is in normalized scientific notation, but $0.1ten *10^{-8}$ and $10.0_{ten} \times 10^{-10}$ are not.

Just as we can show decimal numbers in scientific notation, we can also show binary numbers in scientific notation:

$$1.0_{two} \times 2^{-1}$$

To keep a binary number in normalized form, we need a base that we can increase or decrease by exactly the number of bits the number must be shifted to have one nonzero digit to the left of the decimal point. Only a base of 2 fulfills our need. Since the base is not 10, we also need a new name for decimal point; *binary point* will do fine.

Floating point Computer arithmetic that represents numbers in which the binary point is not fixed.

Computer arithmetic that supports such numbers is called **floating point** because it represents numbers in which the binary point is not fixed, as it is for integers. The programming language C uses the name *fl oat* for such numbers. Just as in scientific notation, numbers are represented as a single nonzero digit to the left of the binary point. In binary, the form is

$$1.xxxxxxxxx\text{two} \times 2^{yyyy}$$

Floating-Point Representation

Fraction The value, generally between 0 and 1, placed in the fraction field. The fraction is also called the *mantissa*.

Exponent In the numerical representation system of floating-point arithmetic, the value that is placed in the exponent field.

Floating-point numbers are usually a multiple of the size of a word. The representation of a MIPS floating-point number is shown below, where s is the sign of the floating-point number (1 meaning negative), *exponent* is the value of the 8-bit exponent field (including the sign of the exponent), and *fraction* is the 23-bit number.

31	30	29	28	27	26	25	24	23	22	21	20	19	18	17	16	15	14	13	12	11	10	9	8	7	6	5	4	3	2	1	0
s	exponent								fraction																						

1 bit   8 bits   23 bits

In general, floating-point numbers are of the form

$$(-1)^{s} \times F \times 2^{E}$$

F involves the value in the fraction field and E involves the value in the exponent Field.

Overflow (floatingpoint) A situation in which a positive exponent becomes too large to fit in the exponent field.

Underflow (floatingpoint) A situation in which a negative exponent becomes too large to fit in the exponent field.

Double precision A floating-point value represented in two 32-bit words.

Single precision A floating-point value represented in a single 32- bit word.

The representation of a double precision floating-point number takes two MIPS words, as shown below, where s is still the sign of the number, *exponent* is the value of the 11-bit exponent field, and *fraction* is the 52-bit number in the fraction field.

31	30	29	28	27	26	25	24	23	22	21	20	19	18	17	16	15	14	13	12	11	10	9	8	7	6	5	4	3	2	1	0
s	exponent												fraction																		

1 bit   11 bits   20 bits

fraction (continued)

32 bits

MIPS double precision allows numbers almost as small as $2.0_{ten} \times 10^{-308}$ and almost as large as $2.0_{ten} \times 10^{308}$. Although double precision does increase the exponent range, its primary advantage is its greater precision because of the much larger fraction.

These formats go beyond MIPS. They are part of the *IEEE 754 floating-point standard*, found in virtually every computer invented since 1980. This standard has greatly improved both the ease of porting floating-point programs and the quality of computer arithmetic.

To pack even more bits into the significand, IEEE 754 makes the leading 1-bit of normalized binary numbers implicit. Hence, the number is actually 24 bits long in single precision (implied 1 and a 23-bit fraction), and 53 bits long in double precision (1 + 52). To be precise, we use the term *significand* to represent the 24- or 53-bit number that is 1 plus the fraction, and *fraction* when we mean the 23- or 52-bit number. Since 0 has no leading 1, it is given the reserved exponent value 0 so that the hardware won't attach a leading 1 to it.

Single precision		Double precision		Object represented
Exponent	Fraction	Exponent	Fraction	
0	0	0	0	0
0	Nonzero	0	Nonzero	± denormalized number
1–254	Anything	1–2046	Anything	± floating-point number
255	0	2047	0	± infinity
255	Nonzero	2047	Nonzero	NaN (Not a Number)

EEE 754 encoding of floating-point numbers. A separate sign bit determines the sign.

Thus 00 ... 00two represents 0; the representation of the rest of the numbers uses the form from before with the hidden 1 added:

$$(-1)^S \times (1 + \text{Fraction}) \times 2^E$$

where the bits of the fraction represent a number between 0 and 1 and E specifies the value in the exponent field, to be given in detail shortly. If we number the bits of the fraction from *left to right* s1, s2, s3, ..., then the value is

$$(-1)^S \times (1 + (s1 \times 2^{-1}) + (s2 \times 2^{-2}) + (s3 \times 2^{-3}) + (s4 \times 2^{-4}) + ...) \times 2^E$$

Negative exponents pose a challenge to simplified sorting. If we use two's complement or any other notation in which negative exponents have a 1 in the most significant bit of the exponent field, a negative exponent will look like a big number. For example, $1.0_{two} \times 2^{-1}$ would be represented as

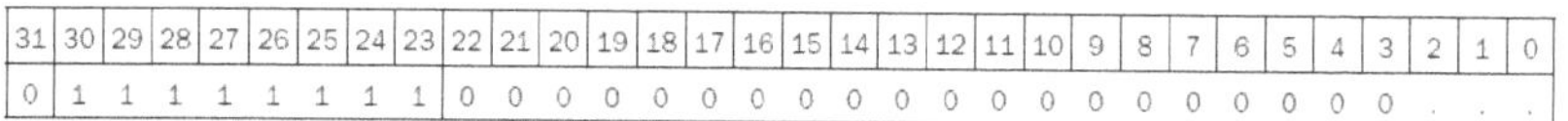

31	30	29	28	27	26	25	24	23	22	21	20	19	18	17	16	15	14	13	12	11	10	9	8	7	6	5	4	3	2	1	0
0	1	1	1	1	1	1	1	1	0	0	0	0	0	0	0	0	0	0	0	0	0	0	0	0	0	0	0	.	.	.	

The value $1.0_{two} \times 2^{-1}$ would look like the smaller binary number

31	30	29	28	27	26	25	24	23	22	21	20	19	18	17	16	15	14	13	12	11	10	9	8	7	6	5	4	3	2	1	0
0	0	0	0	0	0	0	0	1	0	0	0	0	0	0	0	0	0	0	0	0	0	0	0	0	0	0	0	.	.	.	

The desirable notation must therefore represent the most negative exponent as $00 ... 00_{two}$ and the most positive as $11 ... 11_{two}$. This convention is called *biased notation*, with the bias being the number subtracted from the normal, unsigned representation to determine the real value.

IEEE 754 uses a bias of 127 for single precision, so an exponent of -1 is represented by the bit pattern of the value $-1 + 127_{ten}$, or $126_{ten} = 0111\ 1110_{two}$, and +1 is represented by $1 + 127$, or $128_{ten} = 1000\ 0000_{two}$. The exponent bias for double precision is 1023. Biased exponent means that the value represented by a floating-point number is really

$$(-1)^S \times (1 + Fraction) \times 2^{(Exponent - Bias)}$$

The range of single precision numbers is then from as small as

$$\pm 1.00000000000000000000000_{two} \times 2^{-126}$$

to as large as

$$\pm 1.11111111111111111111111_{two} \times 2^{-127}.$$

Floating-Point Representation

Show the IEEE 754 binary representation of the number -0.75_{ten} in single and double precision.

The number -0.75_{ten} is also $-3/4_{ten}$ or $-3/2^2{}_{ten}$

It is also represented by the binary fraction

$$-11_{two} / 2^2_{ten} \text{ or } -0.11_{two}$$

In scientific notation, the value is

$$-0.11_{two} \times 2^0$$

and in normalized scientific notation, it is

$$-1.1_{two} \times 2^{-1}$$

The general representation for a single precision number is

$$(-1)S \times (1 + \text{Fraction}) \times 2^{(\text{Exponent}-127)}$$

Subtracting the bias 127 from the exponent of $-1.1_{two} \times 2^{-1}$ yields

$$(-1)^1 \times (1 + .1000\ 0000\ 0000\ 0000\ 0000\ 000_{two}) \times 2^{(126-127)}$$

The single precision binary representation of -0.75_{ten} is then

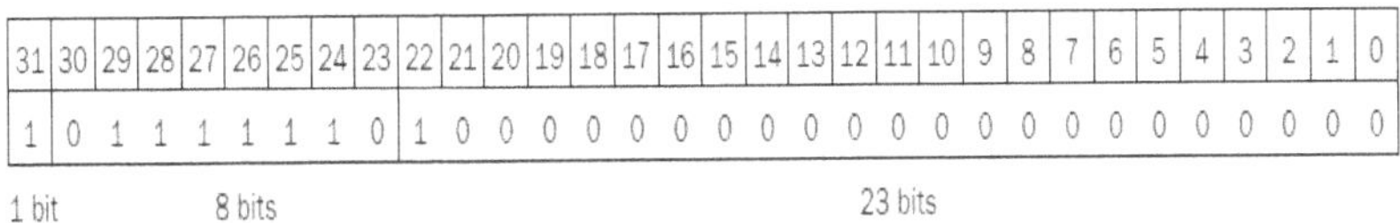

The double precision representation is

$$(-1)^1 \times (1 + .1000\ 0000\ 0000\ 0000\ 0000\ 0000\ 0000\ 0000\ 0000\ 0000\ 0000\ 0000\ 0000_{two})$$
$$\times 2^{(1022-1023)}$$

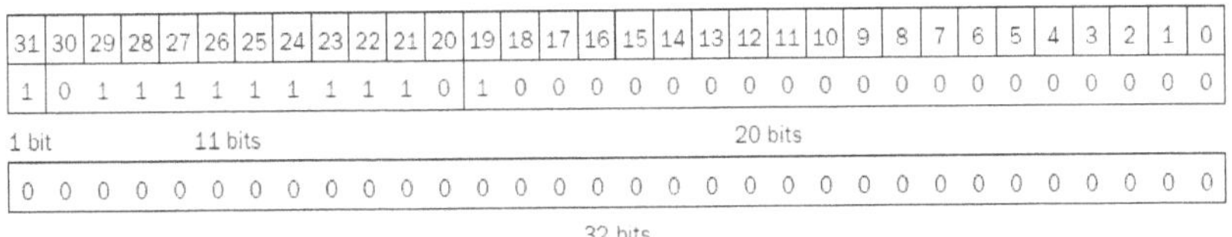

Floating-Point Addition

Let's add numbers in scientific notation by hand to illustrate the problems in floating-point addition: $9.999_{ten} \times 10^1 + 1.610_{ten} \times 10^{-1}$. Assume that we can store only four decimal digits of the significand and two decimal digits of the exponent. Step 1. To be able to add these numbers properly, we must align the decimal point of the number that has the smaller exponent. Hence, we need a form of the smaller number, $1.610_{ten} \times 10^{-1}$, that matches the larger exponent. We obtain this by observing that there are multiple representations of an unnormalized floating-point number in scientific notation:

$$1.610ten \times 10^{-1} = 0.1610ten \times 10^0 = 0.01610ten \times 10^1$$

The number on the right is the version we desire, since its exponent matches the exponent of the larger number, $9.999ten \times 10^1$. Thus, the first step shift s the significand of the smaller number to the right until its corrected exponent matches that of the larger number. But we can represent only four decimal digits so, after shifting, the number is really

$$0.016 \times 10^1$$

Step 2. Next comes the addition of the significands:

$$\begin{array}{r} 9.999_{ten} \\ +\ \ 0.016_{ten} \\ \hline 10.015_{ten} \end{array}$$

The sum is $10.015ten \times 10^1$.

Step 3. This sum is not in normalized scientific notation, so we need to adjust it:

$$10.015ten \times 10^1 = 1.0015ten \times 10^2$$

Thus, after the addition we may have to shift the sum to put it into normalized form, adjusting the exponent appropriately. This example shows shifting to the right, but if one number were positive and the other were negative, it would be possible for the sum to have many leading 0s, requiring left shift s. Whenever the exponent is increased or decreased, we must check for overflow or underflow—that is, we must make sure that the exponent still fits in its field.

Step 4. Since we assumed that the significand can be only four digits long (excluding the sign), we must round the number. In our grammar school algorithm, the rules truncate the number if the digit to the right of the desired point is between 0 and 4 and add 1 to the digit if the number to the right is between 5 and 9. The number,

$$1.0015ten \times 10^2$$

Is rounded to four digits in the significand to,

$$1.002ten \times 10^2$$

Since the fourth digit to the right of the decimal point was between 5 and 9. Notice that if we have bad luck on rounding, such as adding 1 to a string of 9s, the sum may no longer be normalized and we would need to perform step 3 again.

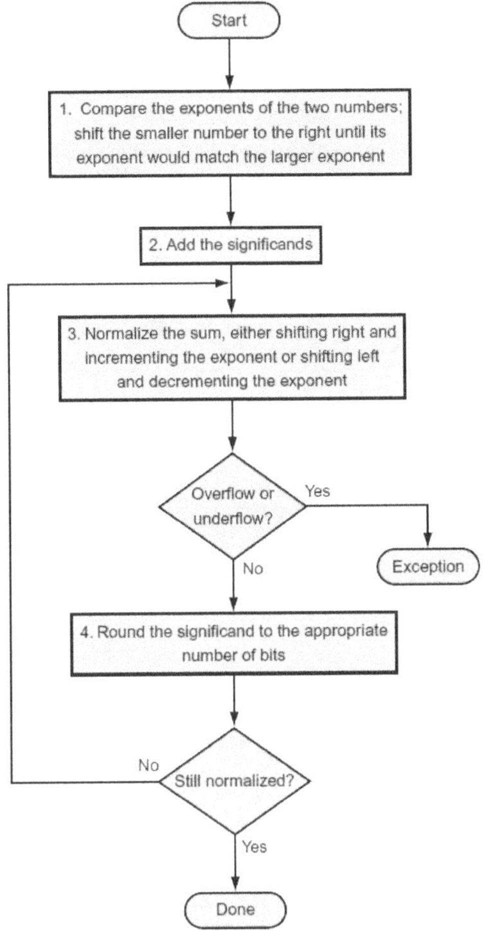

Floating-point addition. The normal path is to execute steps 3 and 4 once, but if rounding causes the sum to be unnormalized, we must repeat step 3.

Floating-Point Multiplication

We start by multiplying decimal numbers in scientific notation by hand: $1.110_{ten} \times 10^{10} \times 9.200_{ten} \times 10^{-5}$. Assume that we can store only four digits of the significand and two digits of the exponent.

Step 1. Unlike addition, we calculate the exponent of the product by simply adding the exponents of the operands together:

$$\text{New exponent} = 10 + (-5) = 5$$

Let's do this with the biased exponents as well to make sure we obtain the same result: 10 + 127 = 137, and -5 + 127 = 122, so

$$\text{New exponent} = 137 + 122 = 259$$

This result is too large for the 8-bit exponent field, so something is amiss! The problem is with the bias because we are adding the biases as well as the exponents:

$$\text{New exponent} = (10 + 127) + (-5 + 127) = (5 + 2 \times 127) = 259$$

Accordingly, to get the correct biased sum when we add biased numbers, we must subtract the bias from the sum:

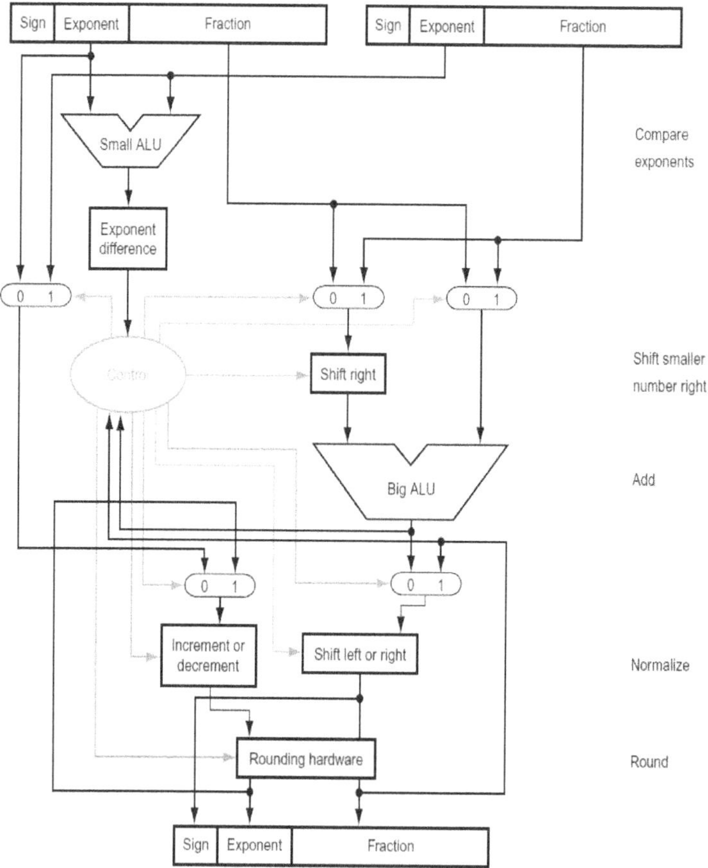

Block Diagram of an Arithmetic Unit Dedicated to Floating-Point Addition

First, the exponent of one operand is subtracted from the other using the small ALU to determine which is larger and by how much. This difference controls the three multiplexors; from left to right, they select the larger exponent, the significand of the smaller number, and the significand of the larger number. The smaller significand is shifted right, and then the significands are added together using the big ALU. The normalization step then shift s the sum left or right and increments or decrements the exponent. Rounding then creates the final result, which may require normalizing again to produce the actual final result.

$$\text{New exponent} = 137 + 122 - 127 = 259 - 127 = 132 = (5 + 127)$$

And 5 is indeed the exponent we calculated initially.

Step 2. Next comes the multiplication of the significands:

$$
\begin{array}{r}
1.110_{ten} \\
\times \quad 9.200_{ten} \\
\hline
0000 \\
0000 \\
2220 \\
9990 \\
\hline
10212000_{ten}
\end{array}
$$

There are three digits to the right of the decimal point for each operand, so the decimal point is placed six digits from the right in the product significand:

$$10.212000_{ten}$$

Assuming that we can keep only three digits to the right of the decimal point, the product is 10.212×10^5.

Step 3. This product is unnormalized, so we need to normalize it:

$$10.212_{ten} \times 10^5 = 1.0212_{ten} \times 10^6$$

Thus, after the multiplication, the product can be shifted right one digit to put it in normalized form, adding 1 to the exponent. At this point, we can check for overflow and underflow. Underflow may occur if both operands are small—that is, if both have large negative exponents.

Step 4. We assumed that the significand is only four digits long (excluding the   sign), so we must round the number. The number $1.0212_{ten} \times 10^6$ is rounded to four digits in the significand to

$$1.021_{ten} \times 10^6$$

Step 5. The sign of the product depends on the signs of the original operands. If they are both the same, the sign is positive; otherwise, it's negative. Hence, the product is

$$+1.021_{ten} \times 10^6$$

The sign of the sum in the addition algorithm was determined by addition of the significands, but in multiplication, the sign of the product is determined by the signs of the operands.

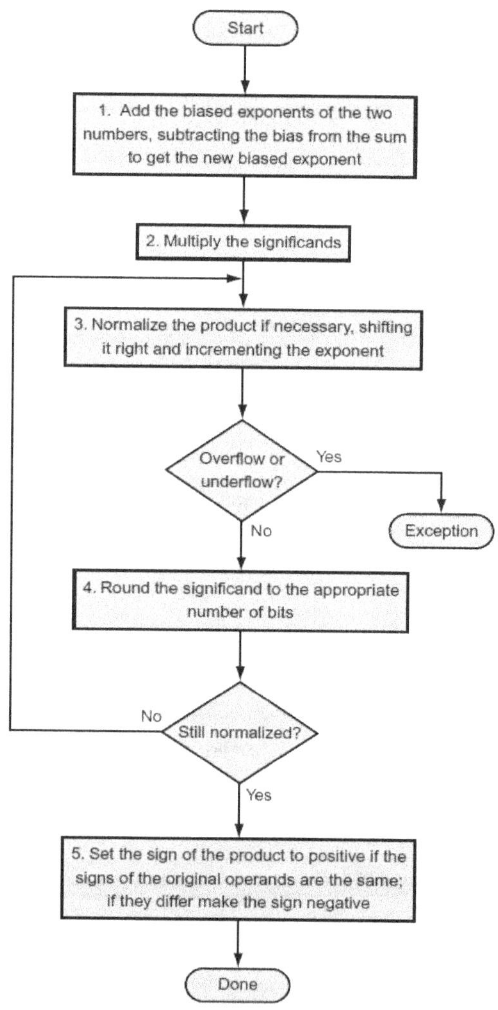

We start with calculating the new exponent of the product by adding the biased exponents, being sure to subtract one bias to get the proper result. Next is multiplication of significands, followed by an optional normalization step. The size of the exponent is checked for overflow or underflow, and then the product is rounded. If rounding leads to further normalization, we once again check for exponent size. Finally, set the sign bit to 1 if the signs of the operands were different (negative product) or to 0 if they were the same (positive product).

Floating-Point Instructions in MIPS

MIPS supports the IEEE 754 single precision and double precision formats with these instructions:

- Floating-point *addition, single* (add.s) and *addition, double* (add.d)
- Floating-point *subtraction, single* (sub.s) and *subtraction, double* (sub.d)
- Floating-point *multiplication, single* (mul.s) and *multiplication, double* (mul.d)
- Floating-point *division, single* (div.s) and *division, double* (div.d)
- Floating-point *comparison, single* (c.x.s) and *comparison, double* (c.x.d), where x may be *equal* (eq), *not equal* (neq), *less than* (lt), *less than or equal* (le), *greater than* (gt), or *greater than or equal* (ge)
- Floating-point *branch, true* (bc1t) and *branch, false* (bc1f)

Floating-point comparison sets a bit to true or false, depending on the comparison condition, and a fl oating-point branch then decides whether or not to branch, depending on the condition.

The MIPS designers decided to add separate floating-point registers—called $f0, $f1, $f2, used either for single precision or double precision. Hence, they included separate loads and stores for floating-point registers: lwc1 and swc1. The base registers for floating-point data transfers which are used for addresses remain integer registers. The MIPS code to load two single precision numbers from memory, add them, and then store the sum might look like this:

lwc1 $f4,c($sp) # Load 32-bit F.P. number into F4

lwc1 $f6,a($sp) # Load 32-bit F.P. number into F6

add.s $f2,$f4,$f6 # F2 = F4 + F6 single precision

swc1 $f2,b($sp) # Store 32-bit F.P. number from F2

A double precision register is really an even-odd pair of single precision registers, using the even register number as its name. Thus, the pair of single precision registers $f2 and $f3 also form the double precision register named $f2.

MIPS floating point operands

Name	Example	Comments
32 floating point registers	$f0, $f1, $f2, ... , $f31	MIPS floating point registers are used in pairs for double precision numbers
2^{30} memory words	Memory[0], Memory[4], ... , Memory[4294967292]	Accessed only by data transfer instructions. MIPS uses byte addresses, so sequential word addresses differ by 4. Memory holds data structures, such as arrays, and spilled registers, such as those saved on procedure calls.

MIPS floating point assembly language

Category	Instruction	Example	Meaning	Comments
Arithmetic	FP add single	add.s $f2,$f4,$f6	$f2 = $f4 + $f6	FP add (single precision)
	FP subtract single	sub.s $f2,$f4,$f6	$f2 = $f4 − $f6	FP sub (single precision)
	FP multiply single	mul.s $f2,$f4,$f6	$f2 = $f4 × $f6	FP multiply (single precision)
	FP divide single	div.s $f2,$f4,$f6	$f2 = $f4 / $f6	FP divide (single precision)
	FP add double	add.d $f2,$f4,$f6	$f2 = $f4 + $f6	FP add (double precision)
	FP subtract double	sub.d $f2,$f4,$f6	$f2 = $f4 − $f6	FP sub (double precision)
	FP multiply double	mul.d $f2,$f4,$f6	$f2 = $f4 × $f6	FP multiply (double precision)
	FP divide double	div.d $f2,$f4,$f6	$f2 = $f4 / $f6	FP divide (double precision)
Data transfer	load word copr. 1	lwc1 $f1,100($s2)	$f1 = Memory[$s2 + 100]	32-bit data to FP register
	store word copr. 1	swc1 $f1,100($s2)	Memory[$s2 + 100] = $f1	32-bit data to memory
Conditional branch	branch on FP true	bc1t 25	if (cond == 1) go to PC + 4 + 100	PC-relative branch if FP cond.
	branch on FP false	bc1f 25	if (cond == 0) go to PC + 4 + 100	PC-relative branch if not cond.
	FP compare single (eq,ne,lt,le,gt,ge)	c.lt.s $f2,$f4	if ($f2 < $f4) cond = 1; else cond = 0	FP compare less than single precision
	FP compare double (eq,ne,lt,le,gt,ge)	c.lt.d $f2,$f4	if ($f2 < $f4) cond = 1; else cond = 0	FP compare less than double precision

MIPS floating point machine language

Name	Format	Example						Comments
add.s	R	17	16	6	4	2	0	add.s $f2,$f4,$f6
sub.s	R	17	16	6	4	2	1	sub.s $f2,$f4,$f6
mul.s	R	17	16	6	4	2	2	mul.s $f2,$f4,$f6
div.s	R	17	16	6	4	2	3	div.s $f2,$f4,$f6
add.d	R	17	17	6	4	2	0	add.d $f2,$f4,$f6
sub.d	R	17	17	6	4	2	1	sub.d $f2,$f4,$f6
mul.d	R	17	17	6	4	2	2	mul.d $f2,$f4,$f6
div.d	R	17	17	6	4	2	3	div.d $f2,$f4,$f6
lwc1	I	49	20	2	100			lwc1 $f2,100($s4)
swc1	I	57	20	2	100			swc1 $f2,100($s4)
bc1t	I	17	8	1	25			bc1t 25
bc1f	I	17	8	0	25			bc1f 25
c.lt.s	R	17	16	4	2	0	60	c.lt.s $f2,$f4
c.lt.d	R	17	17	4	2	0	60	c.lt.d $f2,$f4
Field size		6 bits	5 bits	5 bits	5 bits	5 bits	6 bits	All MIPS instructions 32 bits

op(31:26):

28–26 31–29	0(000)	1(001)	2(010)	3(011)	4(100)	5(101)	6(110)	7(111)
0(000)	Rfmt	Bltz/gez	j	jal	beq	bne	blez	bgtz
1(001)	addi	addiu	slti	sltiu	ANDi	ORi	xORi	lui
2(010)	TLB	FlPt						
3(011)								
4(100)	lb	lh	lwl	lw	lbu	lhu	lwr	
5(101)	sb	sh	swl	sw			swr	
6(110)	lwc0	lwc1						
7(111)	swc0	swc1						

op(31:26) = 010001 (FlPt), (rt(16:16) = 0 => c = f, rt(16:16) = 1 => c = t), rs(25:21):

23–21 25–24	0(000)	1(001)	2(010)	3(011)	4(100)	5(101)	6(110)	7(111)
0(00)	mfc1		cfc1		mtc1		ctc1	
1(01)	bc1.c							
2(10)	f = single	f = double						
3(11)								

op(31:26) = 010001 (FlPt), (f above: 10000 => f = s, 10001 => f = d), funct(5:0):

2–0 5–3	0(000)	1(001)	2(010)	3(011)	4(100)	5(101)	6(110)	7(111)
0(000)	add.f	sub.f	mul.f	div.f		abs.f	mov.f	neg.f
1(001)								
2(010)								
3(011)								
4(100)	cvt.s.f	cvt.d.f			cvt.w.f			
5(101)								
6(110)	c.f.f	c.un.f	c.eq.f	c.ueq.f	c.olt.f	c.ult.f	c.ole.f	c.ule.f
7(111)	c.sf.f	c.ngle.f	c.seq.f	c.ngl.f	c.lt.f	c.nge.f	c.le.f	c.ngt.f

Compiling a Floating-Point C Program into MIPS Assembly Code

Let's convert a temperature in Fahrenheit to Celsius:

float f2c (float fahr)

{

return ((5.0/9.0) *(fahr – 32.0));

}

Assume that the floating-point argument fahr is passed in $f12 and the result should go in $f0. (Unlike integer registers, floating-point register 0 can contain a number.) What is the MIPS assembly code?

We assume that the compiler places the three floating-point constants in memory within easy reach of the global pointer $gp. The first two instructions load the constants 5.0 and 9.0 into floating-point registers:

f2c:

lwc1 $f16,const5($gp) # $f16 = 5.0 (5.0 in memory)

lwc1 $f18,const9($gp) # $f18 = 9.0 (9.0 in memory)

They are then divided to get the fraction 5.0/9.0:

div.s $f16, $f16, $f18 # $f16 = 5.0 / 9.0

(Many compilers would divide 5.0 by 9.0 at compile time and save the single constant 5.0/9.0 in memory, thereby avoiding the divide at runtime.) Next, we load the constant 32.0 and then subtract it from fahr ($f12):

lwc1 $f18, const32($gp)# $f18 = 32.0

sub.s $f18, $f12, $f18 # $f18 = fahr – 32.0

Finally, we multiply the two intermediate results, placing the product in $f0 as the return result, and then return

mul.s $f0, $f16, $f18 # $f0 = (5/9)*(fahr – 32.0)

jr $ra # return

Guard The first of two extra bits kept on the right during intermediate calculations of floating point numbers; used to improve rounding accuracy.

Round Method to make the intermediate floating-point result fit the floating-point format; the goal is typically to find the nearest number that can be represented in the format.

2.5.   Sub Word Parallelism

Since every desktop microprocessor by definition has its own graphical displays, as transistor budgets increased it was inevitable that support would be added for graphics operations.

Many graphics systems originally used 8 bits to represent each of the three primary colors plus 8 bits for a location of a pixel. The addition of speakers and microphones for teleconferencing and video games suggested support of sound as well. Audio samples need more than 8 bits of precision, but 16 bits are sufficient. Architects recognized that many graphics and audio applications would perform the same operation on vectors of this data.

By partitioning the carry chains within a 128-bit adder, a processor could use **parallelism** to perform simultaneous operations on short vectors of sixteen 8-bit operands, eight 16-bit operands, four 32-bit operands, or two 64-bit operands. The cost of such partitioned adders was small. Given that the parallelism occurs within a wide word, the extensions are classified as *subword parallelism*. It is also classified under the more general name of *data level parallelism*.

For example, ARM added more than 100 instructions in the NEON multimedia instruction extension to support subword parallelism, which can be used either with ARMv7 or ARMv8. It added 256 bytes of new registers for NEON that can be viewed as 32 registers 8 bytes wide or 16 registers 16 bytes wide. NEON supports all the subword data types you can imagine *except* 64-bit floating point numbers:

- 8-bit, 16-bit, 32-bit, and 64-bit signed and unsigned integers.
- 32-bit floating point numbers.

Data Transfer	Arithmetic	Logical/Compare
VLDR.F32	VADD.F32, VADD{L,W}{S8,U8,S16,U16,S32,U32}	VAND.64, VAND.128
VSTR.F32	VSUB.F32, VSUB{L,W}{S8,U8,S16,U16,S32,U32}	VORR.64, VORR.128
VLD{1,2,3,4}.{I8,I16,I32}	VMUL.F32, VMULL{S8,U8,S16,U16,S32,U32}	VEOR.64, VEOR.128
VST{1,2,3,4}.{I8,I16,I32}	VMLA.F32, VMLAL{S8,U8,S16,U16,S32,U32}	VBIC.64, VBIC.128
VMOV.{I8,I16,I32,F32}, #imm	VMLS.F32, VMLSL{S8,U8,S16,U16,S32,U32}	VORN.64, VORN.128
VMVN.{I8,I16,I32,F32}, #imm	VMAX.{S8,U8,S16,U16,S32,U32,F32}	VCEQ.{I8,I16,I32,F32}
VMOV.{I64,I128}	VMIN.{S8,U8,S16,U16,S32,U32,F32}	VCGE.{S8,U8,S16,U16,S32,U32,F32}
VMVN.{I64,I128}	VABS.{S8,S16,S32,F32}	VCGT.{S8,U8,S16,U16,S32,U32,F32}
	VNEG.{S8,S16,S32,F32}	VCLE.{S8,U8,S16,U16,S32,U32,F32}
	VSHL.{S8,U8,S16,U16,S32,S64,U64}	VCLT.{S8,U8,S16,U16,S32,U32,F32}
	VSHR.{S8,U8,S16,U16,S32,S64,U64}	VTST.{I8,I16,I32}

Summary of ARM NEON Instructions for Sub Word Parallelism

We use the curly brackets {} to show optional variations of the basic operations: {S8,U8,8} stand for signed and unsigned 8-bit integers or 8-bit data where type doesn't matter, of which 16 fit in a 128-bit register; {S16,U16,16} stand for signed and unsigned 16-bit integers or 16-bit type-less data, of which 8 fit in a 128-bit register; {S32,U32,32} stand for signed and unsigned 32-bit integers or 32-bit type-less data, of which 4 fit in a 128-bit register; {S64,U64,64} stand for signed and unsigned 64-bit integers or type-less 64-bit data, of which 2 fit in a 128-bit register; {F32} stand for signed and unsigned 32-bit floating point numbers, of which 4 fi t in a 128-bit register. Vector Load reads one n-element structure from memory into 1, 2, 3, or 4 NEON registers. It loads a single n-element structure to one lane, and elements of the register that are not loaded are unchanged. Vector Store writes one n-element structure into memory from 1, 2, 3, or 4 NEON registers.

UNIT III

PROCESSOR AND CONTROL UNIT

3.1. A Basic MIPS Implementation

We will be examining an implementation that includes a subset of the core MIPS instruction set:

- The memory-reference instructions *load word* (lw) and *store word* (sw).
- The arithmetic-logical instructions add, sub, AND, OR, and slt.
- The instructions *branch equal* (beq) and *jump* (j), which we add last.

This subset does not include all the integer instructions (for example, shift, multiply, and divide are missing), nor does it include any floating-point instructions. For every instruction, the first two steps are identical:

1. Send the *program counter* (PC) to the memory that contains the code and fetch the instruction from that memory.
2. Read one or two registers, using fields of the instruction to select the registers to read. For the load word instruction, we need to read only one register, but most other instructions require reading two registers.

After these two steps, the actions required to complete the instruction depend on the instruction class. Fortunately, for each of the three instruction classes (memory-reference, arithmetic-logical, and branches), the actions are largely the same, independent of the exact instruction. The simplicity and regularity of the MIPS instruction set simplifies the implementation by making the execution of many of the instruction classes similar.

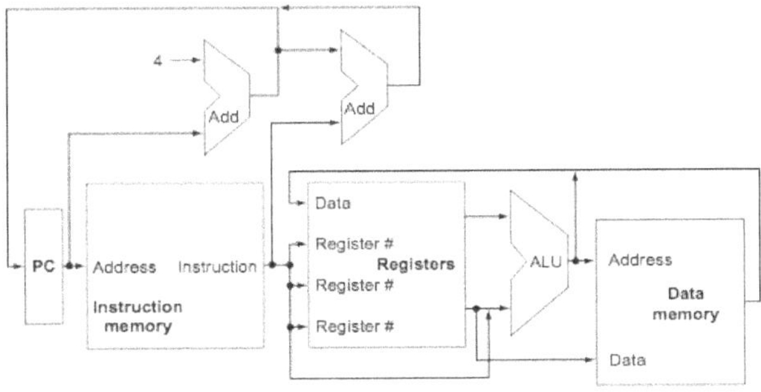

High-Level View of a MIPS Implementation

Above Figure shows the high-level view of a MIPS implementation, focusing on the various functional units and their interconnection. Although this figure shows most of the flow of data through the processor, it omits two important aspects of instruction execution.

All instructions start by using the program counter to supply the instruction address to the instruction memory. After the instruction is fetched, the register operands used by an instruction are specified by fields of that instruction. Once the register operands have been fetched, they can be operated on to compute a memory address (for a load or store), to compute an arithmetic result (for an integer arithmetic-logical instruction), or a compare (for a branch). If the instruction is an arithmetic-logical instruction, the result from the ALU must be written to a register. If the operation is a load or store, the ALU result is used as an address to either store a value from the registers or load a value from memory into the registers. The result from the ALU or memory is written back into the register file. Branches require the use of the ALU output to determine the next instruction address, which comes either from the ALU (where the PC and branch offset are summed) or from an adder that increments the current PC by 4. The thick lines interconnecting the functional units represent buses, which consist of multiple signals. The arrows are used to guide the reader in knowing how information flows. Since signal lines may cross, we explicitly show when crossing lines are connected by the presence of a dot where the lines cross.

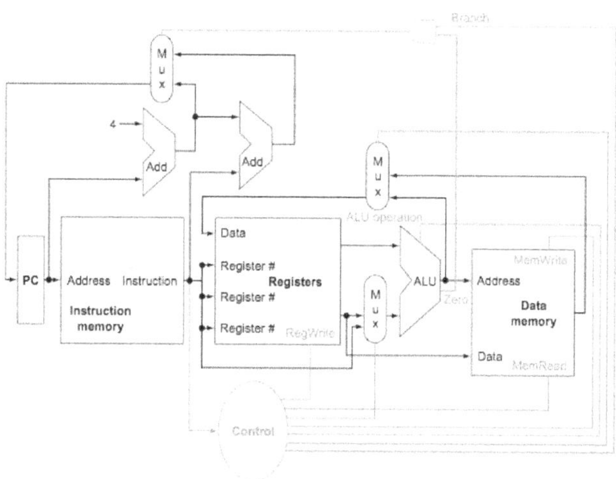

The Basic Implementation of the MIPS Subset, Including the Necessary Multiplexors and Control Lines

The top multiplexor ("Mux") controls what value replaces the PC (PC + 4 or the branch destination address); the multiplexor is controlled by the gate that "ANDs" together the Zero output of the ALU and a control signal that indicates that the instruction is a branch. The middle multiplexor, whose output returns to the register file, is used to steer the output of the ALU (in the case of an arithmetic-logical instruction) or the output of the data memory (in the case of a load) for writing into the register file. Finally, the bottommost multiplexor is used to determine whether the second ALU input is from the registers (for an arithmetic-logical instruction or a branch) or from the offset field of the instruction (for a load or store). The added control lines are straightforward and determine the operation performed at the ALU, whether the data memory should read or write, and whether the registers should perform a write operation. The control lines are shown in color to make them easier to see.

3.2. Building a Datapath

Datapath Element

A unit used to operate on or hold data within a processor. In the MIPS implementation, the datapath elements include the instruction and data memories, the register file, the ALU, and adders.

Program Counter (PC)

The register containing the address of the instruction in the program being executed.

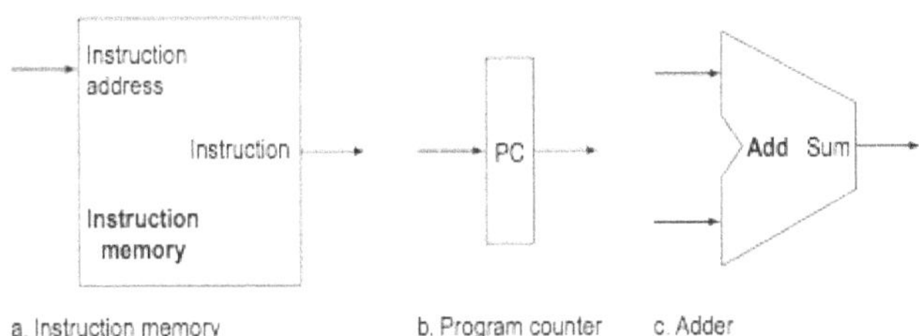

a. Instruction memory   b. Program counter   c. Adder

Two state elements are needed to store and access instructions, and an adder is needed to compute the next instruction address. The state elements are the instruction memory and the program counter. The instruction memory need only provide read access because the datapath does not write instructions. Since the instruction memory only reads, we treat it as combinational logic: the output at any time reflects the contents of the location specified by the address input, and no read control signal is needed. (We will need to write the instruction memory when we load the program; this is not hard to add, and we ignore it for simplicity.) The program counter is a 32-bit register that is written at the end of every clock cycle and thus does not need a write control signal. The adder is an ALU wired to always add its two 32-bit inputs and place the sum on its output.

Register File

A state element that consists of a set of registers that can be read and written by supplying a register number to be accessed.

R-format instructions have three register operands, so we will need to read two data words from the register file and write one data word into the register file for each instruction. For each data word to be read from the registers, we need an input to the register file that specifies the *register number* to be read and an output from the register file that will carry the value that has been read from the registers.

To write a data word, we will need two inputs: one to specify the register number to be written and one to supply the *data* to be written into the register.

The register file always outputs the contents of whatever register numbers are on the Read register inputs. Writes, however, are controlled by the write control signal, which must be asserted for a write to occur at the clock edge.

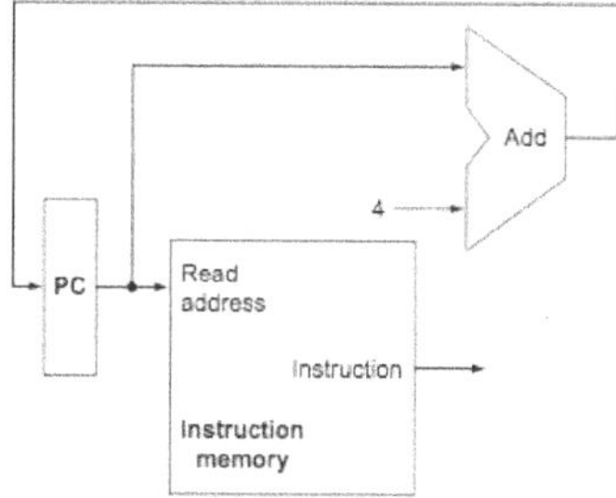

A Portion of the Datapath used for Fetching Instructions and Incrementing the Program Counter

The fetched instruction is used by other parts of the datapath. The register file contains all the registers and has two read ports and one write port. The register file always outputs the contents of the registers corresponding to the Read register inputs on the outputs; no other control inputs are needed. In contrast, a register write must be explicitly indicated by asserting the write control signal. Remember that writes are edge-triggered, so that all the write inputs (i.e., the value to be written, the register number, and the write control signal) must be valid at the clock edge. Since writes to the register file are edge-triggered, our design can legally read and write the same register within a clock cycle: the read will get the value written in an earlier clock cycle, while the value written will be available to a read in a subsequent clock cycle. The inputs carrying the register number to the register file are all 5 bits wide, whereas the lines carrying data values are 32 bits wide.

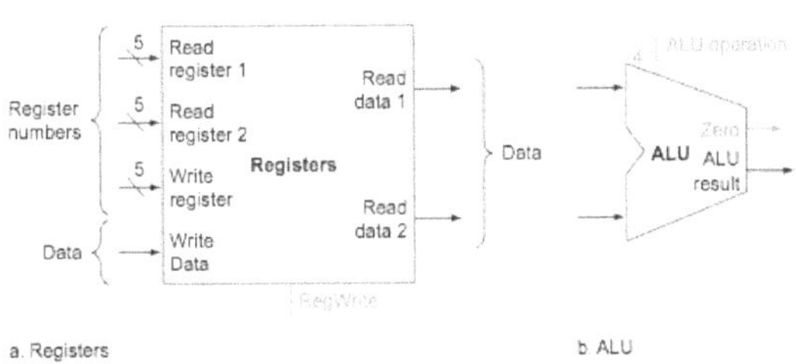

The Two Elements Needed to Implement R-Format ALU Operations are the Register File and the ALU

Sign-Extend

To increase the size of a data item by replicating the high-order sign bit of the original data item in the high- order bits of the larger, destination data item.

Branch

A type of branch where the instruction immediately following the branch is always executed, independent of whether the branch condition is true or false.

Branch Target Address

The address specified in a branch, which becomes the new program counter (PC) if the branch is taken. In the MIPS architecture the branch target is given by the sum of the offset field of the instruction and the address of the instruction following the branch.

Branch Taken

A branch where the branch condition is satisfied and the program counter (PC) becomes the branch target. All unconditional jumps are taken branches.

Branch not Taken or (Untaken Branch)

A branch where the branch condition is false and the program counter (PC) becomes the address of the instruction that sequentially follows the branch.

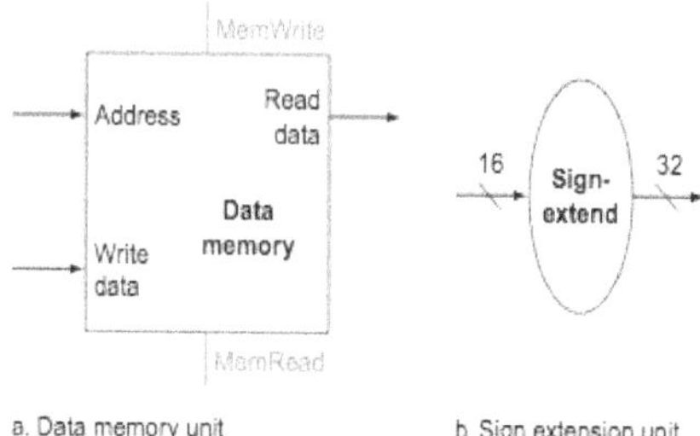

a. Data memory unit   b. Sign extension unit

The Two Units Needed to implement loads and Stores, in Addition to the Register File and ALU are the Data Memory Unit and the Sign Extension Unit

The memory unit is a state element with inputs for the address and the write data, and a single output for the read result. There are separate read and write controls, although only one of these may be asserted on any given clock. The memory unit needs a read signal, since, unlike the register file, reading the value of an invalid address can cause problems. The sign extension unit has a 16-bit input that is sign-extended into a 32-bit result appearing on the output. We assume the data memory is edge-triggered for writes. Standard memory chips actually have a write enable signal that is used for writes. Although the write enable is not edge-triggered, our edge-triggered design could easily be adapted to work with real memory chips.

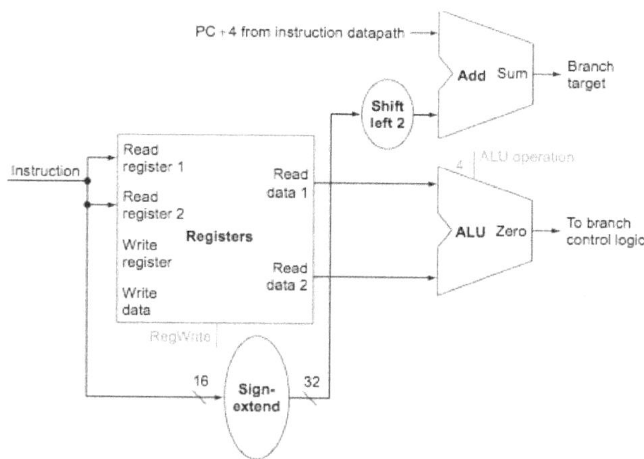

The data path for a branch uses the ALU to evaluate the branch condition and a separate adder to compute the branch target as the sum of the incremented PC and the sign-extended, lower 16 bits of the instruction (the branch displacement), shifted left 2 bits.

The unit labeled *Shift left 2* is simply a routing of the signals between input and output that adds 00 to the low-order end of the sign-extended offset field; no actual shift hardware is needed, since the amount of the "shift" is constant. Since we know that the offset was sign-extended from 16 bits, the shift will throw away only "sign bits." Control logic is used to decide whether the incremented PC or branch target should replace the PC, based on the Zero output of the ALU.

Creating a Single Datapath

The operations of arithmetic-logical (or R-type) instructions and the memory instructions datapath are quite similar. The key differences are the following:

- The arithmetic-logical instructions use the ALU, with the inputs coming from the two registers. The memory instructions can also use the ALU to do the address calculation, although the second input is the sign- extended 16-bit offset field from the instruction.
- The value stored into a destination register comes from the ALU (for an R-type instruction) or the memory (for a load).

Show how to build a datapath for the operational portion of the memory- reference and arithmetic-logical instructions that uses a single register file and a single ALU to handle both types of instructions, adding any necessary multiplexors.

To create a datapath with only a single register file and a single ALU, we must support two different sources for the second ALU input, as well as two different sources for the data stored into the register file. Thus, one multiplexor is placed at the ALU input and another at the data input to the register file. Figure shows the operational portion of the combined datapath.

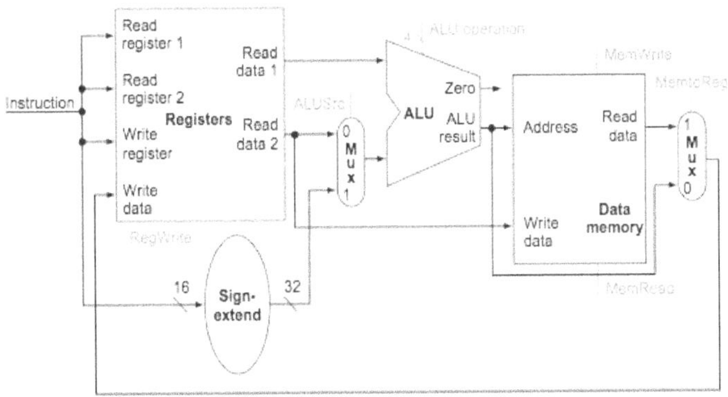

The Datapath for the Memory Instructions and R-type Instructions

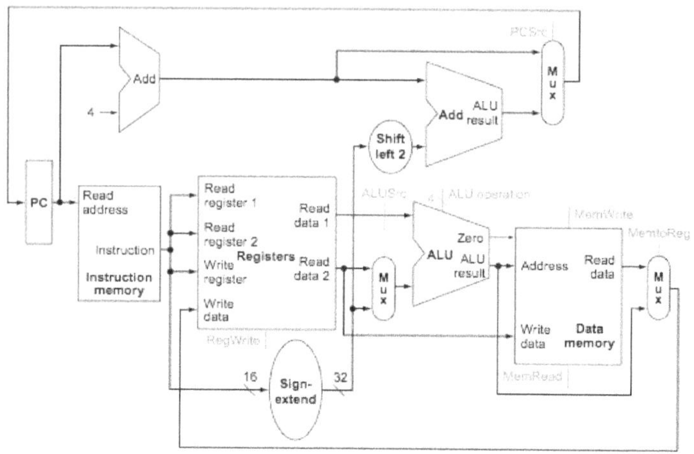

The Simple Datapath for the Core MIPS Architecture Combines the Elements Required by Different Instruction Classes

3.3.   Control Implementation Scheme

The ALU Control

ALU control lines	Function
0000	AND
0001	OR
0010	add
0110	subtract
0111	set on less than
1100	NOR

Depending on the instruction class, the ALU will need to perform one of these first five functions. (NOR is needed for other parts of the MIPS instruction set not found in the subset we are implementing.) For load word and store word instructions, we use the ALU to compute the memory address by addition. For the R-type instructions, the ALU needs to perform one of the five actions (AND, OR, subtract, add, or set on less than), depending on the value of the 6-bit funct (or function) field in the low-order bits of the instruction. For branch equal, the ALU must perform a subtraction.

We can generate the 4-bit ALU control input using a small control unit that has as inputs the function field of the instruction and a 2-bit control field, which we call ALUOp. ALUOp indicates whether the operation to be performed should be add (00) for loads and stores, subtract (01) for beq, or determined by the operation encoded in the funct field (10). The output of the ALU control unit is a 4-bit signal that directly controls the ALU by generating one of the 4-bit combinations shown previously.

Instruction opcode	ALUOp	Instruction operation	Funct field	Desired ALU action	ALU control input
LW	00	load word	XXXXXX	add	0010
SW	00	store word	XXXXXX	add	0010
Branch equal	01	branch equal	XXXXXX	subtract	0110
R-type	10	add	100000	add	0010
R-type	10	subtract	100010	subtract	0110
R-type	10	AND	100100	AND	0000
R-type	10	OR	100101	OR	0001
R-type	10	set on less than	101010	set on less than	0111

How the ALU Control Bits are Set Depends on the ALUOp Control Bits and the Different Function Codes for the R-Type Instruction

The opcode, listed in the first column, determines the setting of the ALUOp bits. All the encodings are shown in binary. Notice that when the ALUOp code is 00 or 01, the desired ALU action does not depend on the function code field; in this case, we say that we "don't care" about the value of the function code, and the funct field is shown as XXXXXX. When the ALUOp value is 10, then the function code is used to set the ALU control input.

Truth table from logic, a representation of a logical operation by listing all the values of the inputs and then in each case showing what the resulting outputs should be.

Don't-care term an element of a logical function in which the output does not depend on the values of all the inputs. Don't-care terms may be specified in different ways.

Designing the Main Control Unit

ALUOp		Funct field						Operation
ALUOp1	ALUOp0	F5	F4	F3	F2	F1	F0	
0	0	X	X	X	X	X	X	0010
X	1	X	X	X	X	X	X	0110
1	X	X	X	0	0	0	0	0010
1	X	X	X	0	0	1	0	0110
1	X	X	X	0	1	0	0	0000
1	X	X	X	0	1	0	1	0001
1	X	X	X	1	0	1	0	0111

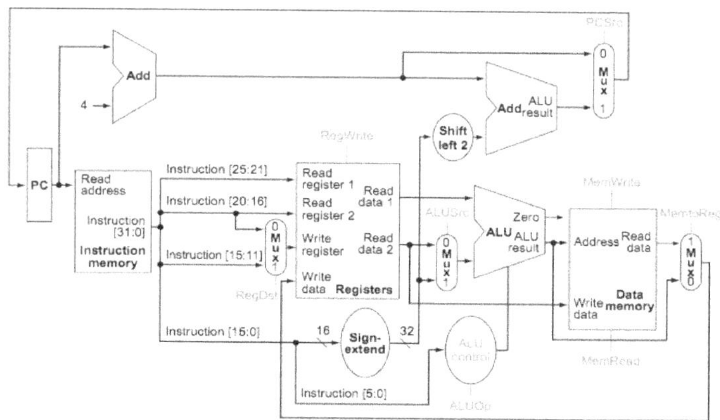

The Truth Table for the 4 ALU Control Bits (called Operation). The inputs are the ALUOp and Function Code Field

Only the entries for which the ALU control is asserted are shown. Some don't-care entries have been added. For example, the ALUOp does not use the encoding 11, so the truth table can contain entries 1X and X1, rather than 10 and 01. Note that when the function field is used, the first 2 bits (F5 and F4) of these instructions are always 10, so they are don't-care terms and are replaced with XX in the truth table.

Field	0	rs	rt	rd	shamt	funct
Bit positions	31:26	25:21	20:16	15:11	10:6	5:0

a. R-type instruction

Field	35 or 43	rs	rt	address
Bit positions	31:26	25:21	20:16	15:0

b. Load or store instruction

Field	4	rs	rt	address
Bit positions	31:26	25:21	20:16	15:0

c. Branch instruction

The Three Instruction Classes (R-Type, Load and Store, and Branch) use Two Different Instruction Formats

The jump instructions use another format, which we will discuss shortly. (a) Instruction format for R-format instructions, which all have an opcode of 0. These instructions have three register operands: rs, rt, and rd. Fields rs and rt are sources, and rd is the destination. The ALU function is in the funct field and is decoded by the ALU control design in the previous section. The R-type instructions that we implement are add, sub, AND, OR, and slt. The shamt field is used only for shifts; we will ignore it in this chapter. (b) Instruction format for load (opcode = 35nd store (opcode = 43instructions. The register rs is the base register that is added to the 16-bit address field to form the memory address. For loads, rt is the destination register for the loaded value. For stores, rt is the source register whose value should be stored into memory. (c) Instruction format for branch equal (opcode =4). The registers rs and rt are the source registers that are compared for equality. The 16-bit address field is sign-extended, shifted, and added to the PC + 4 to compute the branch target address.

There are several major observations about this instruction format that we will rely on:

- The op field, is called the **opcode**, is always contained in bits 31:26. We will refer to this field as Op[5:0].

- The two registers to be read are always specified by the rs and rt fields, at positions 25:21 and 20:16. This is true for the R-type instructions, branch equal, and store.

- The base register for load and store instructions is always in bit positions 25:21 (rs).

- The 16-bit offset for branch equal, load, and store is always in positions 15:0.

- The destination register is in one of two places. For a load it is in bit positions 20:16 (rt), while for an R-type instruction it is in bit positions 15:11 (rd). Thus, we will need to add a multiplexor to select which field of the instruction is used to indicate the register number to be written.

The datapath with all necessary multiplexors and all control lines identified . The control lines are shown in color. The ALU control block has also been added. The PC does not require a write control, since it is written once at the end of every clock cycle; the branch control logic determines whether it is written with the incremented PC or the branch target address.

Signal name	Effect when deasserted	Effect when asserted
RegDst	The register destination number for the Write register comes from the rt field (bits 20:16).	The register destination number for the Write register comes from the rd field (bits 15:11).
RegWrite	None.	The register on the Write register input is written with the value on the Write data input.
ALUSrc	The second ALU operand comes from the second register file output (Read data 2).	The second ALU operand is the sign-extended, lower 16 bits of the instruction.
PCSrc	The PC is replaced by the output of the adder that computes the value of PC + 4.	The PC is replaced by the output of the adder that computes the branch target.
MemRead	None.	Data memory contents designated by the address input are put on the Read data output.
MemWrite	None.	Data memory contents designated by the address input are replaced by the value on the Write data input.
MemtoReg	The value fed to the register Write data input comes from the ALU.	The value fed to the register Write data input comes from the data memory.

Operation of the Datapath

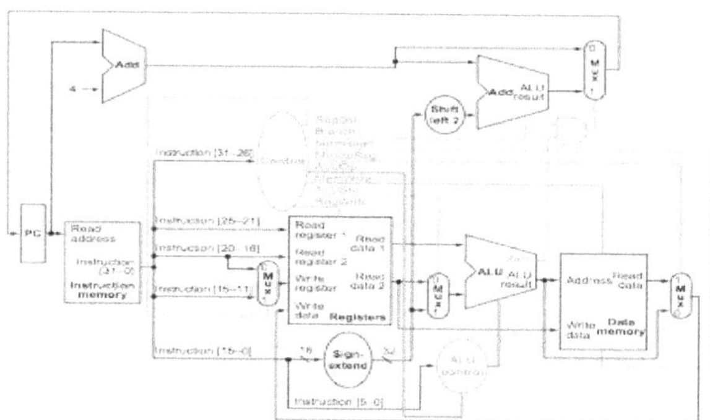

The Simple Datapath with the Control Unit

The input to the control unit is the 6-bit opcode field from the instruction. The outputs of the control unit consist of three 1-bit signals that are used to control multiplexors (RegDst, ALUSrc, and MemtoReg), three signals for controlling reads and writes in the register file and data memory (RegWrite, MemRead, and MemWrite), a 1-bit signal used in determining whether to possibly branch (Branch), and a 2-bit control signal for the ALU (ALUOp). An AND gate is used to combine the branch control signal and the Zero output from the ALU; the AND gate output controls the selection of the next PC. Notice that PCSrc is now a derived signal, rather than one coming directly from the control unit. Thus, we drop the signal name in subsequent figures. These steps are ordered by the flow of information:

1. The instruction is fetched, and the PC is incremented.
2. Two registers, $t2 and $t3, are read from the register file; also, the main control unit computes the setting of the control lines during this step.
3. The ALU operates on the data read from the register file, using the function code (bits 5:0, which is the funct field, of the instruction) to generate the ALU function.
4. The result from the ALU is written into the register file using bits 15:11 of the instruction to select the destination register ($t1).

Instruction	RegDst	ALUSrc	Memto Reg	Reg Write	Mem Read	Mem Write	Branch	ALUOp1	ALUOp0
R-format	1	0	0	1	0	0	0	1	0
lw	0	1	1	1	1	0	0	0	0
sw	X	1	X	0	0	1	0	0	0
beq	X	0	X	0	0	0	1	0	1

The Setting of the Control Lines is Completely Determined by the Opcode Fields of the

Instruction

The first row of the table corresponds to the R-format instructions (add, sub, AND, OR, and slt). For all these instructions, the source register fields are rs and rt, and the destination register field is rd; this defines how the signals ALUSrc and RegDst are set. Furthermore, an R-type instruction writes a register (Reg-Write = 1), but neither reads nor writes data memory. When the Branch control signal is 0, the PC is unconditionally replaced with PC + 4; otherwise, the PC is replaced by the branch target if the Zero output of the ALU is also high. The ALUOp field for R-type instructions is set to 10 to indicate that the ALU control should be generated from the funct field.

The second and third rows of this table give the control signal settings for lw and sw. These ALUSrc and ALUOp fields are set to perform the address calculation. The MemRead and Mem-Write are set to perform the memory access. Finally, RegDst and RegWrite are set for a load to cause the result to be stored into the rt register.

The branch instruction is similar to an R-format operation, since it sends the rs and rt registers to the ALU.

The ALUOp field for branch is set for a subtract (ALU control = 01), which is used to test for equality. Notice that the MemtoReg field is irrelevant when the RegWrite signal is 0: since the register is not being written, the value of the data on the register data write port is not used.

Thus, the entry MemtoReg in the last two rows of the table is replaced with X for don't care. Don't cares can also be added to RegDst when RegWrite is 0. This type of don't care must be added by the designer, since it depends on knowledge of how the datapath works.

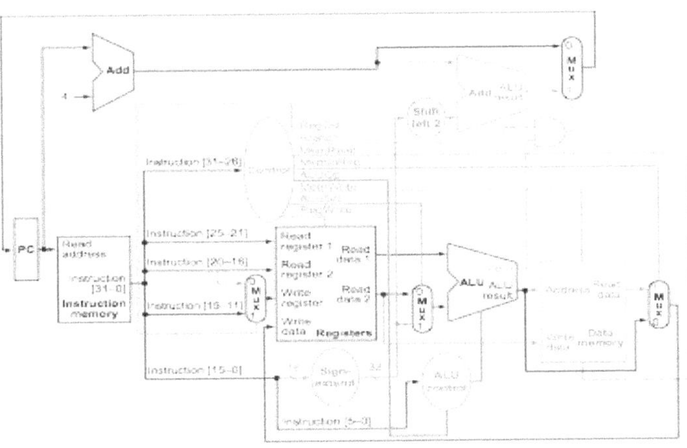

The Datapath in Operation for an R-Type Instruction, such as add $t1,$t2,$t3. The Control Lines, Datapath Units, and Connections that are Active are Highlighted

Similarly, we can illustrate the execution of a load word, such as,

lw $t1, offset($t2)

In a style similar to figure shows the active functional units and asserted control lines for a load. The control lines, datapath units, and connections that are active are highlighted. A store instruction would operate very similarly. The main difference would be that the memory control would indicate a write rather than a read, the second register value read would be used for the data to store, and the operation of writing the data memory value to the register file would not occur.

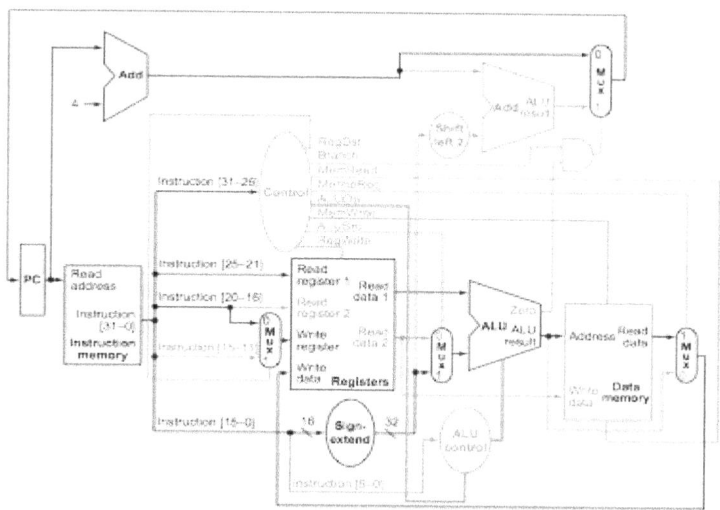

The Datapath in Operation for a Load Instruction

We can think of a load instruction as operating in five steps (similar to how the R-type executed in four):

1. An instruction is fetched from the instruction memory, and the PC is incremented.
2. A register ($t2) value is read from the register file.
3. The ALU computes the sum of the value read from the register file and the sign-extended, lower 16 bits of the instruction (offset).
4. The sum from the ALU is used as the address for the data memory.
5. The data from the memory unit is written into the register file; the register destination is given by bits 20:16 of the instruction ($t1).

Finally, we can show the operation of the branch-on-equal instruction, such as beq $t1,$t2,offset, in the same fashion. It operates much like an R-format instruction, but the ALU output is used to determine whether the PC is written with PC + 4 or the branch target address.

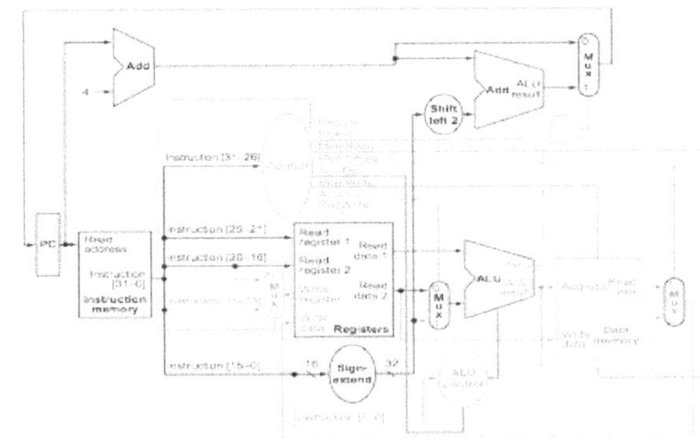

The Datapath in Operation for a Branch-on-Equal Instruction

The control lines, datapath units, and connections that are active are highlighted. After using the register file and ALU to perform the compare, the Zero output is used to select the next program counter from between the two candidates.

Figure shows the four steps in execution:

1. An instruction is fetched from the instruction memory, and the PC is incremented.
2. Two registers, $t1 and $t2, are read from the register file.
3. The ALU performs a subtract on the data values read from the register file. The value of PC + 4 is added to the sign-extended, lower 16 bits of the instruction (offset) shifted left by two; the result is the branch target address.
4. The Zero result from the ALU is used to decide which adder result to store into the PC.

3.4.   An Overview of Pipelining

Pipelining

An implementation technique in which multiple instructions are overlapped in execution, much like an assembly line. MIPS instructions classically take five steps:

1. Fetch instruction from memory.
2. Read registers while decoding the instruction. The regular format of MIPS instructions allows reading and decoding to occur simultaneously.
3. Execute the operation or calculate an address.

4. Access an operand in data memory.

5. Write the result into a register.

We can turn the pipelining speed-up into a formula. If the stages are perfectly balanced, then the time between instructions on the pipelined processor—assuming ideal conditions—is equal to

$$\text{Time between instructions}_{\text{pipelined}} = \frac{\text{Time between instruction}_{\text{nonpipelined}}}{\text{Number of pipe stages}}$$

The formula suggests that a five-stage pipeline should offer nearly a fivefold improvement over the 800 ps non pipelined time, or a 160 ps clock cycle. The example shows, however, that the stages may be imperfectly balanced.

Moreover, pipelining involves some overhead, the source of which will be clearer shortly. Thus, the time per instruction in the pipelined processor will exceed the minimum possible, and speed-up will be less than the number of pipeline stages.

Instruction class	Instruction fetch	Register read	ALU operation	Data access	Register write	Total time
Load word (lw)	200 ps	100 ps	200 ps	200 ps	100 ps	800 ps
Store word (sw)	200 ps	100 ps	200 ps	200 ps		700 ps
R-format (add, sub, AND, OR, slt)	200 ps	100 ps	200 ps		100 ps	600 ps
Branch (beq)	200 ps	100 ps	200 ps			500 ps

Total Time for Each Instruction Calculated from the Time for Each Component

This calculation assumes that the multiplexors, control unit, PC accesses, and sign extension unit have no delay.

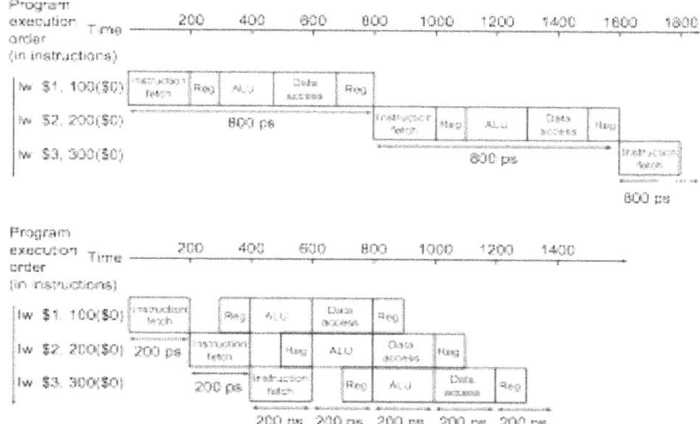

Figure: Single-cycle, nonpipelined execution in top versus pipelined execution in bottom. Both use the same hardware components, whose time is listed in figure. In this case, we see a fourfold speed-up on average time between instructions, from 800 ps down to 200 ps.

Pipeline Hazards

There are situations in pipelining when the next instruction cannot execute in the following clock cycle. These events are called *hazards*, and there are three different types.

Structuralhazard When a planned instruction cannot execute in the proper clock cycle because the hardware does not support the combination of instructions that are set to execute.

Data hazard Also called a **pipeline data hazard**. When a planned instruction cannot execute in the proper clock cycle because data that is needed to execute the instruction is not yet available.

Forwarding Also called **bypassing**. A method of resolving a data hazard by retrieving the missing data element from internal buffers rather than waiting for it to arrive from program- mer- visible registers or memory. In a computer pipeline, data hazards arise from the dependence of one instruction on an earlier one that is still in the pipeline (a relationship that does not really exist when doing laundry). For example, suppose we have an add instruction followed immediately by a subtract instruction that uses the sum ($s0):

$$\text{add} \quad \$s0, \$t0, \$t1$$
$$\text{sub} \quad \$t2, \$s0, \$t3$$

Without intervention, a data hazard could severely stall the pipeline. The add instruction doesn't write its result until the fifth stage, meaning that we would have to waste three clock cycles in the pipeline.

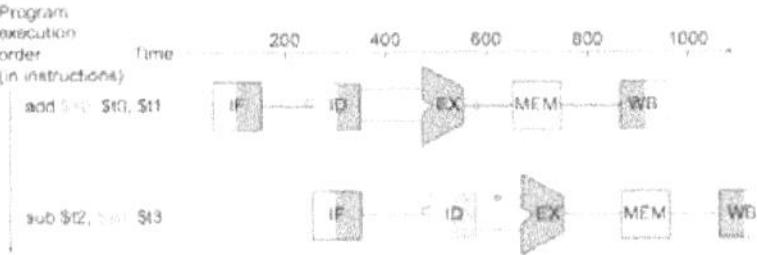

Figure: Graphical representation of forwarding. The connection shows the forwarding path from the output of the EX stage of add to the input of the EX stage for sub, replacing the value from register $s0 read in the second stage of sub.

Control hazard Also called **branch hazard**. When the proper instruction cannot execute in the proper pipeline clock cycle because the instruction that was fetched is not the one that is needed; that is, the flow of instruction addresses is not what the pipeline expected.

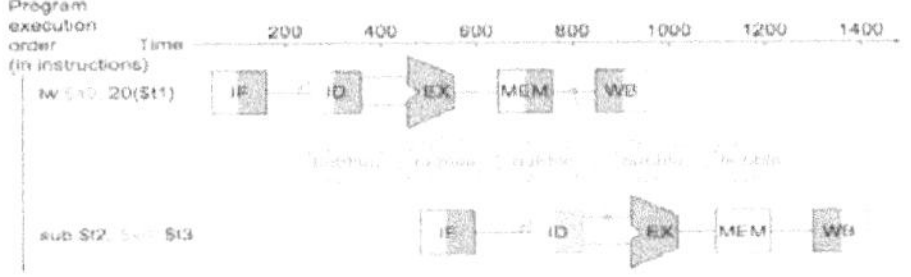

Figure: We need a stall even with forwarding when an R-format instruction following a load tries to use the data. Without the stall, the path from memory access stage output to execution stage input would be going backward in time, which is impossible. This figure is actually a simplification, since we cannot know until after the subtract instruction is fetched and decoded whether or not a stall will be necessary.

Load-Use Data Hazard

A specific form of data hazard in which the data being loaded by a load instruction has not yet become available when it is needed by another instruction.

Pipeline stall Also called **bubble**. A stall initiated in order to resolve a hazard.

Reordering Code to Avoid Pipeline Stalls.

Consider the following code segment in C:

a = b + e;

c = b + f;

Here is the generated MIPS code for this segment, assuming all variables are in memory and are addressable as offsets from $t0:

```
lw    $t1, 0($t0)
lw    $t2, 4($t0)
add   $t3, $t1,$t2
sw    $t3, 12($t0)
lw    $t4, 8($t0)
add   $t5, $t1,$t4
sw    $t5, 16($t0)
```

Find the hazards in the preceding code segment and reorder the instructions to avoid any pipeline stalls.

Both add instructions have a hazard because of their respective dependence on the immediately preceding lw instruction.

Notice that bypassing eliminates several other potential hazards, including the dependence of the first add on the first lw and any hazards for store instructions.

Moving up the third lw instruction to become the third instruction eliminates both hazards:

```
lw  $t1, 0($t0)
lw  $t2, 4($t0)
lw  $t4, 8($t0)
add $t3, $t1,$t2
sw  $t3, 12($t0)
```

add $t5, $t1,$t4

sw $t5, 16($t0)

On a pipelined processor with forwarding, the reordered sequence will complete in two fewer cycles than the original version.

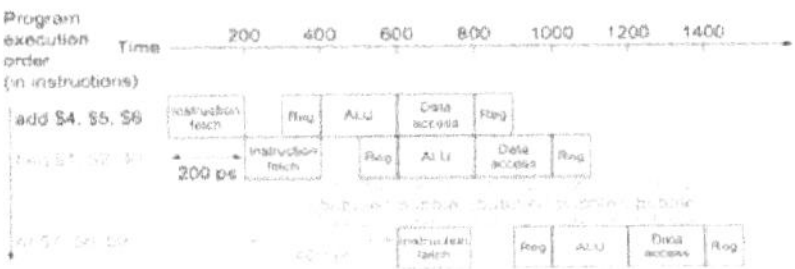

Figure: Pipeline showing stalling on every conditional branch as solution to control hazards. This example assumes the conditional branch is taken, and the instruction at the destination of the branch is the OR instruction. There is a one-stage pipeline stall, or bubble, after the branch. In reality, the process of creating a stall is slightly more complicated. The effect on performance, however, is the same as would occur if a bubble were inserted.

3.5.   Branch Prediction

A method of resolving a branch hazard that assumes a given outcome for the   branch and proceeds from that assumption rather than waiting to ascertain the actual outcome.

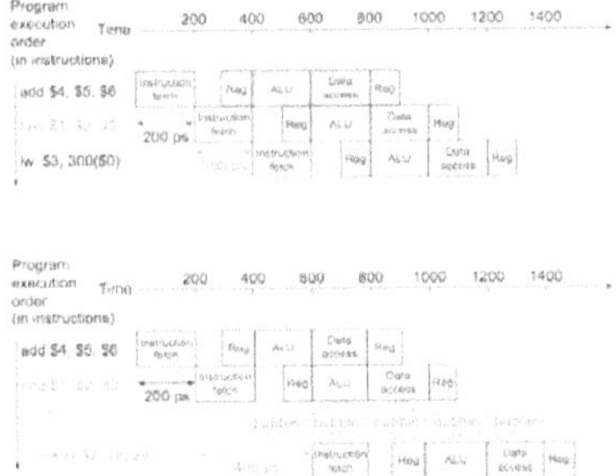

Predicting that Branches are Not Taken as a Solution to Control Hazard

The top drawing shows the pipeline when the branch is not taken. The bottom drawing shows the pipeline when the branch is taken. The insertion of a bubble in this fashion simplifies what actually happens, at least during the first clock cycle immediately following the branch.

Pipelined Datapath and Control

We must separate the datapath into five pieces, with each piece named corresponding to a stage of instruction execution:

1.   IF: Instruction fetch.

2.   ID: Instruction decode and register file read.

3. EX: Execution or address calculation.

4. MEM: Data memory access.

5. WB: Write back

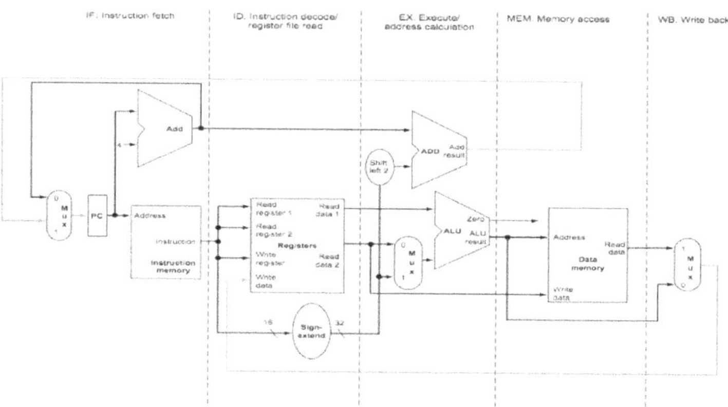

The Single-Cycle Datapath

Each step of the instruction can be mapped onto the datapath from left to right. The only exceptions are the update of the PC and the write-back step, shown in color, which sends either the ALU result or the data from memory to the left to be written into the register file. (Normally we use color lines for control, but these are data lines.). There are, however, two exceptions to this left-to-right flow of instructions:

- The write-back stage, which places the result back into the register file in the middle of the datapath.

- The selection of the next value of the PC, choosing between the incremented PC and the branch address from the MEM stage.

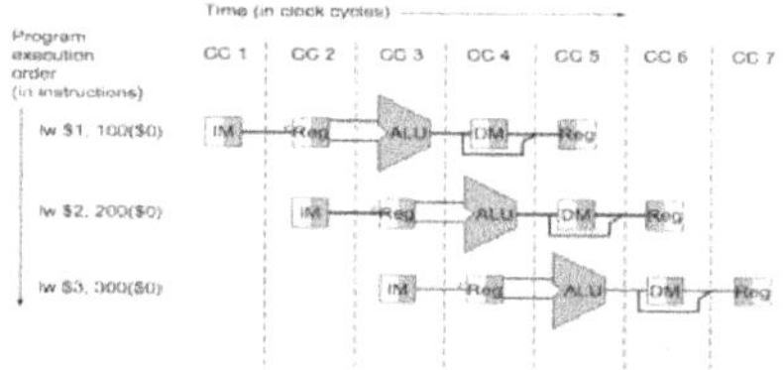

Figure: Instructions being executed using the single-cycle datapath, assuming pipelined execution. This figure pretends that each instruction has its own datapath, and shades each portion according to use.

Unlike those figures, each stage is labeled by the physical resource used in that stage, corresponding to the portions of the datapath .*IM* represents the instruction memory and the PC in the instruction fetch stage, *Reg* stands for the register file and sign extender in the instruction decode/register file read stage (ID), and so on. To maintain proper time order, this stylized datapath breaks the register file into two logical parts: registers read during register fetch (ID) and registers written during write back (WB). This dual use is represented by drawing the unshaded left half of the register file using dashed lines in the ID stage, when it is not being written, and the unshaded right half in dashed lines in the WB stage, when it is not being read. As before, we assume the register file is written in the first half of the clock cycle and the register file is read during the second half.

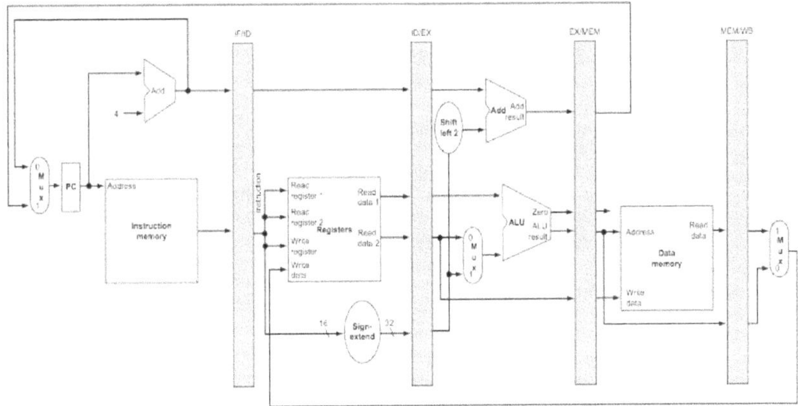

Figure: The pipelined version of the datapath. The pipeline registers, in color, separate each pipeline stage. They are labeled by the stages that they separate; for example, the first is labeled *IF/ID* because it separates the instruction fetch and instruction decode stages. The registers must be wide enough to store all the data corresponding to the lines that go through them. For example, the IF/ID register must be 64 bits wide, because it must hold both the 32-bit instruction fetched from memory and the incremented 32-bit PC address. We will expand these registers over the course of this chapter, but for now the other three pipeline registers contain 128, 97, and 64 bits, respectively. The five stages are the following:

1. *Instruction fetch:* The top portion of figure shows the instruction being read from memory using the address in the PC and then being placed in the IF/ID pipeline register. The PC address is incremented by 4 and then written back into the PC to be ready for the next clock cycle. This incremented address is also saved in the IF/ID pipeline

register in case it is needed later for an instruction, such as beq. The computer cannot know which type of instruction is being fetched, so it must prepare for any instruction, passing potentially needed information down the pipeline.

2. *Instruction decode and register file read:* The bottom portion of figure shows the instruction portion of the IF/ID pipeline register supplying the 16-bit immediate field, which is sign-extended to 32 bits, and the register numbers to read the two registers. All three values are stored in the ID/EX pipeline register, along with the incremented PC address. We again transfer everything that might be needed by any instruction during a later clock cycle.

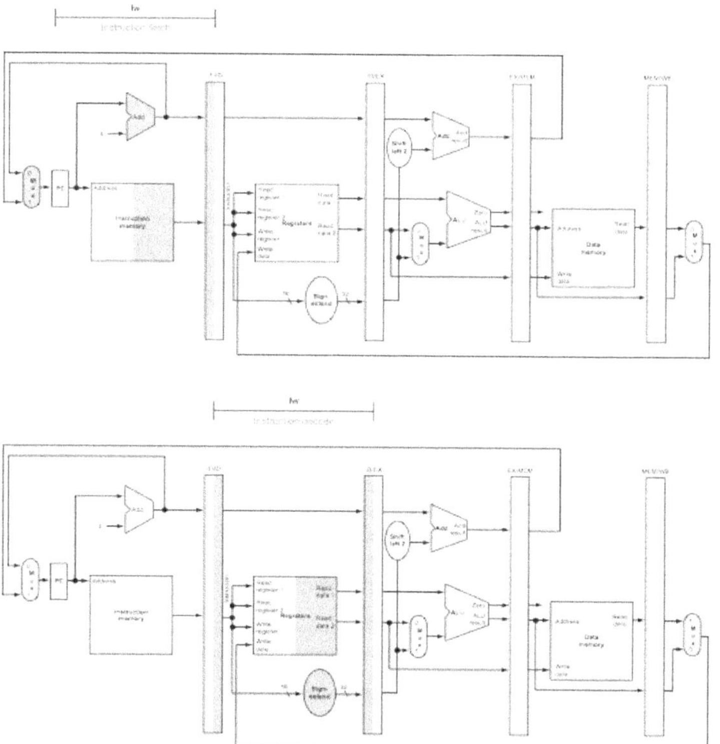

3. *Execute or address calculation:* Figure shows that the load instruction reads the contents of register 1 and the sign-extended immediate from the ID/EX pipeline register and adds them using the ALU. That sum is placed in the EX/MEM pipeline register.

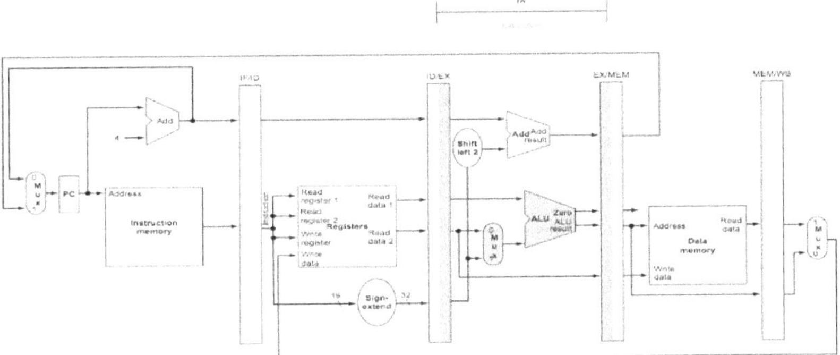

4. *Memory access:* The top portion of figure shows the load instruction reading the data memory using the address from the EX/MEM pipeline register and loading the data into the MEM/WB pipeline register.

5. *Write-back:* The bottom portion of figure shows the final step: reading the data from the MEM/WB pipeline register and writing it into the register file in the middle of the figure.

Here are the Five Pipe Stages of the Store Instruction

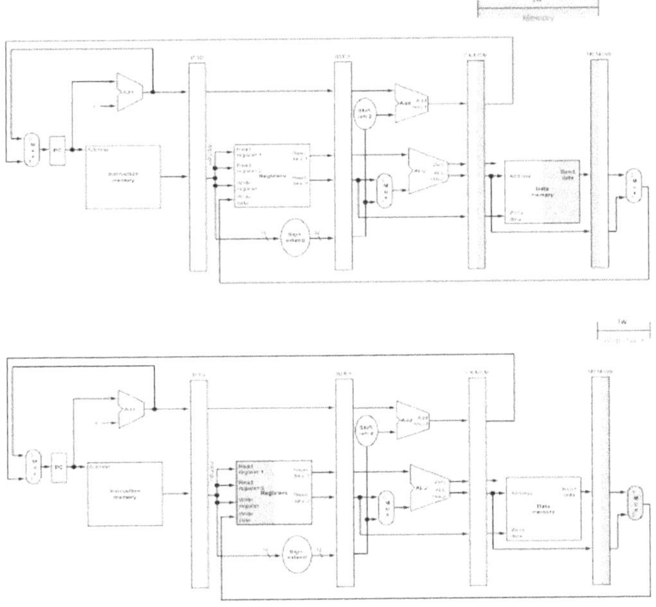

1. *Instruction fetch:* The instruction is read from memory using the address in the PC and then is placed in the IF/ID pipeline register. This stage occurs before the instruction is identified, so the top portion of figure works for store as well as load.

2. *Instruction decode and register file read:* The instruction in the IF/ID pipeline register supplies the register numbers for reading two registers and extends the sign of the 16-bit immediate. These three 32-bit values are all stored in the ID/EX pipeline register. The bottom portion for load instructions also shows the operations of the second stage for stores. These first two stages are executed by all instructions, since it is too early to know the type of the instruction.

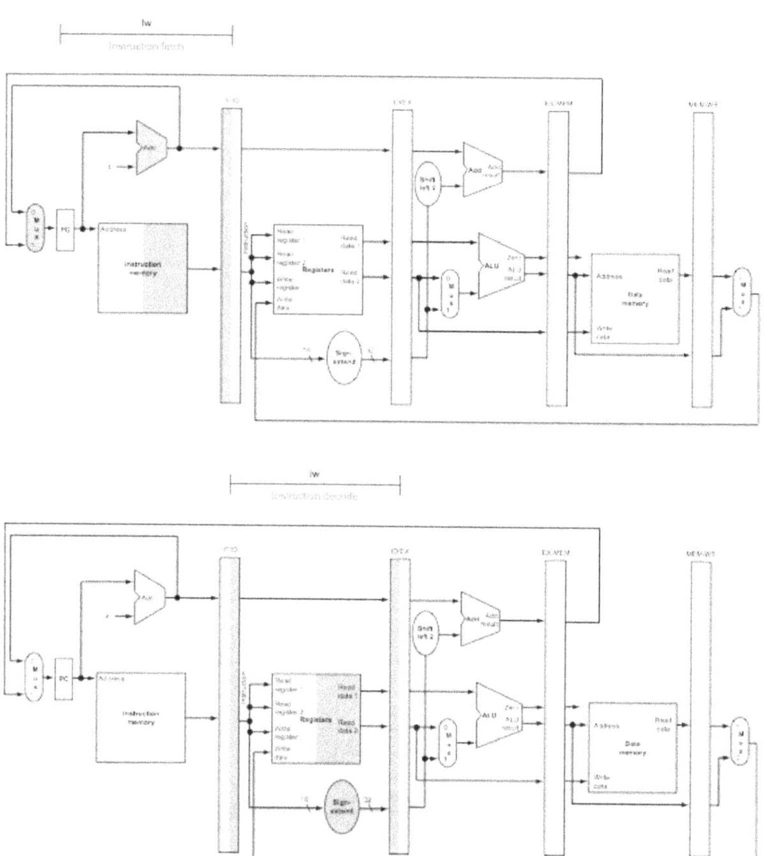

3. *Execute and address calculation:* Figure shows the third step; the effective address is placed in the EX/MEM pipeline register.

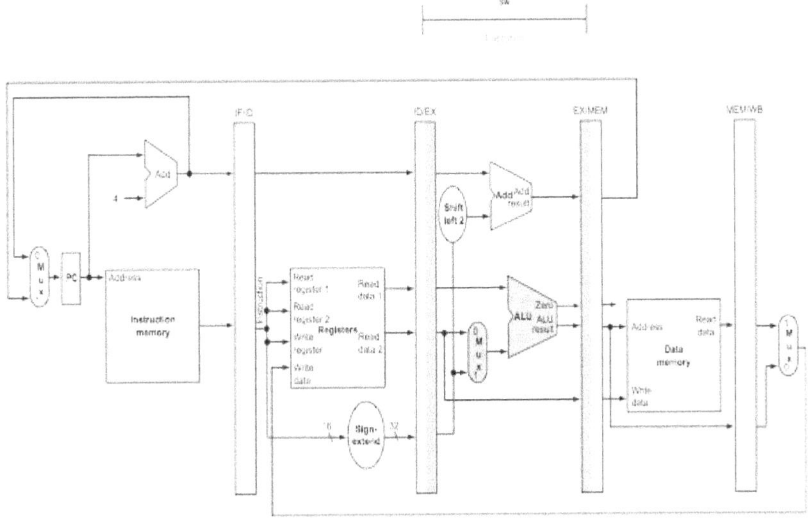

4. *Memory access:* The top portion of Figure shows the data being written to memory. Note that the register containing the data to be stored was read in an earlier stage and stored in ID/EX. The only way to make the data available during the MEM stage is to place the data into the EX/MEM pipeline register in the EX stage, just as we stored the effective address into EX/MEM.

5. *Write-back:* The bottom portion of Figure shows the final step of the store. For this instruction, nothing happens in the write-back stage. Since every instruction behind the store is already in progress, we have no way to accelerate those instructions. Hence, an instruction passes through a stage even if there is nothing to do, because later instructions are already progressing at the maximum rate.

Single-clock-cycle pipeline diagrams show the state of the entire datapath during a single clock cycle, and usually all five instructions in the pipeline are identified by labels above their respective pipeline stages. We use this type of figure to show the details of what is happening within the pipeline during each clock cycle.

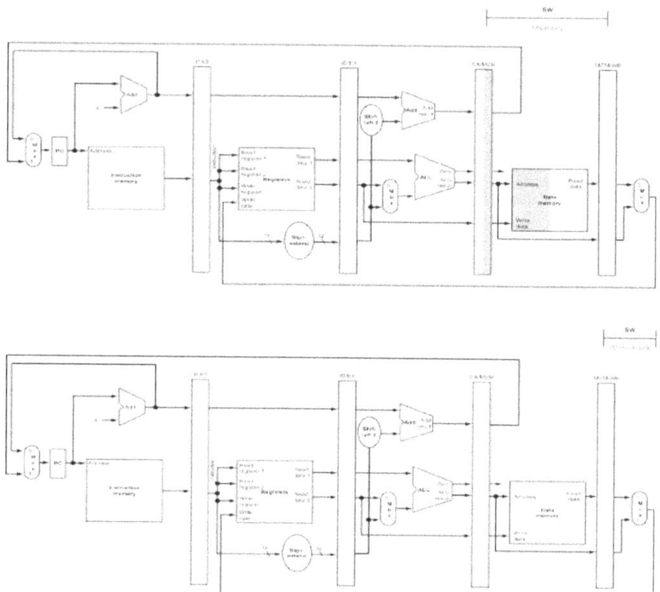

The Portion of the Data Path that is used in all Five Stages of a Load Instruction

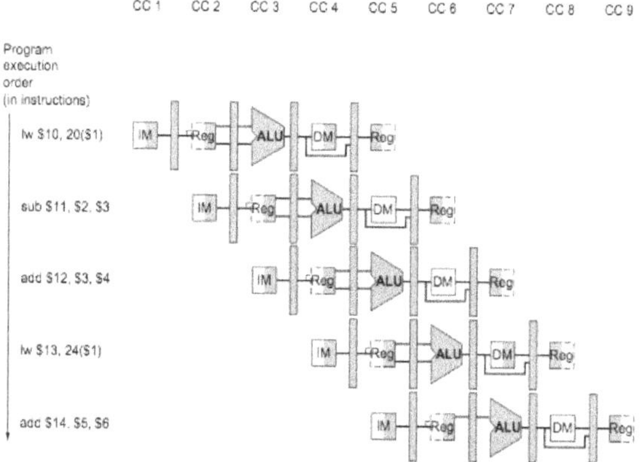

Figure: Multiple-clock-cycle pipeline diagram of five instructions. This style of pipeline representation shows the complete execution of instructions in a single figure. Instructions are listed in instruction execution order from top to bottom, and clock cycles move from left to right.

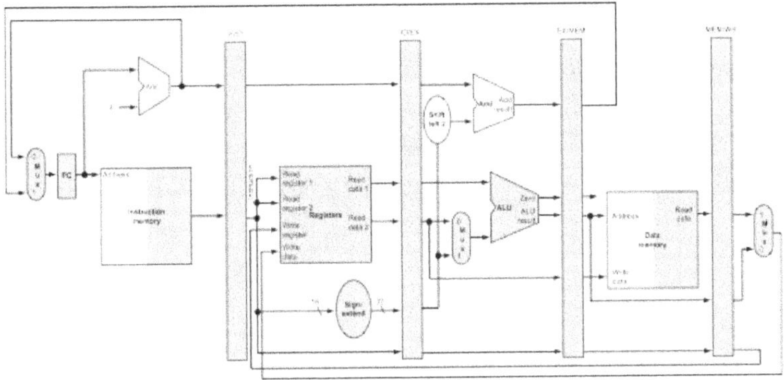

The Pipelined Data Path with the Control Signals Connected to the Control Portions of the Pipe-line Registers

The control values for the last three stages are created during the instruction decode stage and then placed in the ID/EX pipeline register. The control lines for each pipe stage are used, and remaining control lines are then passed to the next pipeline stage.

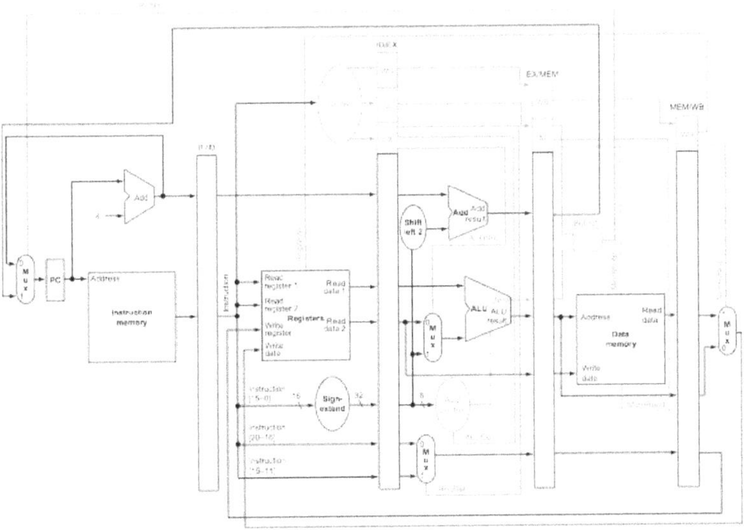

Pipelined Dependences in a Five-Instruction Sequence using Simplified Data Paths to Show the Dependences

All the dependent actions are shown in color, and "CC 1" at the top of the figure means clock cycle 1. The first instruction writes into $2, and all the following instructions read $2. This register is written in clock cycle 5, so the proper value is unavailable before clock cycle 5. (A read of a register during a clock cycle returns the value written at the end of the first half of the cycle, when such a write occurs.) The colored lines from the top datapath to the lower ones show the dependences. Those that must go backward in time are *pipeline data hazards*.

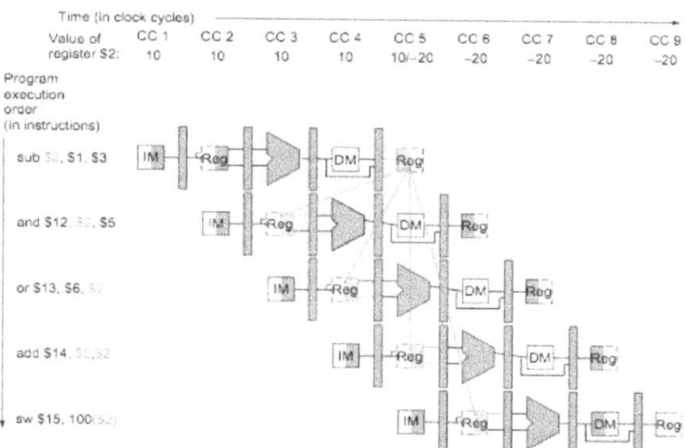

The pipelined datapath of Figure with the control signals identified. Note that we now need the 6-bit funct field (function code) of the instruction in the EX stage as input to ALU control, so these bits must also be included in the ID/EX pipeline register. Recall that these 6 bits are also the 6 least significant bits of the immediate field in the instruction, so the ID/EX pipeline register can supply them from the immediate field since sign extension leaves these bits unchanged.

Go to page 314

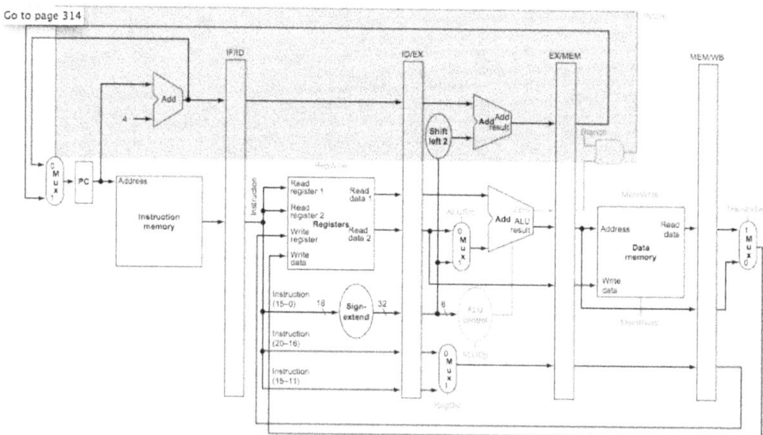

Data Hazards: Forwarding Versus Stalling

Let's look at a sequence with many dependences, shown in color:

The pipelined datapath of Figure 4.46, with the control signals connected to the control portions of

    sub $2, $1,$3
    and $12,$2,$5
    or $13,$6,$2
    add $14,$2,$2
    sw $15,100($2)

    # Register $2 written by sub

    # 1st operand($2) depends on sub

    # 2nd operand($2) depends on sub

    # 1st($2) & 2nd($2) depend on sub

    # Base ($2) depends on sub

The last four instructions are all dependent on the result in register $2 of the first instruction. If register $2 had the value 10 before the subtract instruction and –20 afterwards, the programmer intends that –20 will be used in the following instructions that refer to register $2.

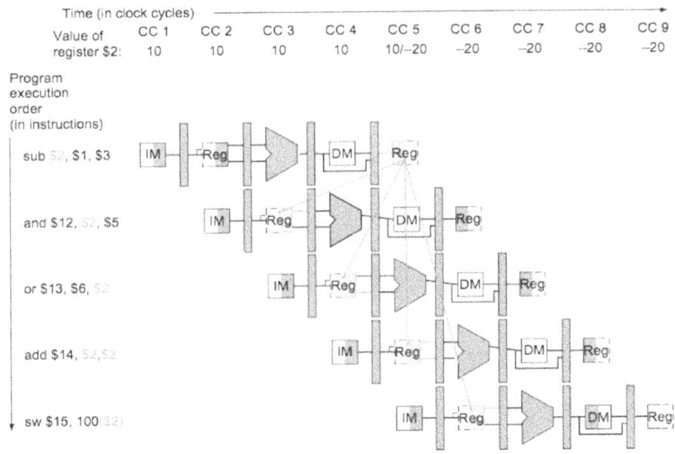

Figure: Pipelined dependences in a five-instruction sequence using simplified datapaths to show the dependences. All the dependent actions are shown in color, and "CC 1" at the top of the figure means clock cycle 1.

The first instruction writes into $2, and all the following instructions read $2. This register is written in clock cycle 5, so the proper value is unavailable before clock cycle 5. (A read of a register during a clock cycle returns the value written at the end of the first half of the cycle, when such a write occurs.) The colored lines from the top datapath to the lower ones show the dependences. Those that must go backward in time are *pipeline data hazards.*

Data Hazards and Stalls

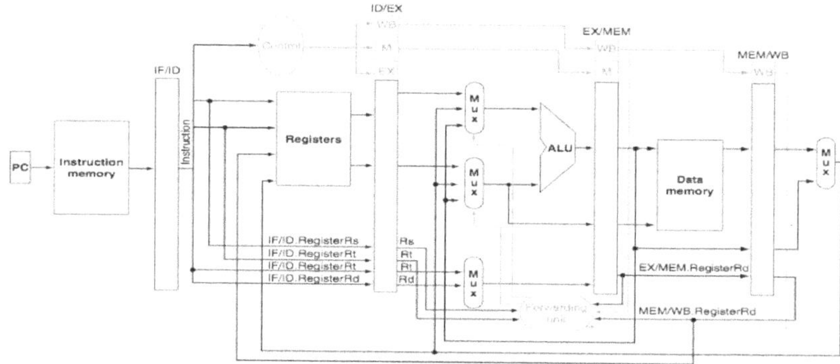

Figure: The datapath modified to resolve hazards via forwarding. This figure is a more stylized drawing, however, leaving out details from the full datapath, such as the branch hardware and the sign extension hardware

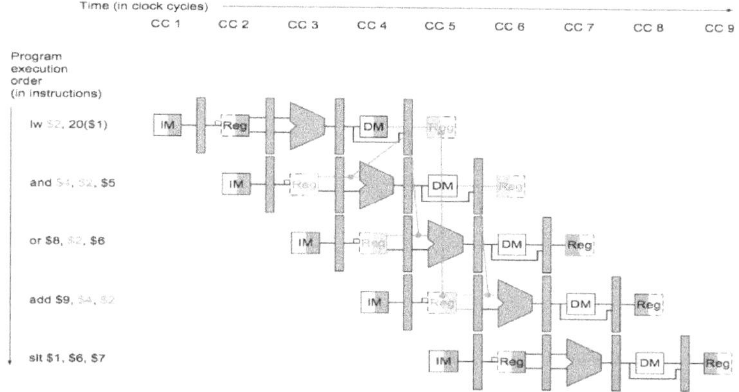

Figure: A pipelined sequence of instructions. Since the dependence between the load and the following instruction (and) goes backward in time, this hazard cannot be solved by forwarding. Hence, this combination must result in a stall by the hazard detection unit.

Nop An instruction that does no operation to change state.

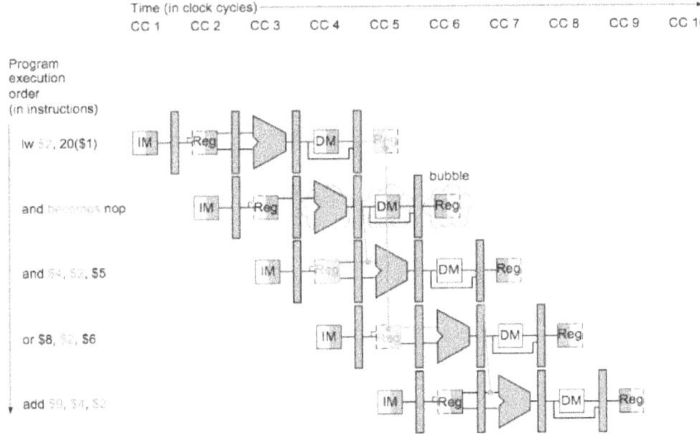

Figure: The way stalls are really inserted into the pipeline. A bubble is inserted beginning in clock cycle 4, by changing the and instruction to a nop. Note that the and instruction is really fetched and decoded in clock cycles 2 and 3, but its EX stage is delayed until clock cycle 5 (versus the unstalled position in clock cycle 4). Likewise the OR instruction is fetched in clock cycle 3, but its ID stage is delayed until clock cycle 5 (versus the unstalled clock cycle 4 position). After insertion of the bubble, all the dependences go forward in time and no further hazards occur.

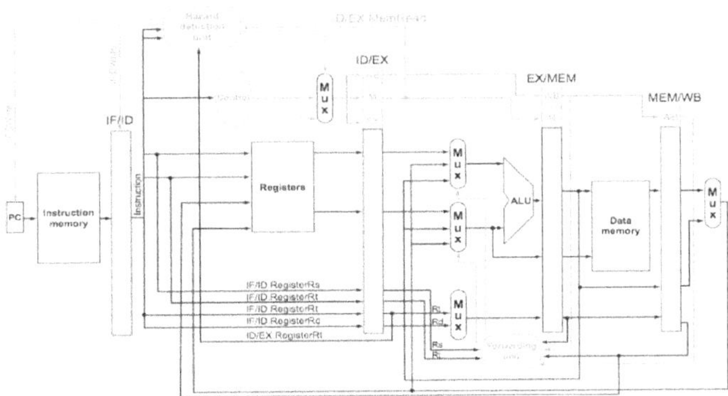

Figure: Pipelined control overview showing the two multiplexors for forwarding, the hazard detection unit, and the forwarding unit. Although the ID and EX stages have been simplified—the sign-extended immediate and branch logic are missing— this drawing gives the essence of the forwarding hardware requirements.

Control Hazards

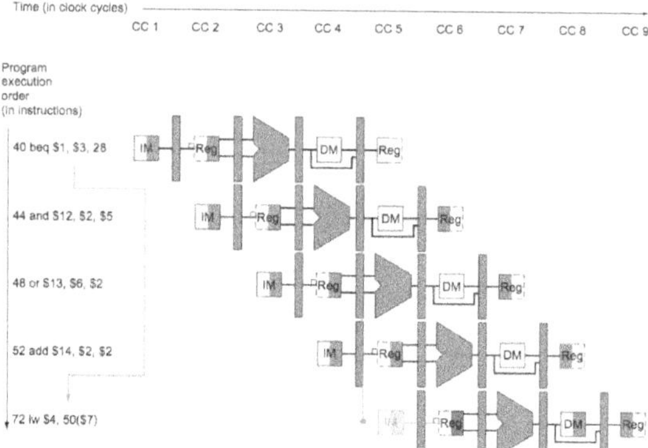

Figure: The impact of the pipeline on the branch instruction. The numbers to the left of the instruction (40, 44, ...) are the addresses of the instructions. Since the branch instruction decides whether to branch in the MEM stage—clock cycle 4 for the beq instruction above—the three sequential instructions that follow the branch will be fetched and begin execution. Without intervention, those three following instructions will begin execution before beq branches to lw at location 72.

Dynamic Branch Prediction

Dynamic branch prediction Prediction of branches at runtime using runtime information.

Branch prediction buffer Also called **branch history table**. A small memory that is indexed by the lower portion of the address of the branch instruction and that contains one or more bits indicating whether the branch was recently taken or not.

Branch delay slot The slot directly aftera delayed branch instruction, which in the MIPS architecture is filled by an instruction that does not affect the branch.

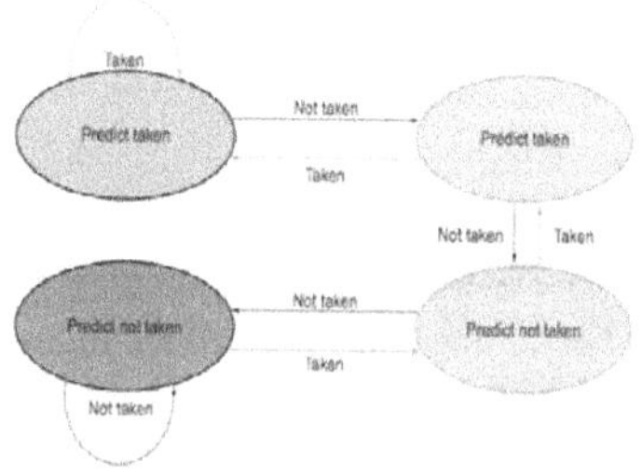

Figure: The states in a 2-bit prediction scheme. By using 2 bits rather than 1, a branch that strongly favors taken or not taken—as many branches do—will be mispredicted only once. The 2 bits are used to encode the four states in the system. The 2-bit scheme is a general instance of a counter-based predictor, which is incremented when the prediction is accurate and decremented otherwise, and uses the mid-point of its range as the division between taken and not taken.

Branch Target Buffer

A structure that caches the destination PC or destination instruction for a branch. It is usually organized as a cache with tags, making it more costly than a simple prediction buffer.

Correlating Predictor

A branch predictor that combines local behavior of a particular branch and global information about the behavior of some recent number of executed branches.

Tournament branch predictor A branch predictor with multiple predictions for each branch and a selection mechanism that chooses which predictor to enable for a given branch.

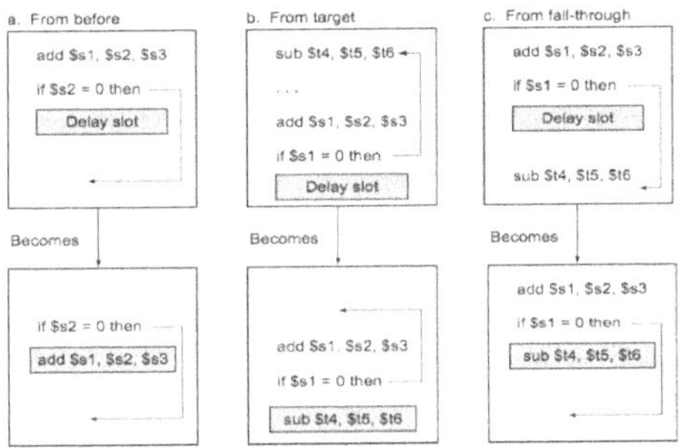

Scheduling the branch delay slot

The top box in each pair shows the code before scheduling; the bottom box shows the scheduled code. In (a), the delay slot is scheduled with an independent instruction from before the branch. This is the best choice. Strategies (b) and (c) are used when (a) is not possible. In the code sequences for (b) and (c), the use of $s1 in the branch condition prevents the add instruction (whose destination is $s1) from being moved into the branch delay slot. In (b) the branch delay slot is scheduled from the target of the branch; usually the target instruction will need to be copied because it can be reached by another path. Strategy (b) is preferred when the branch is taken with high probability, such as a loop branch. Finally, the branch may be scheduled from the not-taken fall-through as in (c). To make this optimization legal for (b) or (c), it must be OK to execute the sub instruction when the branch goes in the unexpected direction. By "OK" we mean that the work is wasted, but the program will still execute correctly. This is the case, for example, if $t4 were an unused temporary register when the branch goes in the unexpected direction.

3.6.   Exceptions

Exception Also called **interrupt**. An unscheduled eventthat disrupts program execution; used to detect overflow.

Interrupt An exception that comes from outside of the processor. (Some architectures use the term *interrupt* for all exceptions.)

Type of event	From where?	MIPS terminology
I/O device request	External	Interrupt
Invoke the operating system from user program	Internal	Exception
Arithmetic overflow	Internal	Exception
Using an undefined instruction	Internal	Exception
Hardware malfunctions	Either	Exception or interrupt

How Exceptions Are Handled in the MIPS Architecture

For the operating system to handle the exception, it must know the reason for the exception, in addition to the instruction that caused it. There are two main methods used to communicate the reason for an exception. The method used in the MIPS architecture is to include a status register (called the *Cause register*), which holds a field that indicates the reason for the exception.

A second method, is to use **vectored interrupts**. In a vectored interrupt, the address to which control is transferred is determined by the cause of the exception. For example, to accommodate the two exception types listed above, we might define the following two exception vector addresses:

Exception type	Exception vector address (in hex)
Undefined instruction	8000 0000$_{hex}$
Arithmetic overflow	8000 0180$_{hex}$

We can perform the processing required for exceptions by adding a few extra registers and control signals to our basic implementation and by slightly extending control. Let's assume that we are implementing the exception system used in the MIPS architecture, with the single entry point being the address 8000 0180$_{hex}$. (Implementing vectored exceptions is no more difficult.) We will need to add two additional registers to our current MIPS implementation:

- *EPC:* A 32-bit register used to hold the address of the affected instruction. (Such a register is needed even when exceptions are vectored.)
- *Cause:* A register used to record the cause of the exception. In the MIPS architecture, this register is 32 bits, although some bits are currently unused. Assume there is a five-bit field that encodes the two possible exception sources mentioned above, with 10 representing an undefined instruction and 12 representing arithmetic overflow.

Exceptions in a Pipelined Implementation

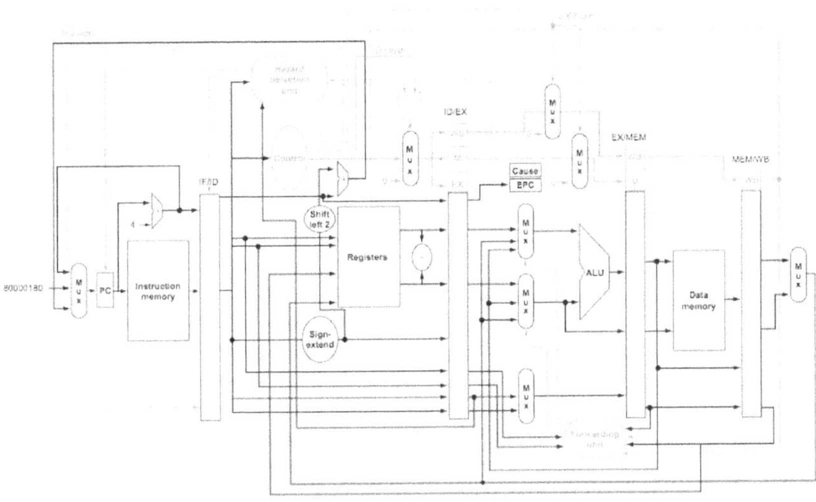

Figure: The datapath with controls to handle exceptions. The key additions include a new input with the value 8000 0180$_{hex}$ in the multiplexor that supplies the new PC value; a Cause register to record the cause of the exception; and an Exception PC register to save the address of the instruction that caused the exception. The 8000 0180$_{hex}$ input to the multiplexor is the initial address to begin fetching instructions in the event of an exception. Although not shown, the ALU overflow signal is an input to the control unit.

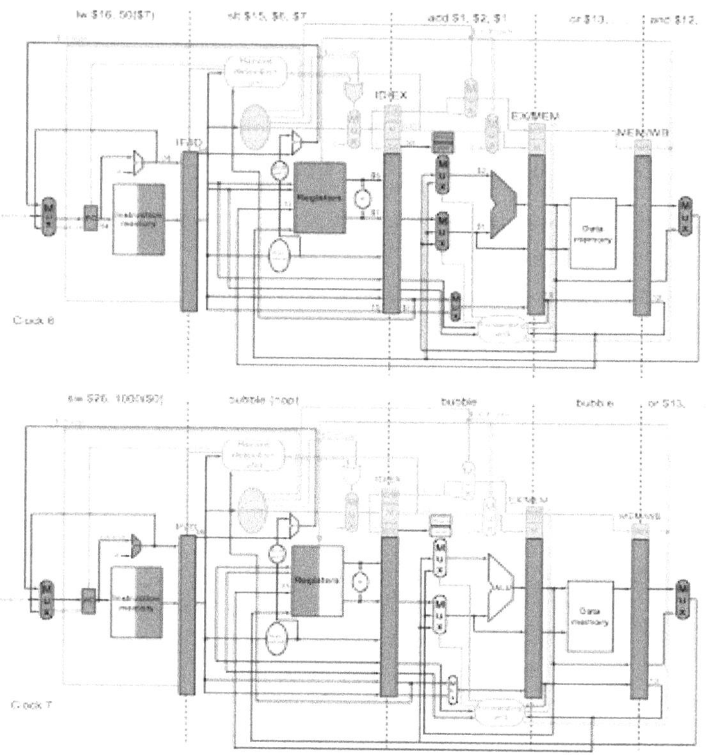

Figure: The result of an exception due to arithmetic overflow in the add instruction. The overflow is detected during the EX stage of clock 6, saving the address following the add in the EPC register ($4C + 4 = 50_{hex}$). Overflow causes all the Flush signals to be set near the end of this clock cycle, deasserting control values (setting them to 0) for the add. Clock cycle 7 shows the instructions converted to bubbles in the pipeline plus the fetching of the first instruction of the exception routine—sw $25,1000($0)—from instruction location 8000 0180$_{hex}$. Note that the AND and OR instructions, which are prior to the add, still complete. Although not shown, the ALU overflow signal is an input to the control unit.

Imprecise interrupt Also called **imprecise exception**. Interrupts or exceptions in pipelined computers that are not associated with the exact instruction that was the cause of the interrupt or exception.

Precise interrupt Also called **precise exception**. An interrupt or exception that is always associated with the correct instruction in pipelined computers.

UNIT IV

PARALLELISM

Instruction-level-parallelism – Parallel processing challenges – Flynn's classification – Hardware multithreading – Multicore processors

4.1. Instruction-Level-Parallelism

Multiprocessor

A computer system with at least two processors. This computer is in contrast to a Uniprocessors, which has one, and is increasingly hard to find today. Since multiprocessor soft ware should scale, some designs support operation in the presence of broken hardware; that is, if a single processor fails in a multiprocessor with n processors, these system would continue to provide service with $n - 1$ processors. Hence, multiprocessors can also improve availability.

High performance can mean high throughput for independent tasks, called **task-level parallelism** or **process-level parallelism**. These tasks are independent single-threaded applications, and they are an important and popular use of multiple processors. This approach is in contrast to running a single job on multiple processors. We use the term **parallel processing program** to refer to a single program that runs on multiple processors simultaneously.

Task-Level Parallelism or Process-Level Parallelism

Utilizing multiple processors by running independent programs simultaneously.

Parallel Processing Program

A single program that runs on multiple processors simultaneously.

Cluster

A set of computers connected over a local area network that function as a single large multiprocessor.

Multicore Microprocessor

A microprocessor containing multiple processors ("cores") in a single integrated circuit. Virtually all microprocessors today in desktops and servers are multicore.

Shared Memory Multiprocessor

(SMP) A parallel processor with a single physical address space.

4.2.   Parallel Processing Challenges

The difficulty with parallelism is not the hardware; it is that too few important application programs have been rewritten to complete tasks sooner on multiprocessors.

It is difficult to write soft ware that uses multiple processors to complete one task faster, and the problem gets worse as the number of processors increases.

The first reason is that you *must* get better performance or better energy efficiency from a parallel processing program on a multiprocessor; otherwise, you would just use a sequential program on a uniprocessor, as sequential programming is simpler.

In fact, uniprocessor design techniques such as superscalar and out-of order execution take advantage of instruction-level parallelism, normally without the involvement of the programmer. Such innovations reduced the demand for rewriting programs for multiprocessors, since programmers could do nothing and yet their sequential programs would run faster on new computers.

Speed-up Challenge

Suppose you want to achieve a speed-up of 90 times faster with 100 processors. What percentage of the original computation can be sequential?

Amdahl's Law says

Execution time after improvement =

$$\frac{\text{Execution time affected by improvement}}{\text{Amount of improvement}} + \text{Execution time unaffected}$$

We can reformulate Amdahl's Law in terms of speed-up versus the original execution time:

$$\text{Speed-up} = \frac{\text{Execution time before}}{(\text{Execution time before} - \text{Execution time affected}) + \dfrac{\text{Execution time affected}}{\text{Amount of improvement}}}$$

This formula is usually rewritten assuming that the execution time before is 1 for some unit of time, and the execution time affected by improvement is considered the fraction of the original execution time:

$$\text{Speed-up} = \cfrac{1}{(1 - \text{Fraction time affected}) + \cfrac{\text{Fraction time affected}}{\text{Amount of improvement}}}$$

Substituting 90 for speed-up and 100 for amount of improvement into the formula above:

$$90 = \cfrac{1}{(1 - \text{Fraction time affected}) + \cfrac{\text{Fraction time affected}}{100}}$$

Then simplifying the formula and solving for fraction time affected:

90× (1 -0.99 Fraction time affected) = 1

90- (90 ×0.99 ×Fraction time affected) = 1

90 -1 = 90 ×0.99× Fraction time affected

Fraction time affected = 89/89.1 = 0.999

Thus, to achieve a speed-up of 90 from 100 processors, the sequential percentage can only be 0.1%.

Speed-Up Challenge: Bigger Problem

Suppose you want to perform two sums: one is a sum of 10 scalar variables, and one is a matrix sum of a pair of two-dimensional arrays, with dimensions 10 by 10.

For now let's assume only the matrix sum is parallelizable; we'll see soon how to parallelize scalar sums. What speed-up do you get with 10 versus 40 processors?

Next, calculate the speed-ups assuming the matrices grow to 20 by 20. If we assume performance is a function of the time for an addition, t, then there are 10 additions that do not benefit from parallel processors and 100 additions that do. If the time for a single processor is 110 t, the execution time for 10 processors is,

Execution time after improvement =

$$\frac{\text{Execution time affected by improvement}}{\text{Amount of improvement}} + \text{Execution time unaffected}$$

$$\text{Execution time after improvement} = \frac{100t}{10} + 10t = 20t$$

So the speed-up with 10 processors is 110t/20t = 5.5. The execution time for 40 processors is,

$$\text{Execution time after improvement} = \frac{100t}{40} + 10t = 12.5t$$

So the speed-up with 40 processors is 110t/12.5t = 8.8. Thus, for this problem size, we get about 55% of the potential speed-up with 10 processors, but only 22% with 40.

Look what happens when we increase the matrix. The sequential program now takes 10t + 400t = 410t.

The execution time for 10 processors is,

$$\text{Execution time after improvement} = \frac{400t}{10} + 10t = 50t$$

So the speed-up with 10 processors is 410t/50t = 8.2. The execution time for 40 processors is,

$$\text{Execution time after improvement} = \frac{400t}{40} + 10t = 20t$$

So the speed-up with 40 processors is 410t/20t = 20.5. Thus, for this larger problem size, we get 82% of the potential speed-up with 10 processors and 51% with 40.

Strong Scaling

Speedup achieved on a multiprocessor without increasing the size of the problem.

Weak Scaling

Speedup achieved on a multiprocessor while increasing the size of the problem proportionally to the increase in the number of processors.

Speed-up Challenge: Balancing Load

To achieve the speed-up of 20.5 on the previous larger problem with 40 processors, we assumed the load was perfectly balanced. That is, each of the 40 processors had 2.5% of the work to do. Instead, show the impact on speed-up if one processor's load is higher than all the rest. Calculate at twice the load (5%) and five times the load (12.5%) for that hardest working processor. How well utilized are the rest of the processors?

If one processor has 5% of the parallel load, then it must do 5% × 400 or 20 additions, and the other 39 will share the remaining 380. Since they are operating simultaneously, we can just calculate the execution time as a maximum.

$$\text{Execution time after improvement} = \text{Max}\left(\frac{380t}{39}, \frac{20t}{1}\right) + 10t = 30t$$

The speed-up drops from 20.5 to $410t/30t = 14$. The remaining 39 processors are utilized less than half the time: while waiting 20t for hardest working processor to finish, they only compute for $380t/39 = 9.7t$.

If one processor has 12.5% of the load, it must perform 50 additions. The formula is:

$$\text{Execution time after improvement} = \text{Max}\left(\frac{350t}{39}, \frac{50t}{1}\right) + 10t = 60t$$

The speed-up drops even further to $410t/60t = 7$. The rest of the processors are utilized less than 20% of the time ($9t/50t$). This example demonstrates the importance of balancing load, for just a single processor with twice the load of the others cuts speed-up by a third, and five times the load on just one processor reduces speed-up by almost a factor of three.

4.3. Flynn's Classification

A conventional uniprocessor has a single instruction stream and single data stream, and a conventional multiprocessor has multiple instruction streams and multiple data streams. These two categories are abbreviated **SISD** and **MIMD**, respectively.

While it is possible to write separate programs that run on different processors on a MIMD computer and yet work together for a grander, coordinated goal, programmers normally write a single program that runs on all processors of an **MIMD** computer, relying on conditional statements when different processors should execute different sections of code. This style is called **Single Program Multiple Data (SPMD)**, but it is just the normal way to program a MIMD computer. **SISD** or Single Instruction stream, Single Data stream.

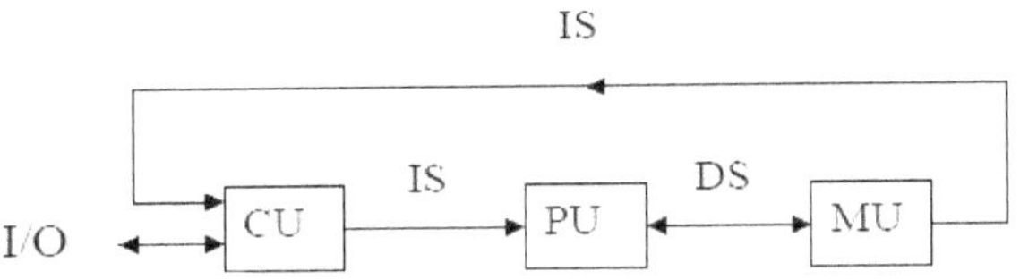

A uniprocessor **MIMD** or Multiple Instruction streams, Multiple Data streams.

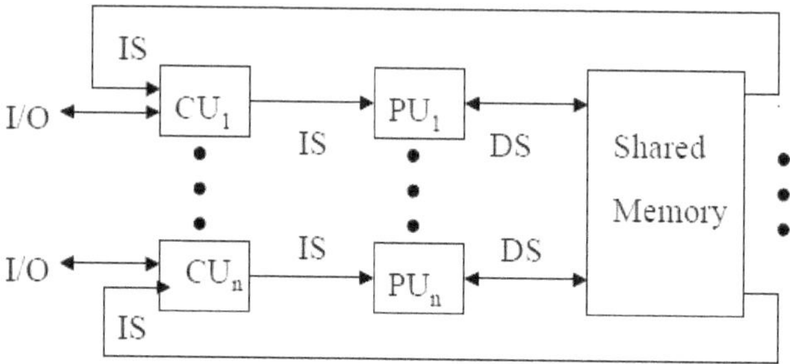

A multiprocessor **SPMD** Single Program, Multiple Data streams. The conventional MIMD programming model, where a single program runs across all processors.

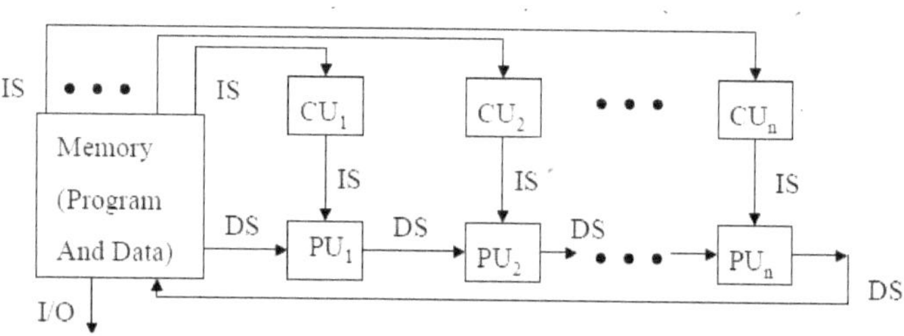

SIMD or Single Instruction stream, Multiple Data streams. The same instruction is applied to many data streams, as in a vector processor.

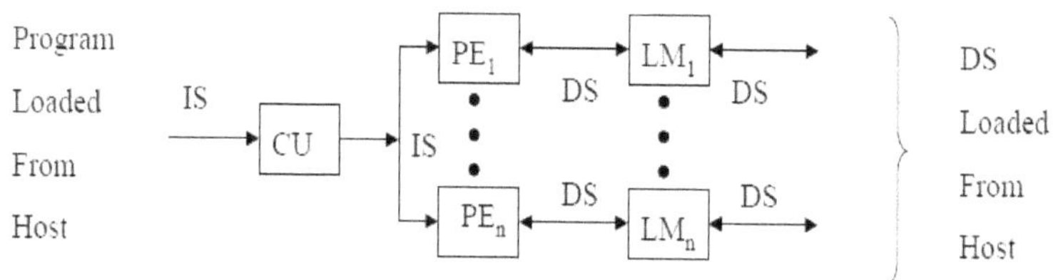

CU -Control Unit.

PU -Processing Unit

MU -Memory Unit.

IS -Instruction Stream

DS -Data Stream.

PE –Processing Element.

LM –Local Memory.

		Data Streams	
		Single	Multiple
Instruction Streams	Single	SISD: Intel Pentium 4	SIMD: SSE instructions of x86
	Multiple	MISD: No examples today	MIMD: Intel Core i7

Data-Level Parallelism

Parallelism achieved by performing the same operation on independent data.

4.4. Hardware Multithreading

Hardware Multithreading

Increasing utilization of a processor by switching to another thread when one thread is stalled.

Thread

A thread includes the program counter, the register state, and the stack. It is a lightweight process; whereas threads commonly share a single address space, processes don't.

Process

A process includes one or more threads, the address space, and the operating system state. Hence, a process switch usually invokes the operating system, but not a thread switch.

Fine-Grained Multithreading

A version of hardware multithreading that implies switching between threads after every instruction.

Coarse-Grained Multithreading

A version of hardware multithreading that implies switching between threads only after significant events, such as a last-level cache miss.

Simultaneous Multithreading

(SMT) A version of multithreading that lowers the cost of multithreading by utilizing the resources needed for multiple issue, dynamically scheduled micro architecture.

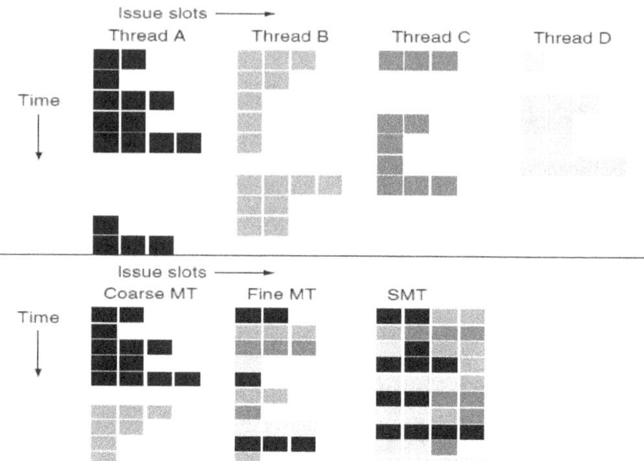

How Four Threads use the Issue Slots of a Superscalar Processor in Different Approaches

The four threads at the top show how each would execute running alone on a standard superscalar processor without multithreading support. The three examples at the bottom show how they would execute running together in three multithreading options. The horizontal dimension represents the instruction issue capability in each clock cycle. The vertical dimension represents a sequence of clock cycles.

An empty (white) box indicates that the corresponding issue slot is unused in that clock cycle. The shades of gray and color correspond to four different threads in the multithreading processors. The additional pipeline start-up effects for coarse multithreading, which are not illustrated in this figure, would lead to further loss in throughput for coarse multithreading.

How four threads would execute independently on a superscalar with no multithreading support. The bottom portion shows how the four threads could be combined to execute on the processor more efficiently using three multithreading options:

- A superscalar with coarse-grained multithreading.
- A superscalar with fine-grained multithreading.
- A superscalar with simultaneous multithreading.

In the superscalar without hardware multithreading support, the use of issue slots is limited by a lack of **instruction-level parallelism**. In addition, a major stall, such as an instruction cache miss, can leave the entire processor idle.

In the coarse-grained multithreaded superscalar, the long stalls are partially hidden by switching to another thread that uses the resources of the processor.

Although this reduces the number of completely idle clock cycles, the pipeline start-up overhead still leads to idle cycles, and limitations to ILP means all issue slots will not be used. In the fine-grained case, the interleaving of threads mostly eliminates idle clock cycles. Because only a single thread issues instructions in a given clock cycle, however, limitations in instruction-level parallelism still lead to idle slots within some clock cycles.

4.5. Multicore Processors

Uniform Memory Access (UMA)

A multiprocessor in which latency to any word in main memory is about the same no matter which processor requests the access.

Non Uniform Memory Access (NUMA)

A type of single address space multiprocessor in which some memory accesses are much faster than others depending on which processor asks for which word.

Synchronization

The process of coordinating the behavior of two or more processes, which may be running on different processors.

Lock

A synchronization device that allows access to data to only one processor at a time.

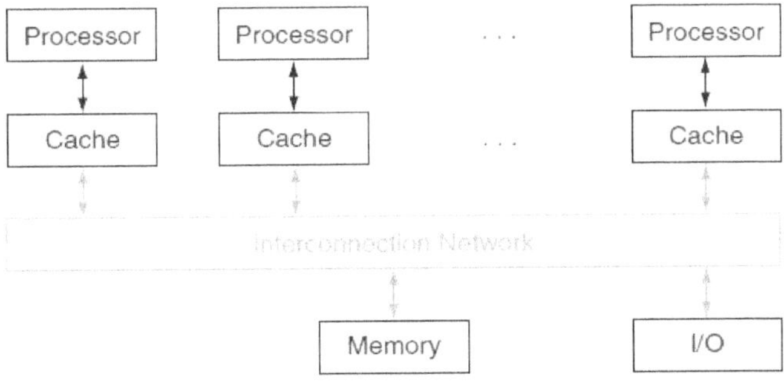

Classic Organization of a Shared Memory Multiprocessor

A Simple Parallel Processing Program for a Shared Address Space.

Suppose we want to sum 64,000 numbers on a shared memory multiprocessor computer with uniform memory access time. Let's assume we have 64 processors.

The first step is to ensure a balanced load per processor, so we split the set of numbers into subsets of the same size. We do not allocate the subsets to a different memory space, since there is a single memory space for this machine; we just give different starting addresses to each processor. Pn is the number that identifies the processor, between 0 and 63. All processors start the program by running a loop that sums their subset of numbers:

sum[Pn] = 0;

for (i = 1000*Pn; i < 1000*(Pn+1); i += 1)

sum[Pn] += A[i]; /*sum the assigned areas*/

The next step is to add these 64 partial sums. This step is called a **reduction**, where we divide to conquer. Half of the processors add pairs of partial sums, and then a quarter add pairs of the new partial sums, and so on until we have the single, final sum.

Reduction

A function that processes a data structure and returns a single value.

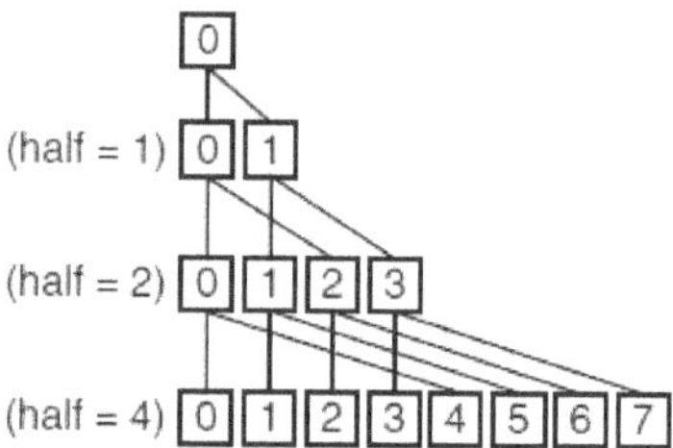

The last four levels of a reduction that sums results from each processor, from bottom to top. For all processors whose number i is less than half, add the sum produced by processor number (i + half) to its sum.

In this example, the two processors must synchronize before the "consumer" processor tries to read the result from the memory location written by the "producer" processor; otherwise, the consumer may read the old value of the data. We want each processor to have its own version of the loop counter variable i, so we must indicate that it is a "private" variable. Here is the code.

(half is private also):

```
half = 64; /*64 processors in multiprocessor*/
do
synch(); /*wait for partial sum completion*/
if (half%2 != 0 && Pn == 0)
sum[0] += sum[half-1];
/*Conditional sum needed when half is
odd; Processor0 gets missing element */
half = half/2; /*dividing line on who sums */
if (Pn < half) sum[Pn] += sum[Pn+half];
while (half > 1); /*exit with final sum in Sum[0] */
```

UNIT V

MEMORY AND I/O SYSTEMS

Memory hierarchy - Memory technologies – Cache basics – Measuring and improving cache performance - Virtual memory, TLBs - Input/output system, programmed I/O, DMA and interrupts, I/O processors.

5.1. Memory Hierarchy

- A structure that uses multiple levels of memories; as the distance from the processor increases, the size of the memories and the access time both increase.

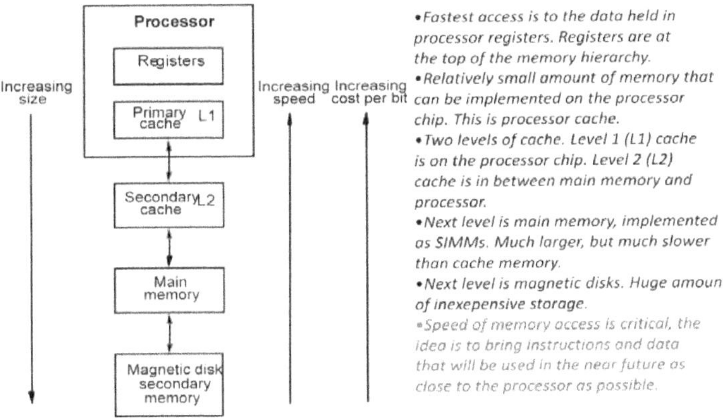

Speed, Size and Cost

- A big challenge in the design of a computer system is to provide a sufficiently large memory, with a reasonable speed at an affordable cost.

- **Static RAM**
  - Very fast, but expensive, because a basic SRAM cell has a complex circuit making it impossible to pack a large number of cells onto a single chip.

- **Dynamic RAM**
  - Simpler basic cell circuit, hence are much less expensive, but significantly slower than SRAMs.

- **Magnetic disks**
  - Storage provided by DRAMs is higher than SRAMs, but is still less than what is necessary.
  - Secondary storage such as magnetic disks provide a large amount of storage, but is much slower than DRAMs.

Locality of Reference

- Analysis of programs indicates that many instructions in localized areas of a program are executed repeatedly during some period of time, while the others are accessed relatively less frequently.
  - These instructions may be the ones in a loop, nested loop or few procedures calling each other repeatedly. This is called "locality of reference".
- **Temporal locality of reference (locality in time):**
  - The principle stating that if a data location is referenced then it will tend to be referenced again soon.
- **Spatial locality of reference(locality in space):**
  - The locality principle stating that if a data location is referenced, data locations with nearby addresses will tend to be referenced again soon.

5.2. Memory Technologies

- Four primary technologies:
  - SRAM (static random access memory)
    Cache memory
  - DRAM (dynamic random access memory)
    Main memory
  - Flash memory
    Secondary memory in Personal Mobile Devices
  - Magnetic disk
    Secondary memory in PC, Servers

Access Time

Memory technology	Typical access time
SRAM semiconductor memory	0.5–2.5 ns
DRAM semiconductor memory	50–70 ns
Flash semiconductor memory	5,000–50,000 ns
Magnetic disk	5,000,000–20,000,000 ns

SRAM

- Two inverters are cross connected to implement a basic flip-flop.
- The cell is connected to one word line and two bits lines by transistors T1 and T2.
- When word line is at ground level, the transistors are turned off and the latch retains its state.
- Read operation: In order to read state of SRAM cell, the word line is activated to close switches T1 and T2. Sense/Write circuits at the bottom monitor the state of b and b'.

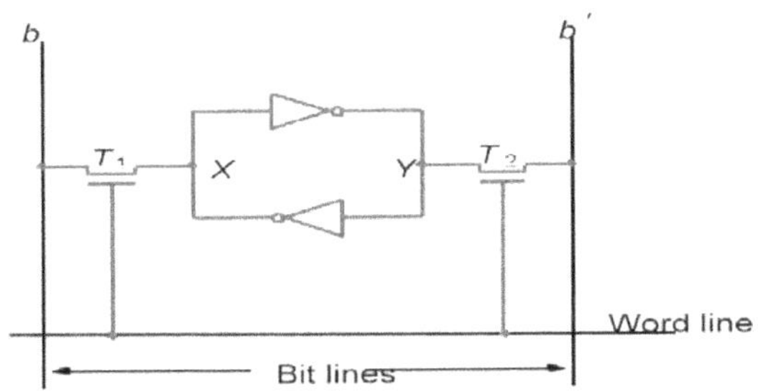

DRAM

- Cells do not retain their state indefinitely.
- Information is stored in a dynamic memory cell in the form of a charge on a capacitor.

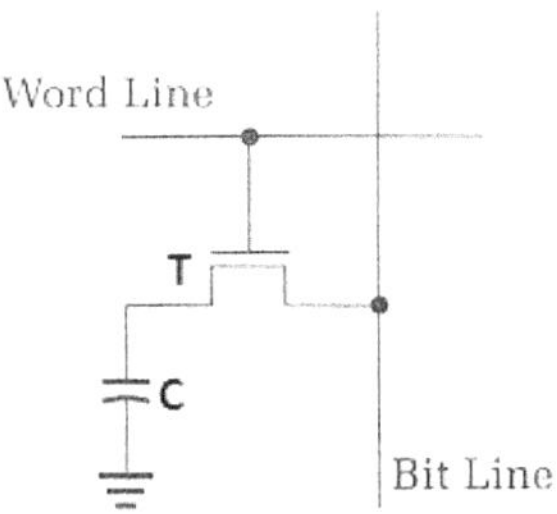

Comparison of SRAM and DRAM

- **Static RAMs (SRAMs)**
    - Consist of circuits that are capable of retaining their state as long as the power is applied.
    - Volatile memories, because their contents are lost when power is interrupted.
    - Access times of static RAMs are in the range of few nanoseconds.
    - However, the cost is usually high.

- **Dynamic RAMs (DRAMs):**
  - Do not retain their state indefinitely.
  - Contents must be periodically refreshed.
  - Contents may be refreshed while accessing them for reading.
  - Cost is low.

Flash Memory

- SRAM and SDRAM chips are volatile:
  - Lose the contents when the power is turned off.
- Many applications need memory devices to retain contents after the power is turned off.
- Non-volatile memory is read in the same manner as volatile memory.
  - Separate writing process is needed to place information in this memory.
- Flash memory is a type of Electrically Erasable Programmable Read-Only Memory (EEPROM)
- Power consumption of flash memory is very low, making it attractive for use in equipment that is battery-driven.
- Usage:
  - Digital Music Device.
  - Smartphones.
  - Digital Cameras.
  - Removable Storage Devices.

Magnetic Disk

- **Purpose**
  - Long-term, nonvolatile, inexpensive storage for files
  - Large, inexpensive, slow level in the memory hierarchy
- Data represented as magnetic spots
  - Magnetized spot = 1
  - Absence of a magnetized spot = 0
- Read
  - Converts the magnetized data to electrical impulses
- Write
  - Converts electrical impulses to magnetized spots on disk

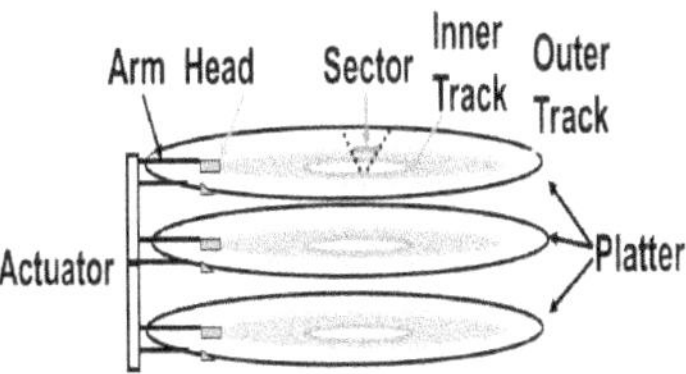

- Several platters, with information recorded magnetically on both surfaces (usually).
- Bits recorded in tracks, which in turn divided into sectors (e.g., 512 Bytes).
- Actuator moves head (end of arm,1/surface) over track ("seek"), select surface, wait for sector rotate under head, then read or write.
  - "Cylinder": all tracks under heads

5.3. Cache Basics

- Processor is much faster than the main memory.
  - As a result, the processor has to spend much of its time waiting while instructions and data are being fetched from the main memory.
  - Major obstacle towards achieving good performance.
- Speed of the main memory cannot be increased beyond a certain point.
- Cache memory is an architectural arrangement which makes the main memory appear faster to the processor than it really is.
- Cache memory is based on the property of computer programs known as "locality of reference".

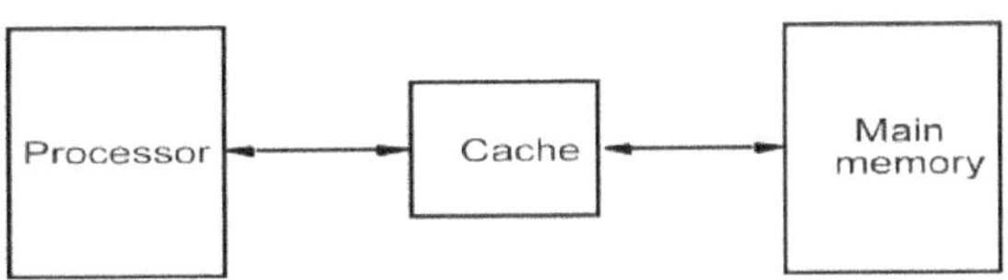

- *Processor issues a Read request, a block of words is transferred from the main memory to the cache, one word at a time.*
- *Subsequent references to the data in this block of words are found in the cache.*
- *At any given time, only some blocks in the main memory are held in the cache. Which blocks in the main memory are in the cache is determined by a **"mapping function".***
- *When the cache is full, and a block of words needs to be transferred from the main memory, some block of words in the cache must be replaced. This is determined by a **"replacement algorithm".***
- ***If the data is in the cache it is called a Read or Write hit.***

- ***Read hit***
  - *The data is obtained from the cache.*
- ***Write hit***
  - *Cache has a replica of the contents of the main memory.*
  - *Contents of the cache and the main memory may be updated simultaneously. This is the **write-through** protocol.*
  - *Update the contents of the cache, and mark it as updated by setting a bit known as the dirty bit or modified bit. The contents of the main memory are updated when this block is replaced. This is **write-back or copy-back** protocol.*
- ***If the data is not present in the cache, then a <u>Read miss or Write miss</u> occurs.***
- ***Read miss***
  - *Block of words containing this requested word is transferred from the memory.*
  - *After the block is transferred, the desired word is forwarded to the processor.*
  - *The desired word may also be forwarded to the processor as soon as it is transferred without waiting for the entire block to be transferred. This is called **<u>load-through or early-restart.</u>***
- ***Write-miss***
  - *Write-through protocol is used, then the contents of the main memory are updated directly.*
  - *If write-back protocol is used, the block containing the addressed word is first brought into the cache. The desired word is overwritten with new information.*

5.4. Mapping Functions

- Mapping functions determine how memory blocks are placed in the cache.
- A simple processor example:
  - Cache consisting of 128 blocks of 16 words each.
  - Total size of cache is 2048 (2K) words.
  - Main memory is addressable by a 16-bit address.
  - Main memory has 64K words.
  - Main memory has 4K blocks of 16 words each.
- **Three mapping functions**
  - Direct mapping.
  - Associative mapping.
  - Set-associative mapping.

1. *Direct Mapping*

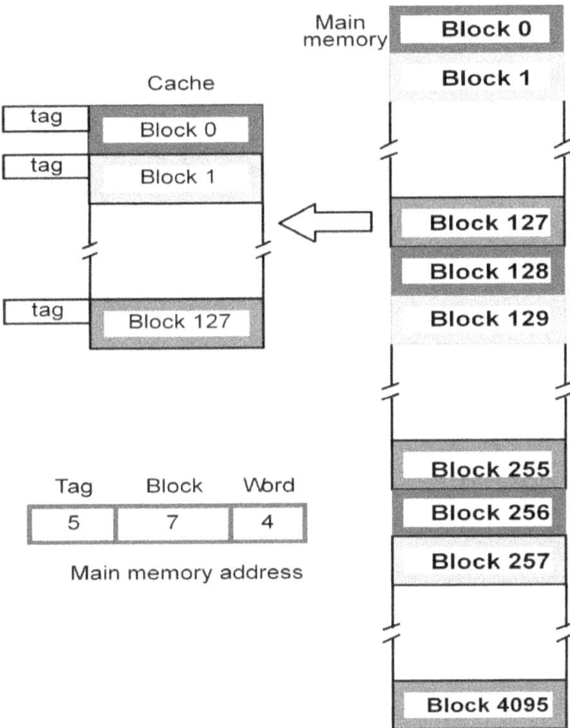

- Block j of the main memory maps to j modulo 128 of the cache.0 maps to 0,129 maps to 1.
- More than one memory block is mapped onto the same position in the cache.
- May lead to contention for cache blocks even if the cache is not full.
- Resolve the contention by allowing new block to replace the old block, leading to a trivial replacement algorithm.
- **Memory address is divided into three fields.**
  - Low order 4 bits determine one of the 16 words in a block.
  - When a new block is brought into the cache, the next 7 bits determine which cache block this new block is placed in.
  - High order 5 bits determine which of the possible 32 blocks is currently present in the cache. These are tag bits.
- Simple to implement but not very flexible.

2. Associative Mapping

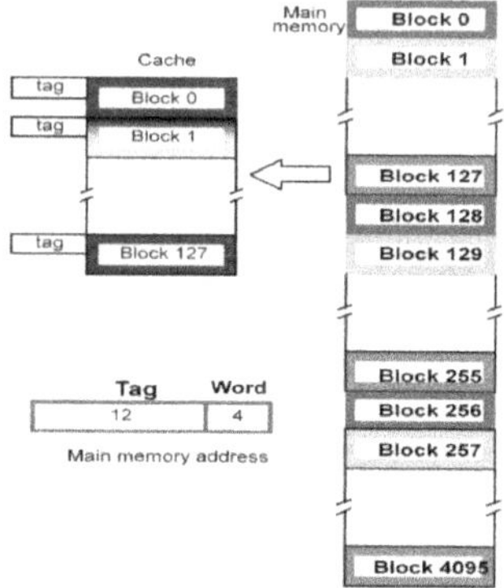

- Main memory block can be placed into any cache position.
- **Memory address is divided into two fields:**
    - Low order 4 bits identify the word within a block.
    - High order 12 bits or tag bits identify a memory block when it is resident in the cache.
- Flexible, and uses cache space efficiently.
- Replacement algorithms can be used to replace an existing block in the cache when the cache is full.
- Cost is higher than direct-mapped cache because of the need to search all 128 patterns to determine whether a given block is in the cache.

3. Set – Associative Mapping

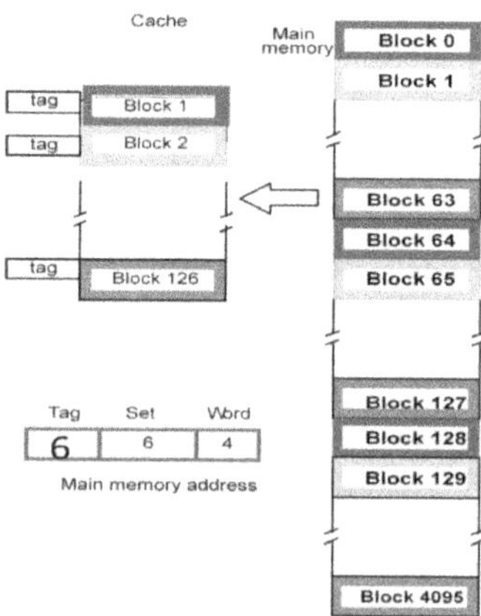

- Blocks of cache are grouped into sets.
- Mapping function allows a block of the main memory to reside in any block of a specific set.
- Divide the cache into 64 sets, with two blocks per set.
- Memory block 0, 64, 128 etc. map to block 0, and they can occupy either of the two positions.
- **Memory address is divided into three fields:**
    - 6 bit field determines the set number.
    - High order 6 bit fields are compared to the tag fields of the two blocks in a set.
- Set-associative mapping combination of direct and associative mapping.
- Number of blocks per set is a design parameter.
    - One extreme is to have all the blocks in one set, requiring no set bits (fully associative mapping).
    - Other extreme is to have one block per set, is the same as direct mapping.

Virtual Memory

- Techniques that automatically move program and data between main memory and secondary storage when they are required for execution are called **virtual-memory** techniques.
- Recall that an important challenge in the design of a computer system is to provide a large, fast memory system at an affordable cost.
- Architectural solutions to increase the effective speed and size of the memory system.
- **Cache memories were developed to increase the effective speed of the memory system.**
- **Virtual memory is an architectural solution to increase the effective size of the memory system.**
- Recall that the addressable memory space depends on the number of address bits in a computer.
    - For example, if a computer issues 32-bit addresses, the addressable memory space is 4G bytes.
- Physical main memory in a computer is generally not as large as the entire possible addressable space.
    - Physical memory typically ranges from a few hundred megabytes to 1G bytes.

- Large programs that cannot fit completely into the main memory have their parts stored on secondary storage devices such as magnetic disks.
  - Pieces of programs must be transferred to the main memory from secondary storage before they can be executed.
- When a new piece of a program is to be transferred to the main memory, and the main memory is full, then some other piece in the main memory must be replaced.
  - Recall this is very similar to what *we* studied in case of cache memories.
- Operating system automatically transfers data between the main memory and secondary storage.

- Programs and processors reference an instruction or data independent of the size of the main memory.
- Processor issues binary addresses for instructions and data.
  - These binary addresses are called logical or virtual addresses.
- Virtual addresses are translated into physical addresses by a combination of hardware and software subsystems.
  - If virtual *address* refers to a part of the program that is currently in the main memory, it is accessed immediately.
  - If the address refers to a part of the program that is not currently in the main memory, it is first transferred to the main memory before it can be used.

Virtual Memory Organization

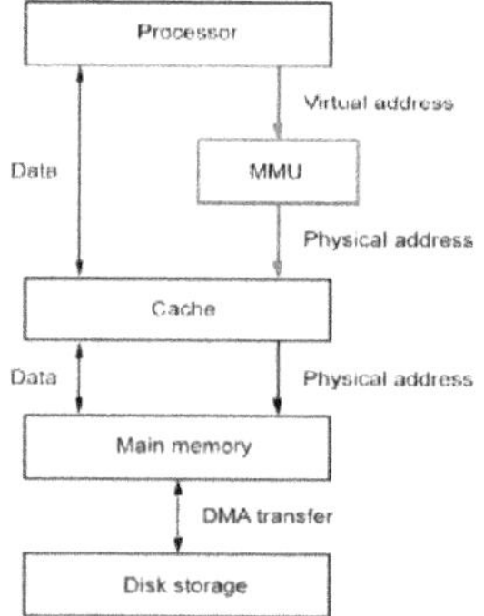

- Memory management unit (MMU) translates virtual addresses into physical addresses.
- If the desired data or instructions are in the main memory they are fetched.
- If the desired data or instructions are not in the main memory, they must be transferred from secondary storage to the main memory.

- MMU causes the operating system to bring the data from the secondary storage into the main memory.

Virtual Memory Address Translation

- Assume that program and data are composed of fixed-length units called pages.
- A page consists of a block of words that occupy contiguous locations in the main memory.
- Page is a basic unit of information that is transferred between secondary storage and main memory.
- Size of a page commonly ranges from 2K to 16K bytes.
    - Pages should not be too small, because the access time of a secondary storage device is *much* larger than the main memory.
    - Pages should not be too large, else a large portion of the page may not be used, and it will occupy valuable space in the main memory.
- Concepts of virtual memory are similar to the concepts of cache memory.
- Cache memory:
    - Introduced to bridge the speed gap between the processor and the main memory.
    - Implemented in hardware.
- Virtual memory:
    - Introduced to bridge the speed gap between the main memory and secondary storage.
    - Implemented in part by software.

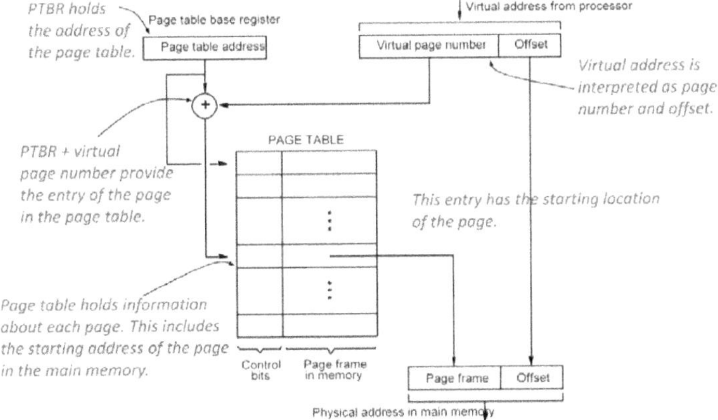

- Each virtual or logical address generated by a processor is interpreted as a virtual page number (high-order bits) plus an offset (low-order bits) that specifies the location of a particular byte within that page.
- Information about the main memory location of each page is kept in the **page table.**
    - Main memory address where the page is stored.
    - Current status of the page.
- Area of the main memory that can hold a page is called as **page frame.**
- Starting address of the page table is kept in a **page table base register.**
- Virtual page number generated by the processor is added to the contents of the page table base register.
    - This provides the address of the corresponding entry in the page table.
- The contents of this location in the page table give the starting address of the page if the page is currently in the main memory.
- Page table entry for a page also includes some control bits which describe the status of the page while it is in the main memory.
- One bit indicates the validity of the page.
    - Indicates whether the page is actually loaded into the main memory.
    - Allows the operating system to invalidate the page without actually removing it.
- One bit indicates whether the page has been modified during its residency in the main memory.
    - This bit determines whether the page should be written back to the disk when it is removed from the main memory.
    - Similar to the dirty or modified bit in case of cache memory.
- Other control bits for various other types of restrictions that may be imposed.
    - For example, a program may only have read permission for a page, but not write or modify permissions.

5.5. Translation Look a Side Buffer (TLBs)

- Where should the page table be located?
- Recall that the page table is used by the MMU for every read and write access to the memory.
    - Ideal location for the page table is within the MMU.
- Page table is quite large.
- MMU is implemented as part of the processor chip.

- Impossible to include a complete page table on the chip.

- Page table is kept in the main memory.

- A copy of a small portion of the page table can be accommodated within the MMU.

  - Portion consists of page table entries that correspond to the most recently accessed pages

- **A small cache called as** Translation **Look a side Buffer (TLB) is included in the MMU.**

  - **TLB holds page table entries of the most recently accessed pages.**

- Recall that cache memory holds most recently accessed blocks from the main memory.

  - Operation of the TLB and page table in the main memory is similar to the operation of the cache and main memory.

- Page table entry for a page includes:

  - Address of the page frame where the page resides in the main memory.

  - Some control bits.

- In addition to the above for each page, TLB must hold the virtual page number for each page.

Associative-Mapped TLB

- *High-order bits of the virtual address generated by the processor select the virtual page.*

- *These bits are compared to the virtual page numbers in the TLB.*

- *If there is a match, a hit occurs and the corresponding address of the page frame is read.*

- *If there is no match, a miss occurs and the page table within the main memory must be consulted.*

- *Set-associative mapped TLBs are found in commercial processors.*

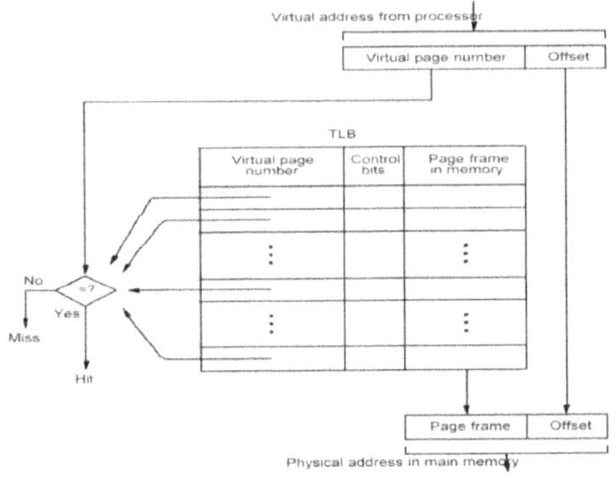

- What happens if a program generates an access to a page that is not in the main memory?
- In this case, a **page fault** is said to occur.
  - Whole page must be brought into the main memory from the disk, before the execution can proceed.
- Upon detecting a page fault by the MMU, following actions occur:
  - MMU asks the operating system to intervene by raising an exception.
  - Processing of the active task which caused the page fault is interrupted.
  - Control is transferred to the operating system.
  - Operating system copies the requested page from secondary storage to the main memory.
  - Once the page is copied, control is returned to the task which was interrupted.
- When a new page is to be brought into the main memory from secondary storage, the main memory may be full.
  - Some page from the main memory must be replaced with this new page.
- How to choose which page to replace?
  - This is similar to the replacement that occurs when the cache is full.
  - The principle of locality of reference (?) can also be applied here.
  - A replacement strategy similar to LRU can be applied.
- Since the size of the main memory is relatively larger compared to cache, a relatively large amount of programs and data can be held in the main memory.
  - Minimizes the frequency of transfers between secondary storage and main memory.

5.6. Input/Output System

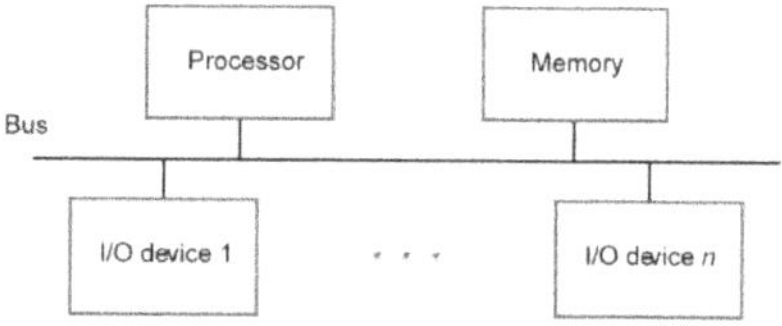

- *Multiple I/O devices may be connected to the processor and the memory via a bus.*
- *Bus consists of three sets of lines to carry address, data and control signals.*
- *Each I/O device is assigned an unique address.*
- *To access an I/O device, the processor places the address on the address lines.*
- *The device recognizes the address, and responds to the control signals.*

- I/O devices and the memory may share the same address space:
  - Memory-mapped I/O.
  - Any machine instruction that can access memory can be used to transfer data to or from an I/O device.
  - Simpler software.
- I/O devices and the memory may have different address spaces:
  - Special instructions to transfer data to and from I/O devices.
  - I/O devices may have to deal with fewer address lines.
  - I/O address lines need not be physically separate from memory address lines.
  - In fact, address lines may be shared between I/O devices and memory, with a control signal to indicate whether it is a memory address or an I/O address.

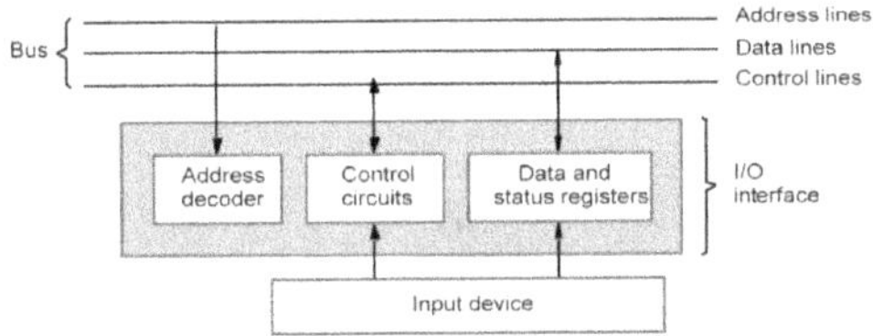

- *I/O device is connected to the bus using an I/O interface circuit which has:*
  - *Address decoder, control circuit, and data and status registers.*
- *Address decoder decodes the address placed on the address lines thus enabling the device to recognize its address.*
- *Data register holds the data being transferred to or from the processor.*
- *Status register holds information necessary for the operation of the I/O device.*
- *Data and status registers are connected to the data lines, and have unique addresses.*
- *I/O interface circuit coordinates I/O transfers.*
- Recall that the rate of transfer to and from I/O devices is slower than the speed of the processor. This creates the need for mechanisms to synchronize data transfers between them.
- Program-controlled I/O:
  - Processor repeatedly monitors a status flag to achieve the necessary synchronization.
  - Processor polls the I/O device.
- Two other mechanisms used for synchronizing data transfers between the processor and memory:

- Interrupts.
- Direct Memory Access.

5.7. Interrupts

- **An interrupt is an event that causes the execution of one program to be suspended and execution of another program to be begin.**
- **In general, the term exception is used to refer to any event that causes an interruption.**
- In program-controlled I/O, when the processor continuously monitors the status of the device, it does not perform any useful tasks.
- An alternate approach would be for the I/O device to alert the processor when it becomes ready.
    - Do so by sending a hardware signal called an interrupt to the processor.
    - At least one of the bus control lines, called an interrupt-request line is dedicated for this purpose.
- Processor can perform other useful tasks while it is waiting for the device to be ready.

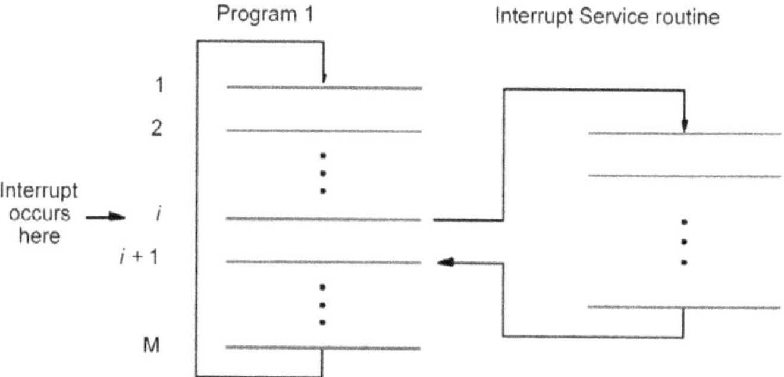

- Processor is executing the instruction located at address i when an interrupt occurs.
- Routine executed in response to an interrupt request is called the interrupt-service routine.
- When an interrupt occurs, control must be transferred to the interrupt service routine.
- But before transferring control, the current contents of the PC (i+1), must be saved in a known location.
- This will enable the return-from-interrupt instruction to resume execution at i+1.
- Return address, or the contents of the PC are usually stored on the processor stack.

Vectored Interrupts

- The device requesting an interrupt may identify itself directly to the processor.
    - Device can do so by sending a special code (4 to 8 bits) the processor over the bus.
    - Code supplied by the device may represent a part of the starting address of the interrupt-service routine.
    - The remainder of the starting address is obtained by the processor based on other information such as the range of memory addresses where interrupt service routines are located.
- Usually the location pointed to by the interrupting device is used to store the starting address of the interrupt-service routine.

Interrupt Nesting

- Previously, before the processor started executing the interrupt service routine for a device, it disabled the interrupts from the device.
- In general, same arrangement is used when multiple devices can send interrupt requests to the processor.
    - During the execution of an interrupt service routine of device, the processor does not accept interrupt requests from any other device.
    - Since the interrupt service routines are usually short, the delay that this causes is generally acceptable.
- However, for certain devices this delay may not be acceptable.
    - Which devices can be allowed to interrupt a processor when it is executing an interrupt service routine of another device?
- I/O devices are organized in a priority structure:
    - An interrupt request from a high-priority device is accepted while the processor is executing the interrupt service routine of a low priority device.
- A priority level is assigned to a processor that can be changed under program control.
    - Priority level of a processor is the priority of the program that is currently being executed.
    - When the processor starts executing the interrupt service routine of a device, its priority is raised to that of the device.
    - If the device sending an interrupt request has a higher priority than the processor, the processor accepts the interrupt request.
- Processor's priority is encoded in a few bits of the processor status register.

- Priority can be changed by instructions that write into the processor status register.
  - Usually, these are privileged instructions, or instructions that can be executed only in the supervisor mode.
  - Privileged instructions cannot be executed in the user mode.
  - Prevents a user program from accidentally or intentionally changing the priority of the processor.
- If there is an attempt to execute a privileged instruction in the user mode, it causes a special type of interrupt called as privilege exception.

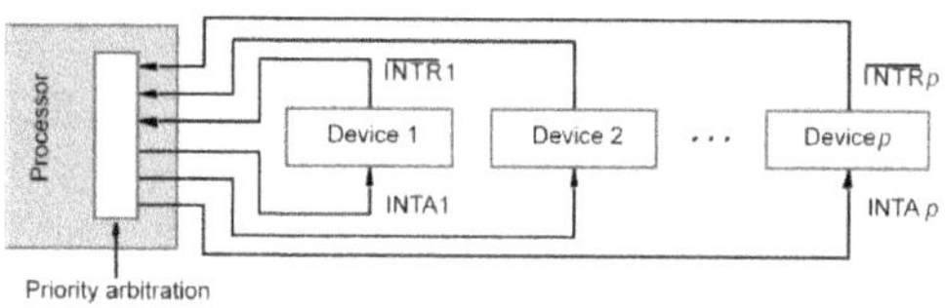

- *Each device has a separate interrupt-request and interrupt-acknowledge line.*
- *Each interrupt-request line is assigned a different priority level.*
- *Interrupt requests received over these lines are sent to a priority arbitration circuit in the processor.*
- *If the interrupt request has a higher priority level than the priority of the processor, then the request is accepted.*

Polling Scheme

- *If the processor uses a polling mechanism to poll the status registers of I/O devices to determine which device is requesting an interrupt.*
- *In this case the priority is determined by the order in which the devices are polled.*
- *The first device with status bit set to 1 is the device whose interrupt request is accepted.*

Daisy Chain Scheme

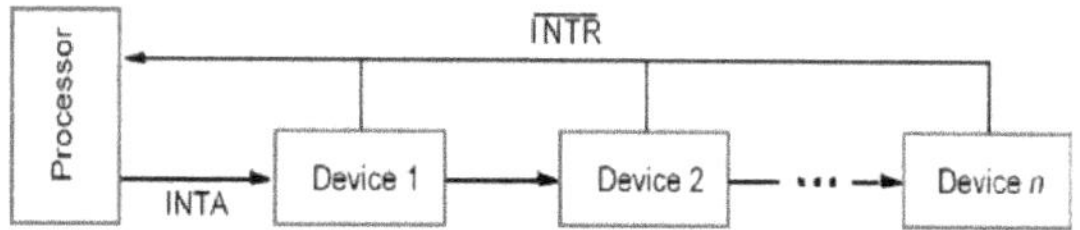

- *Devices are connected to form a daisy chain.*
- *Devices share the interrupt-request line, and interrupt-acknowledge line is connected to form a daisy chain.*

- *When devices raise an interrupt request, the interrupt-request line is activated.*
- *The processor in response activates interrupt-acknowledge.*
- *Received by device 1, if device 1 does not need service, it passes the signal to device 2.*
- *Device that is electrically closest to the processor has the highest priority.*
- *When I/O devices were organized into a priority structure, each device had its own interrupt-request and interrupt-acknowledge line.*
- *When I/O devices were organized in a daisy chain fashion, the devices shared an interrupt-request line, and the interrupt-acknowledge propagated through the devices.*
- *A combination of priority structure and daisy chain scheme can also used.*

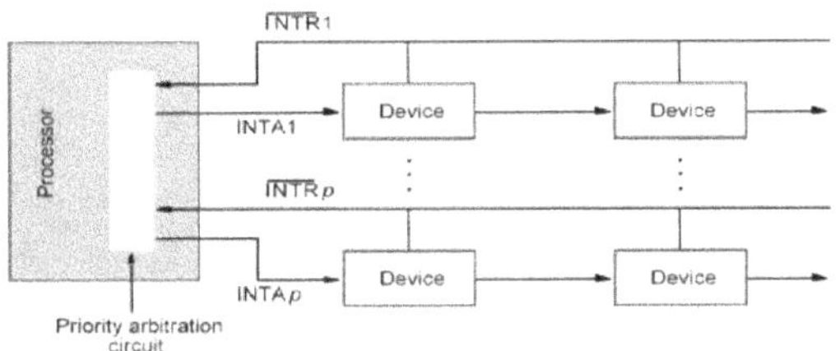

- *Devices are organized into groups.*
- *Each group is assigned a different priority level.*
- *All the devices within a single group share an interrupt-request line, and are connected to form a daisy chain.*

5.8.   Direct Memory Access (DMA)

- **Direct Memory Access**
  - **A special control unit may be provided to transfer a block of data directly between an I/O device and the main memory, without continuous intervention by the processor.**
- Control unit which performs these transfers is a part of the I/O device's interface circuit. This control unit is called as a DMA controller.
- DMA controller performs functions that would be normally carried out by the processor:
  - For each word, it provides the memory address and all the control signals.
  - To transfer a block of data, it increments the memory addresses and keeps track of the number of transfers.
- DMA controller can transfer a block of data from an external device to the processor, without any intervention from the processor.

- However, the operation of the DMA controller must be under the control of a program executed by the processor. That is, the processor must initiate the DMA transfer.
- To initiate the DMA transfer, the processor informs the DMA controller of:
  - Starting address,
  - Number of words in the block.
  - Direction of transfer (I/O device to the memory, or memory to the I/O device).
- Once the DMA controller completes the DMA transfer, it informs the processor by raising an interrupt signal.

Registers in a DMA Interface

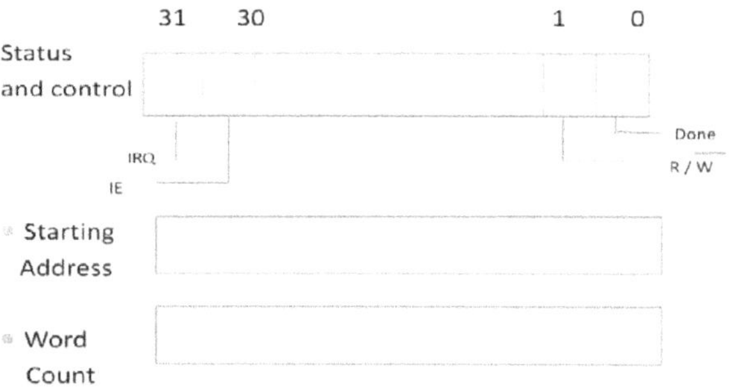

- *DMA controller connects a high-speed network to the computer bus.*
- *Disk controller, which controls two disks also has DMA capability. It provides two DMA channels.*
- *It can perform two independent DMA operations, as if each disk has its own DMA controller. The registers to store the memory address, word count and status and control information are duplicated.*

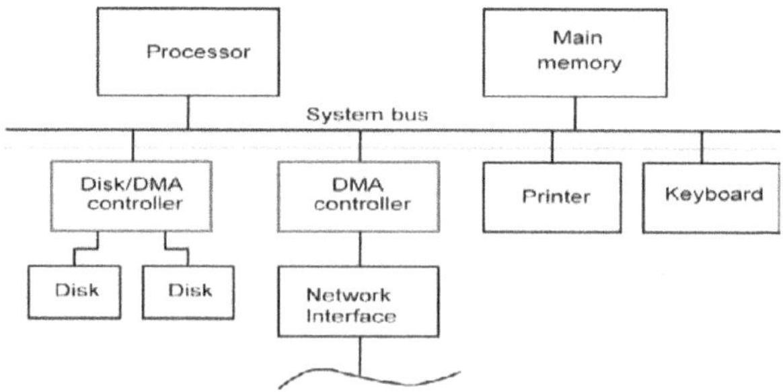

Bus Arbitration

- Processor and DMA controllers both need to initiate data transfers on the bus and access main memory.
- The device that is allowed to initiate transfers on the bus at any given time is called the **bus master.**
- When the current bus master relinquishes its status as the bus master, another device can acquire this status.
    - The process by which the next device to become the bus master is selected and bus mastership is transferred to it is called **bus arbitration.**
- **Two Approaches:**
- **Centralized arbitration:**
    - A single bus arbiter performs the arbitration.
- **Distributed arbitration:**
    - All devices participate in the selection of the next bus master.

Centralized Bus Arbitration

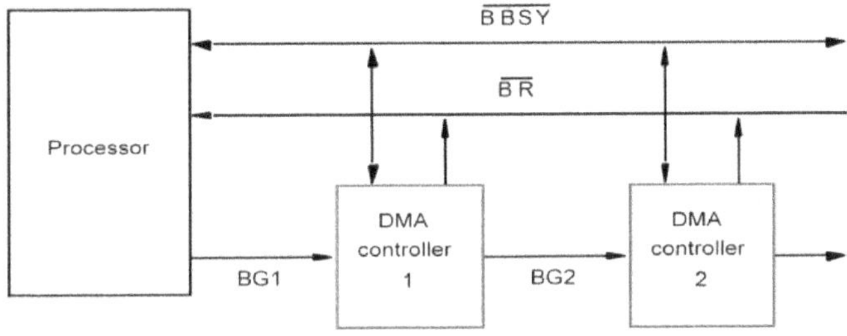

- *Bus arbiter may be the processor or a separate unit connected to the bus.*
- *Normally, the processor is the bus master, unless it grants bus membership to one of the DMA controllers.*
- *DMA controller requests the control of the bus by asserting the Bus Request (BR) line.*
- *In response, the processor activates the Bus-Grant1 (BG1) line, indicating that the controller may use the bus when it is free.*
- *BG1 signal is connected to all DMA controllers in a daisy chain fashion.*
- *BBSY signal is 0, it indicates that the bus is busy. When BBSY becomes 1, the DMA controller which asserted BR can acquire control of the bus.*

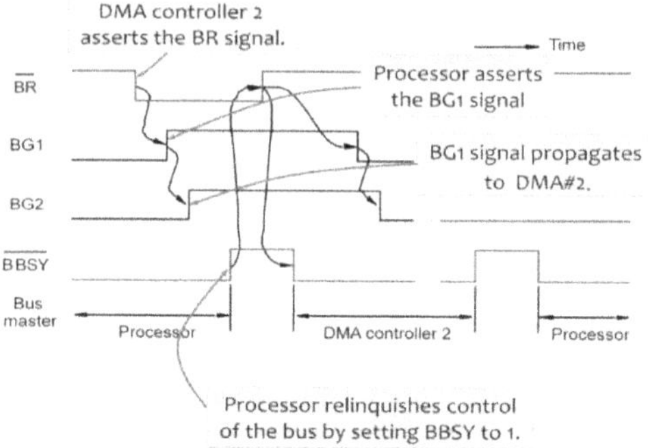

Distributed Arbitration

- All devices waiting to use the bus share the responsibility of carrying out the arbitration process.

    - Arbitration process does not depend on a central arbiter and hence distributed arbitration has higher reliability.

- Each device is assigned a 4-bit ID number.

- All the devices are connected using 5 lines, 4 arbitration lines to transmit the ID, and one line for the Start-Arbitration signal.

- To request the bus a device:

    - Asserts the Start-Arbitration signal.

    - Places its 4-bit ID number on the arbitration lines.

- The pattern that appears on the arbitration lines is the logical-OR of all the 4-bit device IDs placed on the arbitration lines.

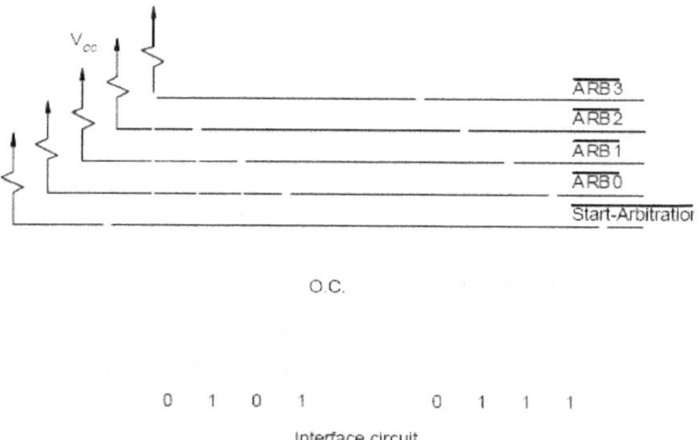

- *Arbitration process*
  - Each device compares the pattern that appears on the arbitration lines to its own ID, starting with MSB.
  - If it detects a difference, it transmits 0's on the arbitration lines for that and all lower bit positions.
  - The pattern that appears on the arbitration lines is the logical-OR of all the 4-bit device IDs placed on the arbitration lines.

Example

- Device A has the ID 5 and wants to request the bus:
  - Transmits the pattern 0101 on the arbitration lines.
- Device B has the ID 6 and wants to request the bus:
  - Transmits the pattern 0110 on the arbitration lines.
- Pattern that appears on the arbitration lines is the logical OR of the patterns:
  - Pattern 0111 appears on the arbitration lines.

Arbitration Process

- Each device compares the pattern that appears on the arbitration lines to its own ID, starting with MSB.
- If it detects a difference, it transmits 0s on the arbitration lines for that and all lower bit positions.
- Device A compares its ID 5 with a pattern 0101 to pattern 0111.
- It detects a difference at bit position 0, as a result, it transmits a pattern 0100 on the arbitration lines.
- The pattern that appears on the arbitration lines is the logical-OR of 0100 and 0110, which is 0110.
- This pattern is the same as the device ID of B, and hence B has won the arbitration.

Velammal Engineering College

Dept of CSE

Cs6303-Computer Architecture

Question Bank – II Year CSE

UNIT I

OVERVIEW AND INSTRUCTIONS

Part A

1. What are the Eight Great Ideas in Computer Architecture?

    - Design for Moore's Law.

    - Use Abstraction to Simplify Design.

    - Make the Common Case Fast.

    - Performance via Parallelism.

    - Performance via Pipelining.

    - Performance via Prediction.

    - Hierarchy of Memories.

    - Dependability via Redundancy.

2. What are the components of computer system?

    The five classic components of a computer are input, output, memory, datapath, and control, with the last two sometimes combined and called the processor.

3. Define input device.

    A mechanism through which the computer is fed information, such as a keyboard.

4. Define output device

    A mechanism that conveys the result of a computation to a user, such as a display, or to another computer.

5. Define liquid crystal display

    A display technology using a thin layer of liquid polymers that can be used to transmit or block light according to whether a charge is applied.

6. Define active matrix display

    A liquid crystal display using a transistor to control the transmission of light at each individual pixel.

7. Define pixel

The smallest individual picture element. Screens are composed of hundreds of thousands to millions of pixels, organized in a matrix.

8. What is integrated circuit/chip?

A device combining dozens to millions of transistors.

9. Define central processor unit.

The active part of the computer, which contains the datapath and control and which adds numbers, tests numbers, signals I/O devices to activate, and so on.

10. What is datapath?

The component of the processor that performs arithmetic operations control The component of the processor that commands the datapath, memory, and I/O devices according to the instructions of the program.

11. Compare Relative performance per unit cost of technologies used in computers over time.

Year	Technology used in computers	Relative performance/unit cost
1951	Vacuum tube	1
1965	Transistor	35
1975	Integrated circuit	900
1995	Very large-scale Integrated circuit	2,400,000
2013	Ultra large-scale integrated circuit	250,000,000,000

12. Define silicon crystal ingot.

A rod composed of a silicon crystal that is between 8 and 12 inches in diameter and about 12 to 24 inches long.

13. Define wafer

A slice from a silicon ingot no more than 0.1 inches thick, used to create chips.

14. What is defect?

A microscopic flaw in a wafer or in patterning steps that can result in the failure of the die containing that defect.

15. What is die and yield?

Die the individual rectangular sections that are cut from a wafer, more informally known as chips. Yield the percentage of good dies from the total number of dies on the wafer.

16. Define response time.

Response time also called execution time. The total time required for the computer to complete a task, including disk accesses, memory accesses, I/O activities, operating system overhead, CPU execution time, and so on.

17. Define throughput.

Throughput also called bandwidth. Another measure of performance, it is the number of tasks completed per unit time.

18. Define CPU execution time.

The actual time the CPU spends computing for a specific task. User CPU time The CPU time spent in a program itself. system CPU time The CPU time spent in the operating system performing tasks on behalf of the program.

19. Define clock cycle.

The time for one clock period, usually of the processor clock, which runs at a constant rate. clock period

20. The length of each clock cycle. Suppose we developed a new, simpler processor that has 85% of the capacitive load of the more complex older processor. Further, assume that it has adjustable voltage so that it can reduce voltage 15% compared to processor B, which results in a 15% shrink in frequency. What is the impact on dynamic power?

$$\frac{\text{Power}_{\text{new}}}{\text{Power}_{\text{old}}} = \frac{(\text{Capacitive load} \times 0.85) \times (\text{Voltage} \times 0.85)^2 \times (\text{Frequency switched} \times 0.85)}{\text{Capacitive load} \times \text{Voltage}^2 \times \text{Frequency switched}}$$

Thus the power ratio is

$$0.85^4 = 0.52$$

Hence, the new processor uses about half the power of the old processor.

21. Define stored-program concept.

The idea that instructions and data of many types can be stored in memory as numbers, leading to the stored program computer.

22. List various logical operators and its MIPS instructions.

Logical operations	C operators	Java operators	MIPS instructions
Shift left	<<	<<	sll
Shift right	>>	>>>	srl
Bit-by-bit AND	&	&	and, andi
Bit-by-bit OR	|	|	or, ori
Bit-by-bit NOT	~	~	nor

23. Define conditional branch.

An instruction that requires the comparison of two values and that allows for a subsequent transfer of control to a new address in the program based on the outcome of the comparison.

24. Define jump address table.

A table of addresses of alternative instruction sequences.

25. Give MIPS instruction format.

Name	Fields						Comments
Field size	6 bits	5 bits	5 bits	5 bits	5 bits	6 bits	All MIPS instructions are 32 bits long
R-format	op	rs	rt	rd	shamt	funct	Arithmetic instruction format
I-format	op	rs	rt	address/immediate			Transfer, branch, imm. format
J-format	op	target address					Jump instruction format

Part B

1. Explain about Eight Great Ideas in Computer Architecture.

Design for Moore's Law

The one constant for computer designers is rapid change, which is driven largely by Moore's Law. It states that integrated circuit resources double every 18–24 months. Moore's Law resulted from a 1965 prediction of such growth in IC capacity made by Gordon Moore, one of the founders of Intel. As computer designs can take years, the resources available per chip can easily double or quadruple between the start and finish of the project. Like a skeet shooter, computer architects must anticipate where the technology will be when the design finishes rather than design for where it starts. We use an "up and to the right" Moore's Law graph to represent designing for rapid change.

Use Abstraction to Simplify Design

Both computer architects and programmers had to invent techniques to make themselves more productive, for otherwise design time would lengthen as dramatically as resources grew by Moore's Law. A major productivity technique for hardware and soft ware is to use abstractions to represent the design at different levels of representation; lower-level details are hidden to offer a simpler model at higher levels. We'll use the abstract painting icon to represent this second great idea.

Make the Common Case Fast

Making the common case fast will tend to enhance performance better than optimizing the rare case. Ironically, the common case is oft en simpler than the rare case and hence is oft en easier to enhance. This common sense advice implies that you know what the common case is, which is only possible with careful experimentation and measurement (see Section 1.6). We use a sports car as the icon for making the common case fast, as the most common trip has one or two passengers, and it's surely easier to make a fast sports car than a fast minivan!

Performance Via Parallelism

Since the dawn of computing, computer architects have offered designs that get more performance by performing operations in parallel. We'll see many examples of parallelism in this book. We use multiple jet engines of a plane as our icon for parallel performance.

Performance Via Pipelining

A particular pattern of parallelism is so prevalent in computer architecture that it merits its own name: pipelining. For example, before fire engines, a "bucket brigade" would respond to a fire, which many cowboy movies show in response to a dastardly act by the villain.

The townsfolk form a human chain to carry a water source to fi re, as they could much more quickly move buckets up the chain instead of individuals running back and forth. Our pipeline icon is a sequence of pipes, with each section representing one stage of the pipeline.

Performance Via Prediction

Following the saying that it can be better to ask for forgiveness than to ask for permission, the final great idea is prediction. In some cases it can be faster on average to guess and start working rather than wait until you know for sure, assuming that the mechanism to recover from a misprediction is not too expensive and your prediction is relatively accurate. We use the fortune-teller's crystal ball as our prediction icon.

Hierarchy of Memories

Programmers want memory to be fast, large, and cheap, as memory speed often shapes performance, capacity limits the size of problems that can be solved, and the cost of memory today is oft en the majority of computer cost. Architects have found that they can address these conflicting demands with a hierarchy of memories, with the fastest, smallest, and most expensive memory per bit at the top of the hierarchy and the slowest, largest, and cheapest per bit at the bottom. Caches give the programmer the illusion that main memory is nearly as fast as the top of the hierarchy and nearly as big and cheap as the bottom of the hierarchy. We use a layered triangle icon to represent the memory hierarchy.

The shape indicates speed, cost, and size: the closer to the top, the faster and more expensive per bit the memory; the wider the base of the layer, the bigger the memory.

Dependability via Redundancy

Computers not only need to be fast; they need to be dependable. Since any physical device can fail, we make systems dependable by including redundant components that can take over when a failure occurs *and* to help detect failures. We use the tractor-trailer as our icon, since the dual tires on each side of its rear axels allow the truck to continue driving even when one tire fails. (Presumably, the truck driver heads immediately to a repair facility so the fl at tire can be fi xed, thereby restoring redundancy!)

2.   Explain in detail about components of computer system.

The five classic components of a computer are input, output, memory, datapath, and control, with the last two sometimes combined and called the processor.

The processor gets instructions and data from memory. Input writes data to memory, and output reads data from memory. Control sends the signals that determine the operations of the datapath, memory, input, and output. Two key components of computers are input devices, such as the microphone, and output devices, such as the speaker. input feeds the computer, and output is the result of computation sent to the user. Some devices, such as wireless networks, provide both input and output to the computer.

Input device

A mechanism through which the computer is fed information, such as a keyboard.

Output device

A mechanism that conveys the result of a computation to a user, such as a display, or to another computer.

Liquid crystal display

A display technology using a thin layer of liquid polymers that can be used to transmit or block light according to whether a charge is applied.

Active matrix display

A liquid crystal display using a transistor to control the transmission of light at each individual pixel.

Pixel

The smallest individual picture element. Screens are composed of hundreds of thousands to millions of pixels, organized in a matrix.

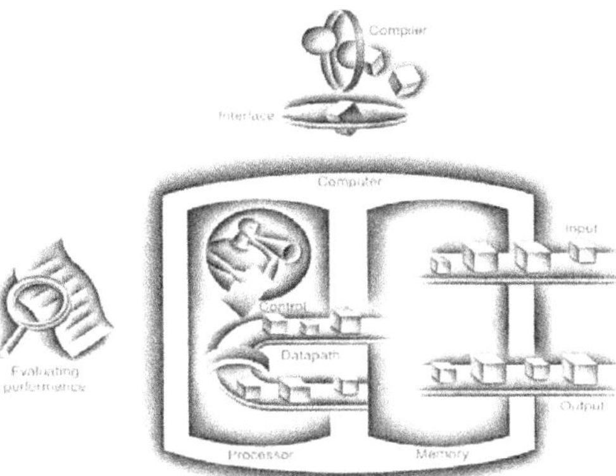

3. Describe basic components of performance and how it is measured?

Components of performance	Units of measure
CPU execution time for a program	Seconds for the program
Instruction count	Instructions executed for the program
Clock cycles per instruction (CPI)	Average number of clock cycles per instruction
Clock cycle time	Seconds per clock cycle

Hardware or software component	Affects what?	How?
Algorithm	Instruction count, possibly CPI	The algorithm determines the number of source program instructions executed and hence the number of processor instructions executed. The algorithm may also affect the CPI, by favoring slower or faster instructions. For example, if the algorithm uses more divides, it will tend to have a higher CPI.
Programming language	Instruction count, CPI	The programming language certainly affects the instruction count, since statements in the language are translated to processor instructions, which determine instruction count. The language may also affect the CPI because of its features; for example, a language with heavy support for data abstraction (e.g., Java) will require indirect calls, which will use higher CPI instructions.
Compiler	Instruction count, CPI	The efficiency of the compiler affects both the instruction count and average cycles per instruction, since the compiler determines the translation of the source language instructions into computer instructions. The compiler's role can be very complex and affect the CPI in complex ways.
Instruction set architecture	Instruction count, clock rate, CPI	The instruction set architecture affects all three aspects of CPU performance, since it affects the instructions needed for a function, the cost in cycles of each instruction, and the overall clock rate of the processor.

4. Describe in detail about MIPS Operands.

MIPS operands

Name	Example	Comments
32 registers	$s0-$s7, $t0-$t9, $zero, $a0-$a3, $v0-$v1, $gp, $fp, $sp, $ra, $at	Fast locations for data. In MIPS, data must be in registers to perform arithmetic, register $zero always equals 0, and register$at is reserved by the assembler to handle large constants.
2^{30} memory words	Memory[0], Memory[4],..... Memory[4294967292]	Accessed only by data transfer instructions. MIPS uses byte addresses, so sequential word addresses differ by 4. Memory holds data structures, arrays, and spilled registers.

5. Describe in detail about MIPS Instruction set.

MIPS assembly language

Category	Instruction	Example	Meaning	Comments
Arithmetic	add	add $s1,$s2,$s3	$s1 = $s2 + $s3	Three register operands
	subtract	sub $s1,$s2,$s3	$s1 = $s2 – $s3	Three register operands
	add immediate	addi $s1,$s2,20	$s1 = $s2 + 20	Used to add constants
Data transfer	load word	lw $s1,20($s2)	$s1 = Memory[$s2 + 20]	Word from memory to register
	store word	sw $s1,20($s2)	Memory[$s2 + 20] = $s1	Word from register to memory
	load half	lh $s1,20($s2)	$s1 = Memory[$s2 + 20]	Halfword memory to register
	load half unsigned	lhu $s1,20($s2)	$s1 = Memory[$s2 + 20]	Halfword memory to register
	store half	sh $s1,20($s2)	Memory[$s2 + 20] = $s1	Halfword register to memory
	load byte	lb $s1,20($s2)	$s1 = Memory[$s2 + 20]	Byte from memory to register
	load byte unsigned	lbu $s1,20($s2)	$s1 = Memory[$s2 + 20]	Byte from memory to register
	store byte	sb $s1,20($s2)	Memory[$s2 + 20] = $s1	Byte from register to memory
	load linked word	ll $s1,20($s2)	$s1 = Memory[$s2 + 20]	Load word as 1st half of atomic swap
	store condition. word	sc $s1,20($s2)	Memory[$s2+20]=$s1;$s1=0 or 1	Store word as 2nd half of atomic swap
	load upper immed.	lui $s1,20	$s1 = 20 * 2^{16}	Loads constant in upper 16 bits
Logical	and	and $s1,$s2,$s3	$s1 = $s2 & $s3	Three reg. operands; bit-by-bit AND
	or	or $s1,$s2,$s3	$s1 = $s2	$s3	Three reg. operands; bit-by-bit OR
	nor	nor $s1,$s2,$s3	$s1 = ~ ($s2 | $s3)	Three reg. operands; bit-by-bit NOR
	and immediate	andi $s1,$s2,20	$s1 = $s2 & 20	Bit-by-bit AND reg with constant
	or immediate	ori $s1,$s2,20	$s1 = $s2	20	Bit-by-bit OR reg with constant
	shift left logical	sll $s1,$s2,10	$s1 = $s2 << 10	Shift left by constant
	shift right logical	srl $s1,$s2,10	$s1 = $s2 >> 10	Shift right by constant
Conditional branch	branch on equal	beq $s1,$s2,25	if ($s1 == $s2) go to PC + 4 + 100	Equal test; PC-relative branch
	branch on not equal	bne $s1,$s2,25	if ($s1!= $s2) go to PC + 4 + 100	Not equal test; PC-relative
	set on less than	slt $s1,$s2,$s3	if ($s2 < $s3) $s1 = 1; else $s1 = 0	Compare less than; for beq, bne
	set on less than unsigned	sltu $s1,$s2,$s3	if ($s2 < $s3) $s1 = 1; else $s1 = 0	Compare less than unsigned
	set less than immediate	slti $s1,$s2,20	if ($s2 < 20) $s1 = 1; else $s1 = 0	Compare less than constant
	set less than immediate unsigned	sltiu $s1,$s2,20	if ($s2 < 20) $s1 = 1; else $s1 = 0	Compare less than constant unsigned
Unconditional jump	jump	j 2500	go to 10000	Jump to target address
	jump register	jr $ra	go to $ra	For switch, procedure return
	jump and link	jal 2500	$ra = PC + 4; go to 10000	For procedure call

6. Explain in details about Uniprocessors to Multiprocessors

Rather than continuing to decrease the response time of a single program running on the single processor, as of 2006 all desktop and server companies are shipping microprocessors with multiple processors per chip, where the benefit is oft en more on throughput than on response time. To reduce confusion between the words processor and microprocessor, companies refer to processors as "cores," and such microprocessors are generically called multicore microprocessors. Hence, a "quadcore" microprocessor is a chip that contains four processors or four cores.

In the past, programmers could rely on innovations in hardware, architecture, and compilers to double performance of their programs every 18 months without having to change a line of code.

Today, for programmers to get significant improvement in response time, they need to rewrite their programs to take advantage of multiple processors. Moreover, to get the historic benefit of running faster on new microprocessors, programmers will have to continue to improve performance of their code as the number of cores increases.

7. Explain various MIPS addressing mode.
    1. *Immediate addressing,* where the operand is a constant within the instruction itself.
    2. *Register addressing,* where the operand is a register.
    3. *Base* or *displacement addressing,* where the operand is at the memory location whose address is the sum of a register and a constant in the instruction.
    4. *PC-relative addressing,* where the branch address is the sum of the PC and a constant in the instruction.
    5. *Pseudodirect addressing,* where the jump address is the 26 bits of the instruction concatenated with the upper bits of the PC.

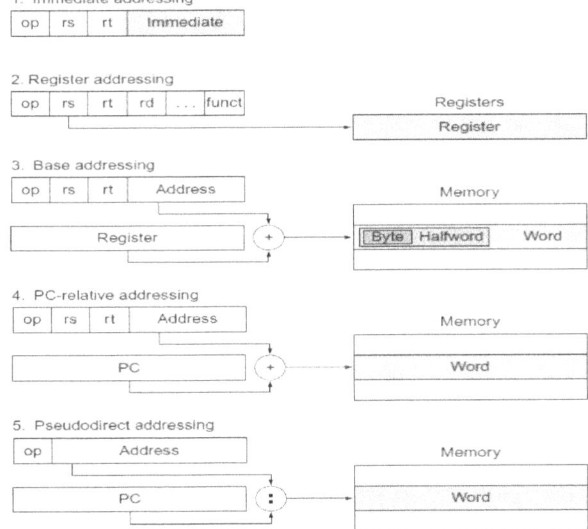

UNIT II

ARITHMETIC OPERATIONS

Part A

1. Add 6ten to 7ten in binary.

$$
\begin{array}{r}
0000\ 0000\ 0000\ 0000\ 0000\ 0000\ 0000\ 0111_{two} = 7_{ten} \\
+\quad 0000\ 0000\ 0000\ 0000\ 0000\ 0000\ 0000\ 0110_{two} = 6_{ten} \\
\hline
=\quad 0000\ 0000\ 0000\ 0000\ 0000\ 0000\ 0000\ 1101_{two} = 13_{ten}
\end{array}
$$

2. Subtract 6ten from 7ten in binary.

$$
\begin{array}{r}
0000\ 0000\ 0000\ 0000\ 0000\ 0000\ 0000\ 0111_{two} = 7_{ten} \\
+\quad 1111\ 1111\ 1111\ 1111\ 1111\ 1111\ 1111\ 1010_{two} = -6_{ten} \\
\hline
=\quad 0000\ 0000\ 0000\ 0000\ 0000\ 0000\ 0000\ 0001_{two} = 1_{ten}
\end{array}
$$

3. Give overflow conditions for addition and subtraction.

Operation	Operand A	Operand B	Result Indicating overflow
$A + B$	≥ 0	≥ 0	< 0
$A + B$	< 0	< 0	≥ 0
$A - B$	≥ 0	< 0	< 0
$A - B$	< 0	≥ 0	≥ 0

4. Define Arithmetic Logic Unit (ALU).

    Hardware that performs addition, subtraction, and usually logical operations such as

    AND and OR.

5. Define Exception.

    Exception Also called interrupt on many computers. An unscheduled event that disrupts program execution; used to detect overflow.

6. Define interrupt.

    An exception that comes from outside of the processor. (Some architectures use the term *interrupt* for all exceptions.)

7. Multiply 1000ten by 1001ten

$$
\begin{array}{lr}
\text{Multiplicand} & 1000_{ten} \\
\text{Multiplier} \quad \times & 1001_{ten} \\
\hline
 & 1000 \\
 & 0000 \\
 & 0000 \\
 & 1000 \\
\hline
\text{Product} & 1001000_{ten}
\end{array}
$$

8. Divide $1{,}001{,}010_{ten}$ by 1000_{ten}

$$
\begin{array}{r}
1001_{ten} \quad \text{Quotient} \\
\text{Divisor } 1000_{ten}\,\overline{)\,1001010_{ten}} \quad \text{Dividend} \\
-1000 \\ \hline
10 \\
101 \\
1010 \\
-1000 \\ \hline
10_{ten} \quad \text{Remainder}
\end{array}
$$

9. Define dividend and divisor.

A number being divided. Divisor A number that the dividend is divided by.

10. Define quotient.

The primary result of a division; a number that when multiplied by the divisor and added to the remainder produces the dividend.

11. Define remainder.

The secondary result of a division; a number that when added to the product of the quotient and the divisor produces the dividend.

12. Define scientific notation.

A notation that renders numbers with a single digit to the left of the decimal point.

13. Define normalization.

A number in floating-point notation that has no leading 0s.

14. Define floating point.

Computer arithmetic that represents numbers in which the binary point is not fixed.

15. Define Fraction.

The value, generally between 0 and 1, placed in the fraction field. The fraction is also called the *mantissa*.

16. Define exponent.

In the numerical representation system of floating-point arithmetic, the value that is placed in the exponent field.

17. Define overflow (floatingpoint)

A situation in which a positive exponent becomes too large to fit in the exponent field.

18. Define underflow (floatingpoint)

A situation in which a negative exponent becomes too large to f t in the exponent field.

19. Define double precision.

A floating-point value represented in two 32-bit words.

20. Define single precision.

A floating-point value represented in a single 32- bit word.

21. Floating-Point Instructions in MIPS

MIPS supports the IEEE 754 single precision and double precision formats with these instructions:

- Floating-point *addition, single* (add.s) and *addition, double* (add.d)
- Floating-point *subtraction, single* (sub.s) and *subtraction, double* (sub.d)
- Floating-point *multiplication, single* (mul.s) and *multiplication, double* (mul.d)
- Floating-point *division, single* (div.s) and *division, double* (div.d)
- Floating-point *comparison, single* (c.x.s) and *comparison, double* (c.x.d),

  where x may be *equal* (eq), *not equal* (neq), *less than* (lt), *less than or equal* (le), *greater than* (gt), or *greater than or equal* (ge)
- Floating-point *branch, true* (bc1t) and *branch, false* (bc1f)

22. Give MIPS floating point operands.

Name	Example	Comments
32 floating point registers	$f0, $f1, $f31	MIPS floating point registers are used in pairs for double precision numbers.
2^{30} memory words	Memory[0], Memory[4], ... Memory[4294967292]	Accessed only by data transfer instructions. MIPS uses byte addresses, so sequential word addresses differ by 4. Memory holds data structures, such as arrays, and spilled registers, such as those saved on procedure calls.

23. Give MIPS floating point assembly instructions.

Category	Instruction	Example	Meaning	Comments
Arithmetic	FP add single	[illegible]	[illegible]	FP add (single precision)
	FP subtract single	[illegible]	[illegible]	FP sub (single precision)
	FP multiply single	[illegible]	[illegible]	FP multiply (single precision)
	FP divide single	div.s [illegible]	[illegible]	FP divide single precision
	FP add double	[illegible]	[illegible]	FP add (double precision)
	FP subtract double	[illegible]	[illegible]	FP sub (double precision)
	FP multiply double	[illegible]	[illegible]	FP multiply (double precision)
	FP divide double	[illegible]	[illegible]	FP divide (double precision)
Data transfer	load word copr. 1	[illegible]	[illegible] = Memory[...]	32-bit data to FP register
	store word copr. 1	[illegible]	Memory[...] = [illegible]	32-bit data to memory
Cond. branch	branch on FP true	[illegible]	if (cond == 1) go to PC + 4 + 100	PC-relative branch if FP cond
	branch on FP false	[illegible]	if (cond == 0) go to PC + 4 + 100	PC-relative branch if not cond
	FP compare single (eq,ne,lt,le,gt,ge)	[illegible]	if (...) cond = 1; else cond = 0	FP compare less than single precision
	FP compare double (eq,ne,lt,le,gt,ge)	[illegible]	if (...) cond = 1; else cond = 0	FP compare less than double precision

24. Define subword parallelism.

Given that the parallelism occurs within a wide word, the extensions are classified as *subword parallelism*. It is also classifi ed under the more general name of *data level parallelism*. Th ey have been also called vector or SIMD, for single instruction, multiple data.

25. Give the summary of basic NEON instructions.

Data transfer	Arithmetic	Logical/Compare
VLDR.F32	VADD.F32, VADD{L,W}{S8,U8,S16,U16,S32,U32}	VAND.64, VAND.128
VSTR.F32	VSUB.F32, VSUB{L,W}{S8,U8,S16,U16,S32,U32}	VORR.64, VORR.128
VLD{1,2,3,4}.{I8,I16,I32}	VMUL.F32, VMULL{S8,U8,S16,U16,S32,U32}	VEOR.64, VEOR.128
VST{1,2,3,4}.{I8,I16,I32}	VMLA.F32, VMLAL{S8,U8,S16,U16,S32,U32}	VBIC.64, VBIC.128
VMOV.{I8,I16,I32,F32}, #Imm	VMLS.F32, VMLSL{S8,U8,S16,U16,S32,U32}	VORN.64, VORN.128
VMVN.{I8,I16,I32,F32}, #Imm	VMAX.{S8,U8,S16,U16,S32,U32,F32}	VCEQ.{I8,I16,I32,F32}
VMOV.{I64,I128}	VMIN.{S8,U8,S16,U16,S32,U32,F32}	VCGE.{S8,U8,S16,U16,S32,U32,F32}
VMVN.{I64,I128}	VABS.{S8,S16,S32,F32}	VCGT.{S8,U8,S16,U16,S32,U32,F32}
	VNEG.{S8,S16,S32,F32}	VCLE.{S8,U8,S16,U16,S32,U32,F32}
	VSHL.{S8,U8,S16,U16,S32,S64,U64}	VCLT.{S8,U8,S16,U16,S32,U32,F32}
	VSHR.{S8,U8,S16,U16,S32,S64,U64}	VTST.{I8,I16,I32}

Part B

1. Explain in detail about 1 bit ALU logical design.

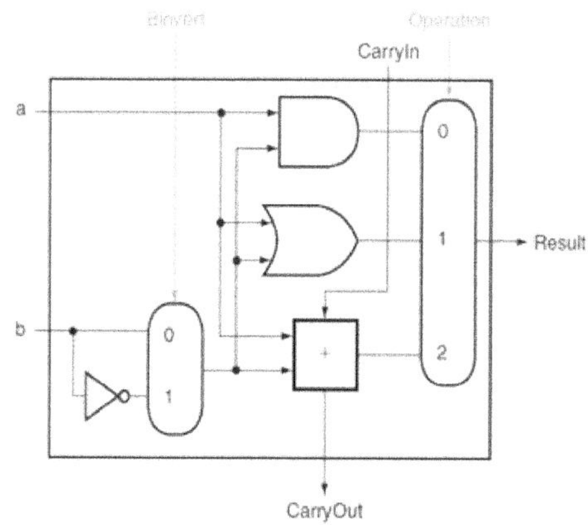

A 1-bit ALU that performs AND, OR, and addition on a and b or a and b̄. By selecting b̄ (Binvert = 1) and setting CarryIn to 1 in the least significant bit of the ALU, we get two's complement subtraction of b from a instead of addition of b to a.

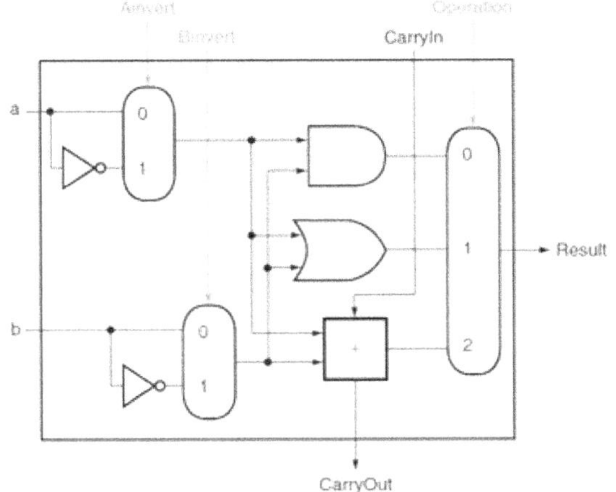

A 1-bit ALU that performs AND, OR, and addition on a and b or ā and b̄. By selecting ā (Ainvert = 1) and b̄ (Binvert = 1), we get a NOR b instead of a AND b.

2. Give the architecture for multiplication hardware.

First version

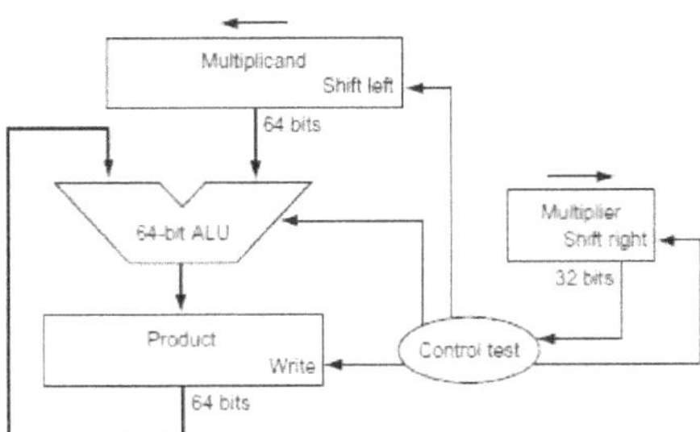

Refined version

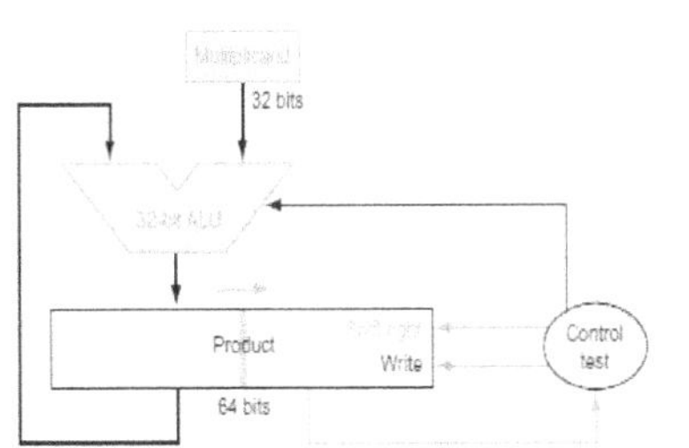

Fast multiplication hardware

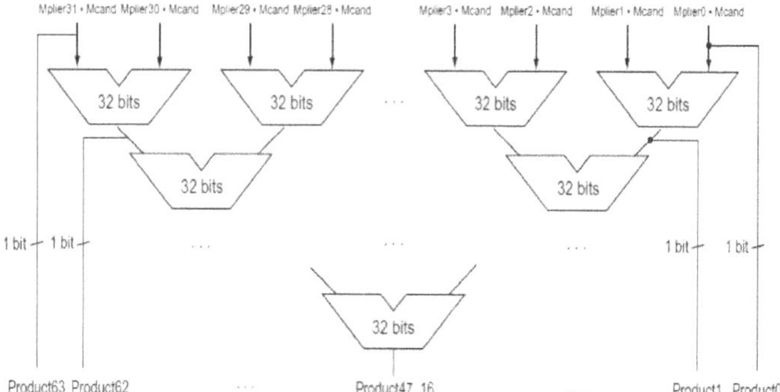

3. Give the architecture for division hardware.

First version

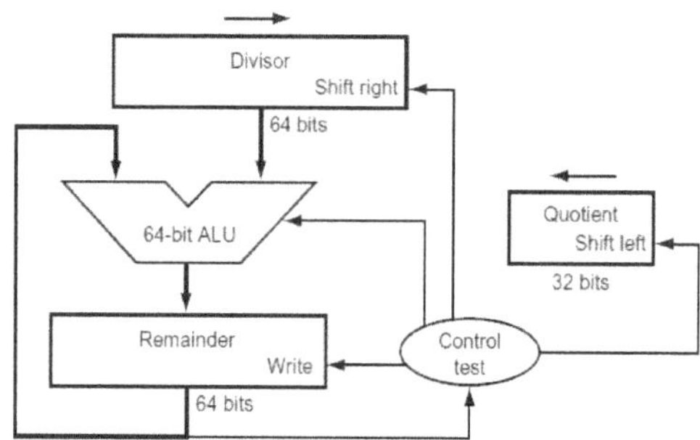

Improved Version

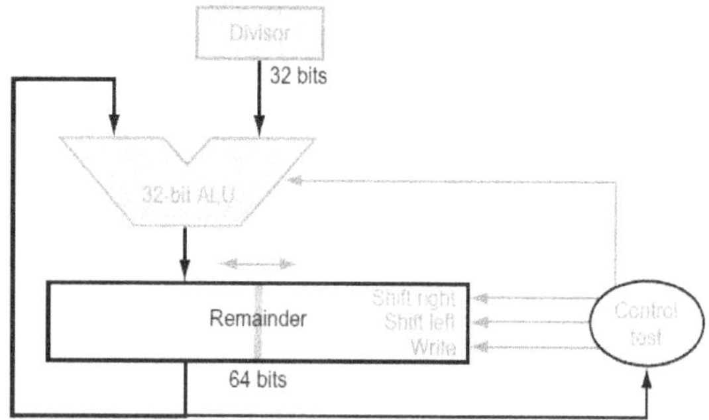

4. Explain in detail about floating point representations.

Floating-Point Representation

Show the IEEE 754 binary representation of the number -0.75_{ten} in single an double precision.

The number -0.75_{ten} is also

$$-3/4_{ten} \text{ or } -3/2^2_{ten}$$

It is also represented by the binary fraction

$$-11_{two}/2^2_{ten} \text{ or } -0.11_{two}$$

In scientific notation, the value is

$$-0.11_{two} \times 2^0$$

and in normalized scientific notation, it is

$$-1.1_{two} \times 2^{-1}$$

The general representation for a single precision number is

$$(-1)^S \times (1 + \text{Fraction}) \times 2^{(\text{Exponent} - 127)}$$

Subtracting the bias 127 from the exponent of $-1.1_{two} \times 2^{-1}$ yields

$$(-1)^1 \times (1 + .1000\ 0000\ 0000\ 0000\ 0000\ 000_{two}) \times 2^{(126 - 127)}$$

The single precision binary representation of -0.75_{ten} is then

31	30	29	28	27	26	25	24	23	22	21	20	19	18	17	16	15	14	13	12	11	10	9	8	7	6	5	4	3	2	1	0
1	0	1	1	1	1	1	1	0	1	0	0	0	0	0	0	0	0	0	0	0	0	0	0	0	0	0	0	0	0	0	0

1 bit	8 bits	23 bits

The double precision representation is

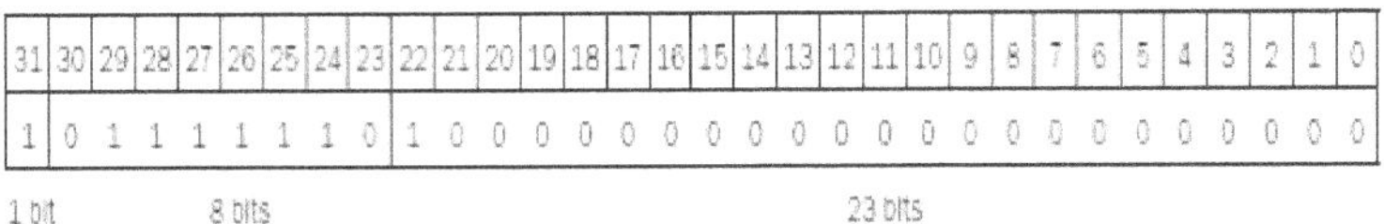

$$(-1)^1 \times (1 + .1000\ 0000\ 0000\ 0000\ 0000\ 0000\ 0000\ 0000\ 0000\ 0000\ 0000\ 0000\ 0000_{two}) \times 2^{(1022 - 1023)}$$

31	30	29	28	27	26	25	24	23	22	21	20	19	18	17	16	15	14	13	12	11	10	9	8	7	6	5	4	3	2	1	0
1	0	1	1	1	1	1	1	1	1	1	0	1	0	0	0	0	0	0	0	0	0	0	0	0	0	0	0	0	0	0	0

1 bit	11 bits	20 bits

0	0	0	0	0	0	0	0	0	0	0	0	0	0	0	0	0	0	0	0	0	0	0	0	0	0	0	0	0	0	0	0

32 bits

5. Explain the steps for floating point addition.

Step 1. To be able to add these numbers properly, we must align the decimal point of the number that has the smaller exponent. Hence, we need a form of the smaller number, $1.610_{ten} \times 10^{-1}$, that matches the larger exponent. We obtain this by observing that there are multiple representations of an unnormalized floating-point number in scientific notation:

$$1.610_{ten} \times 10^{-1} = 0.1610_{ten} \times 10^{0} = 0.01610_{ten} \times 10^{1}$$

The number on the right is the version we desire, since its exponent matches the exponent of the larger number, $9.999_{ten} \times 10^{1}$. Thus, the first step shifts the significand of the smaller number to the right until its corrected exponent matches that of the larger number. But we can represent only four decimal digits so, after shifting, the number is really

$$0.016 \times 10^{1}$$

Step 2. Next comes the addition of the significands:

$$
\begin{array}{r}
9.999_{ten} \\
+ \quad 0.016_{ten} \\
\hline
10.015_{ten}
\end{array}
$$

The sum is $10.015_{ten} \times 10^{1}$.

Step 3. This sum is not in normalized scientific notation, so we need to adjust it:

$$10.015_{ten} \times 10^{1} = 1.0015_{ten} \times 10^{2}$$

Thus, after the addition we may have to shift the sum to put it into normalized form, adjusting the exponent appropriately. This example shows shifting to the right, but if one number were positive and the other were negative, it would be possible for the sum to have many leading 0s, requiring left shifts. Whenever the exponent is increased or decreased, we must check for overflow or underflow—that is, we must make sure that the exponent still fits in its field.

Step 4. Since we assumed that the significand can be only four digits long (excluding the sign), we must round the number. In our grammar school algorithm, the rules truncate the number if the digit to the right of the desired point is between 0 and 4 and add 1 to the digit if the number to the right is between 5 and 9. The number

$$1.0015_{ten} \times 10^{2}$$

is rounded to four digits in the significand to

$$1.002_{ten} \times 10^{2}$$

since the fourth digit to the right of the decimal point was between 5 and 9. Notice that if we have bad luck on rounding, such as adding 1 to a string of 9s, the sum may no longer be normalized and we would need to perform step 3 again.

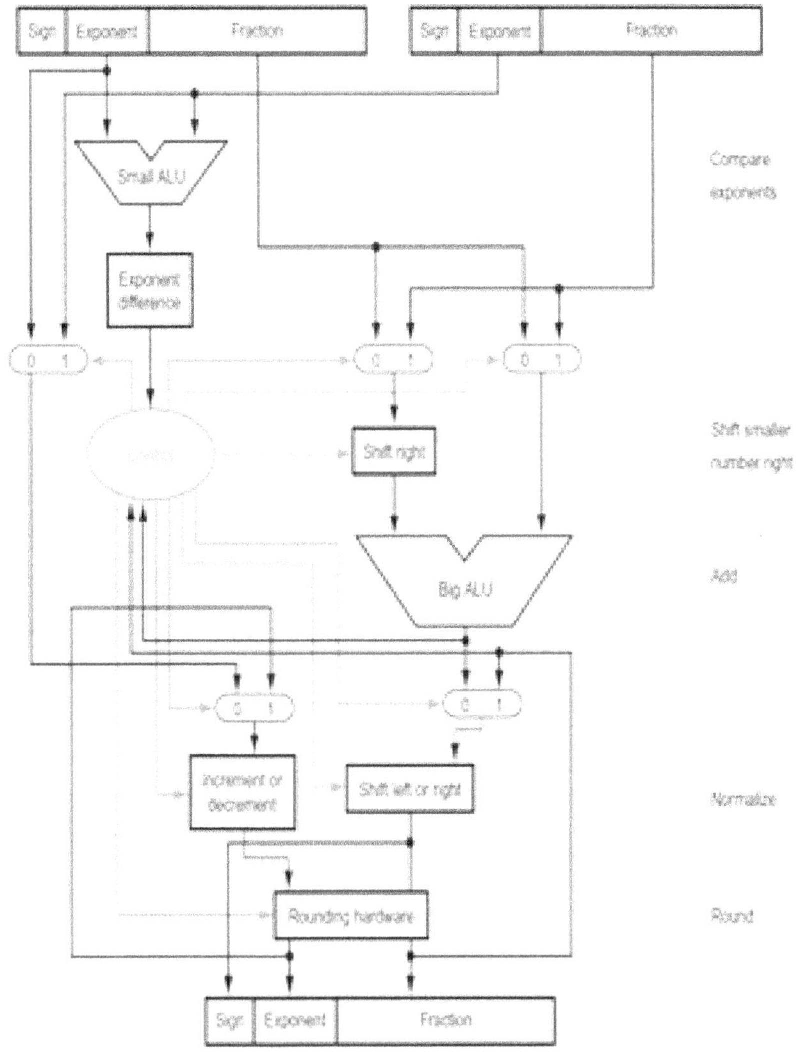

Block diagram of an arithmetic unit dedicated to floating-point addition. The steps of Figure 3.14 correspond to each block, from top to bottom. First, the exponent of one operand is subtracted from the other using the small ALU to determine which is larger and by how much. This difference controls the three multiplexors; from left to right, they select the larger exponent, the significand of the smaller number, and the significand of the larger number. The smaller significand is shifted right, and then the significands are added together using the big ALU. The normalization step then shifts the sum left or right and increments or decrements the exponent. Rounding then creates the final result, which may require normalizing again to produce the actual final result.

6. Explain about floating point operand and instructions

MIPS floating-point **operands**

Name	Example	Comments
32 floating-point registers	$f0, $f1, $f2, ... $f31	MIPS floating-point registers are used in pairs for double precision numbers.
2^{30} memory words	Memory[0], Memory[4], ... , Memory[4294967292]	Accessed only by data transfer instructions. MIPS uses byte addresses, so sequential word addresses differ by 4. Memory holds data structures, such as arrays, and spilled registers, such as those saved on procedure calls.

MIPS floating-point **assembly language**

Category	Instruction	Example	Meaning	Comments
Arithmetic	FP add single	add.s $f2,$f4,$f6	$f2 = $f4 + $f6	FP add (single precision)
	FP subtract single	sub.s $f2,$f4,$f6	$f2 = $f4 - $f6	FP sub (single precision)
	FP multiply single	mul.s $f2,$f4,$f6	$f2 = $f4 × $f6	FP multiply (single precision)
	FP divide single	div.s $f2,$f4,$f6	$f2 = $f4 / $f6	FP divide (single precision)
	FP add double	add.d $f2,$f4,$f6	$f2 = $f4 + $f6	FP add (double precision)
	FP subtract double	sub.d $f2,$f4,$f6	$f2 = $f4 - $f6	FP sub (double precision)
	FP multiply double	mul.d $f2,$f4,$f6	$f2 = $f4 × $f6	FP multiply (double precision)
	FP divide double	div.d $f2,$f4,$f6	$f2 = $f4 / $f6	FP divide (double precision)
Data transfer	load word copr. 1	lwc1 $f1,100($s2)	$f1 = Memory[$s2 + 100]	32-bit data to FP register
	store word copr. 1	swc1 $f1,100($s2)	Memory[$s2 + 100] = $f1	32-bit data to memory
Conditional branch	branch on FP true	bc1t 25	if (cond == 1) go to PC + 4 + 100	PC-relative branch if FP cond
	branch on FP false	bc1f 25	if (cond == 0) go to PC + 4 + 100	PC-relative branch if not cond
	FP compare single (eq,ne,lt,le,gt,ge)	c.lt.s $f2,$f4	if ($f2 < $f4) cond = 1; else cond = 0	FP compare less than single precision
	FP compare double (eq,ne,lt,le,gt,ge)	c.lt.d $f2,$f4	if ($f2 < $f4) cond = 1; else cond = 0	FP compare less than double precision

MIPS floating-point **machine language**

Name	Format	Example						Comments
add.s	R	17	16	6	4	2	0	add.s $f2,$f4,$f6
sub.s	R	17	16	6	4	2	1	sub.s $f2,$f4,$f6
mul.s	R	17	16	6	4	2	2	mul.s $f2,$f4,$f6
div.s	R	17	16	6	4	2	3	div.s $f2,$f4,$f6
add.d	R	17	17	6	4	2	0	add.d $f2,$f4,$f6
sub.d	R	17	17	6	4	2	1	sub.d $f2,$f4,$f6
mul.d	R	17	17	6	4	2	2	mul.d $f2,$f4,$f6
div.d	R	17	17	6	4	2	3	div.d $f2,$f4,$f6
lwc1	I	49	20	2	100			lwc1 $f2,100($s4)
swc1	I	57	20	2	100			swc1 $f2,100($s4)
bc1t	I	17	8	1	25			bc1t 25
bc1f	I	17	8	0	25			bc1f 25
c.lt.s	R	17	16	4	2	0	60	c.lt.s $f2,$f4
c.lt.d	R	17	17	4	2	0	60	c.lt.d $f2,$f4
Field size		6 bits	5 bits	5 bits	5 bits	5 bits	6 bits	All MIPS instructions 32 bits

7. Explain about subword parallelism.

Many graphics systems originally used 8 bits to represent each of the three primary colors plus 8 bits for a location of a pixel. The addition of speakers and microphones for teleconferencing and video games suggested support of sound as well. Audio samples need more than 8 bits of precision, but 16 bits are sufficient. Every microprocessor has special support so that bytes and halfwords take up less space when stored in memory, but due to the infrequency of arithmetic operations on these data sizes in typical integer programs, there was little support beyond data transfers. Architects recognized that many graphics and audio applications would perform the same operation on vectors of this data.

By partitioning the carry chains within a 128-bit adder, a processor could use parallelism to perform simultaneous operations on short vectors of sixteen 8-bit operands, eight 16-bit operands, four 32-bit *operands*, or two 64-bit operands. The cost of such partitioned adders was small.

8. Give the summary of basic NEON instructions.

Data transfer	Arithmetic	Logical/Compare
VLDR.F32	VADD.F32, VADD{L.W}{S8,U8,S16,U16,S32,U32}	VAND.64, VAND.128
VSTR.F32	VSUB.F32, VSUB{L.W}{S8,U8,S16,U16,S32,U32}	VORR.64, VORR.128
VLD{1,2,3,4}.{I8,I16,I32}	VMUL.F32, VMULL{S8,U8,S16,U16,S32,U32}	VEOR.64, VEOR.128
VST{1,2,3,4}.{I8,I16,I32}	VMLA.F32, VMLAL{S8,U8,S16,U16,S32,U32}	VBIC.64, VBIC.128
VMOV.{I8,I16,I32,F32}, #Imm	VMLS.F32, VMLSL{S8,U8,S16,U16,S32,U32}	VORN.64, VORN.128
VMVN.{I8,I16,I32,F32}, #Imm	VMAX.{S8,U8,S16,U16,S32,U32,F32}	VCEQ.{I8,I16,I32,F32}
VMOV.{I64,I128}	VMIN.{S8,U8,S16,U16,S32,U32,F32}	VCGE.{S8,U8,S16,U16,S32,U32,F32}
VMVN.{I64,I128}	VABS.{S8,S16,S32,F32}	VCGT.{S8,U8,S16,U16,S32,U32,F32}
	VNEG.{S8,S16,S32,F32}	VCLE.{S8,U8,S16,U16,S32,U32,F32}
	VSHL.{S8,U8,S16,U16,S32,S64,U64}	VCLT.{S8,U8,S16,U16,S32,U32,F32}
	VSHR.{S8,U8,S16,U16,S32,S64,U64}	VTST.{I8,I16,I32}

Unit III

Processor and Control Unit

Part A

1. What are the core MIPS instruction set?
   - The memory-reference instructions *load word* (lw) and *store word* (sw).
   - The arithmetic-logical instructions add, sub, AND, OR, and slt.
   - The instructions *branch equal* (beq) and *jump* (j), which we add last.

2. Define Control unit.
   - A *control unit*
   - Which has the instruction as an input, is used to determine how to set the control
   - Lines for the functional units and two of the multiplexors.

3. Define Combination element.

   Combinational *element* An operational element, such as an AND gate or an ALU.

4. Define state element.

   State *element* A memory element, such as a register or a memory.

5. Define clocking methodology.

   The *approach* used to determine when data is valid and stable relative to the clock.

6. Define edge-triggered clocking.

   A clocking *scheme* in which all state changes occur on a clock edge.

7. Define control signal.

   A signal used for multiplexor selection or for directing the operation of a functional unit; contrasts with a *data signal*, which contains information that is operated on by a functional unit.

8. Define asserted signal and deasserted signal.

   The signal is *logically* high or true. deasserted signal is logically low or false.

9. Define datapath element.

   A unit used to operate on or hold data within a processor. In the MIPS implementation, the datapath *elements* include the instruction and data memories, the register file, the ALU, and adders.

10. Define program counter.

(PC) The register containing the address of the instruction in the program being executed.

11. Define register file.

A state element *that* consists of a set of registers that can be read and written by supplying a register number to be accessed.

12. Define sign-extend.

To increase the size of a data item by replicating the high-order sign bit of the original data item in the *highorder* bits of the larger, destination data item.

13. Define branch target address.

The address specified in a branch, which becomes the new program counter (PC) if the branch is taken.

14. Define branch not taken or (untaken branch)

A branch where the branch condition is false and the program counter (PC) becomes the address of the instruction that sequentially follows the branch.

15. Define branch.

A type of branch where the instruction immediately following the branch is always executed, *independent* of whether the branch condition is true or false.

16. Define truth table.

From logic, a representation of a logical operation by listing all the values of the inputs and then in each case showing what the resulting outputs should be.

17. Define don't-care term.

An element of a logical function in which the output does not depend on the values of all the inputs. Don't-*care* terms may be specified in different ways.

18. Define pipelining.

Pipelining An implementation technique in which multiple instructions are overlapped in execution, *much* like an assembly line.

19. Define structural hazard.

When a planned instruction cannot execute in the proper clock cycle because the hardware does not support the combination of instructions that are set to execute.

20. Define data hazard.

Pipeline data hazard, When a planned instruction cannot execute in the proper clock cycle because data that is needed to execute the instruction is not yet available.

21. Define forwarding /bypassing.

A method of resolving a data hazard by retrieving the missing data element from internal buffers rather than waiting for it to arrive from programmer visible registers or memory.

22. Define load-use data hazard.

A specific form of data hazard in which the data being loaded by a load instruction has not yet become available when it is needed by another instruction.

23. Define pipeline stall /bubble.

A stall initiated in *order* to resolve a hazard.

24. Define control hazard /branch hazard.

25. When the proper instruction cannot execute in the proper pipeline clock cycle because the instruction that was fetched is not the one that is needed; that is, the flow of instruction addresses is not what the pipeline expected.

26. Define branch prediction.

A method of resolving a branch hazard that assumes a given outcome for the branch and proceeds from *that* assumption rather than waiting to ascertain the actual outcome.

Part B

1. Explain about Basic MIPS implementation.

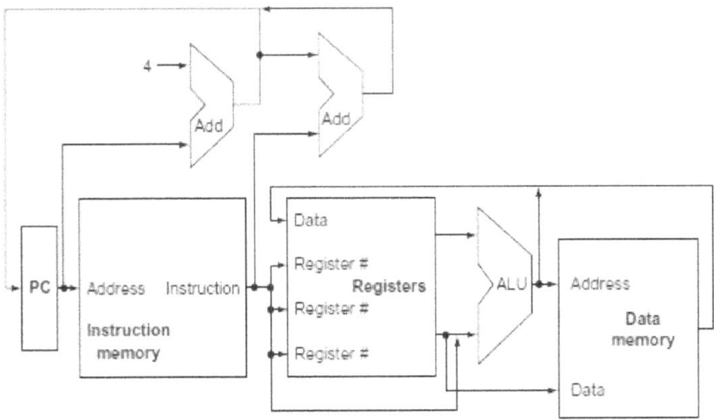

- The memory-reference instructions *load word* (lw) and *store word* (sw).
- The arithmetic-logical instructions add, sub, AND, OR, and slt.
- The instructions *branch equal* (beq) and *jump* (j), which we add last.

2. Components of building datapath.

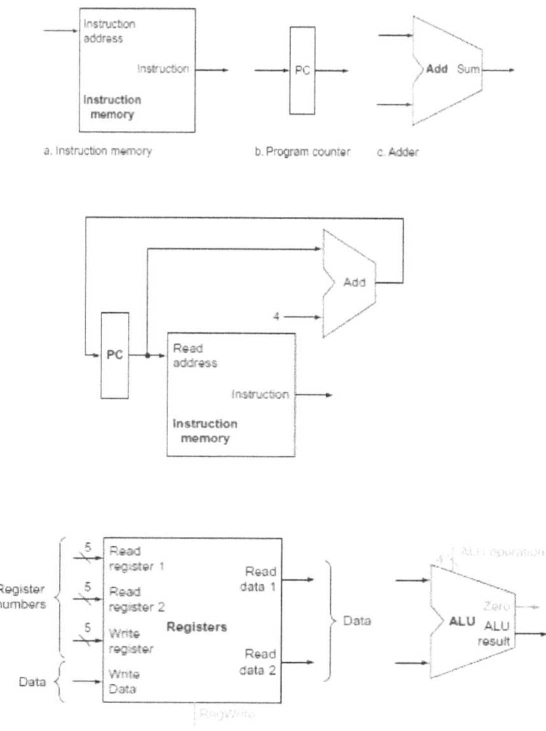

3. Give the datapath architecture for memory instructions and R type instructions.

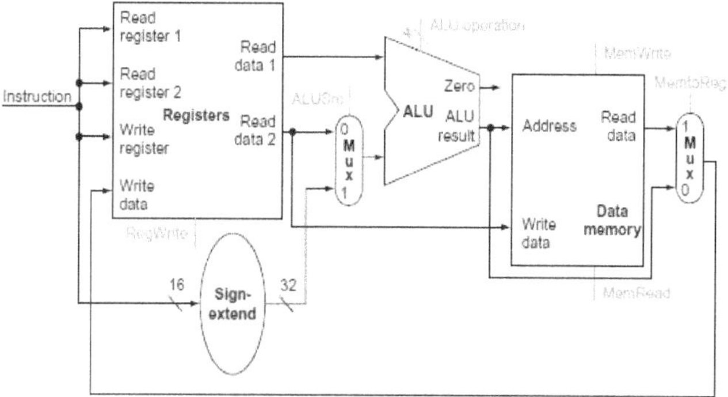

4. Give the datapath architecture with all necessary multiplexers.

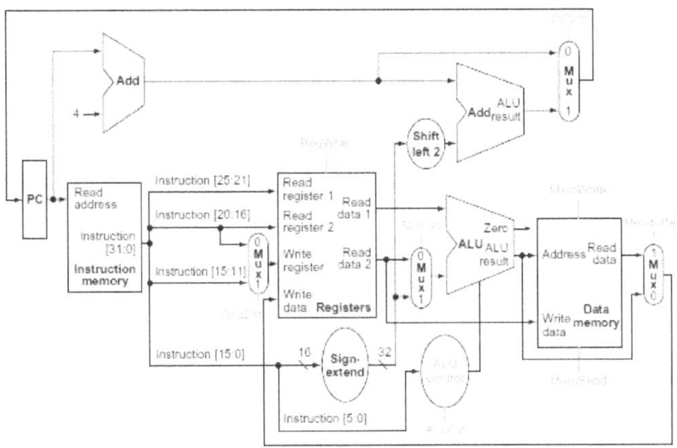

5. Explain the effect of seven control signals.

Signal name	Effect when deasserted	Effect when asserted
RegDst	The register destination number for the Write register comes from the rt field (bits 20:16).	The register destination number for the Write register comes from the rd field (bits 15:11).
RegWrite	None.	The register on the Write register input is written with the value on the Write data input.
ALUSrc	The second ALU operand comes from the second register file output (Read data 2).	The second ALU operand is the sign-extended, lower 16 bits of the instruction.
PCSrc	The PC is replaced by the output of the adder that computes the value of PC + 4.	The PC is replaced by the output of the adder that computes the branch target.
MemRead	None.	Data memory contents designated by the address input are put on the Read data output.
MemWrite	None.	Data memory contents designated by the address input are replaced by the value on the Write data input.
MemtoReg	The value fed to the register Write data input comes from the ALU.	The value fed to the register Write data input comes from the data memory.

6. Explain the pipelining basic concepts.

Pipelining is an implementation technique in which multiple instructions are overlapped in execution. Today, pipelining is nearly universal. MIPS instructions classically take five steps:

1. Fetch instruction from memory.
2. Read registers while decoding the instruction. The regular format of MIPS instructions allows reading and decoding to occur simultaneously.
3. Execute the operation or calculate an address.
4. Access an operand in data memory.
5. Write the result into a register.

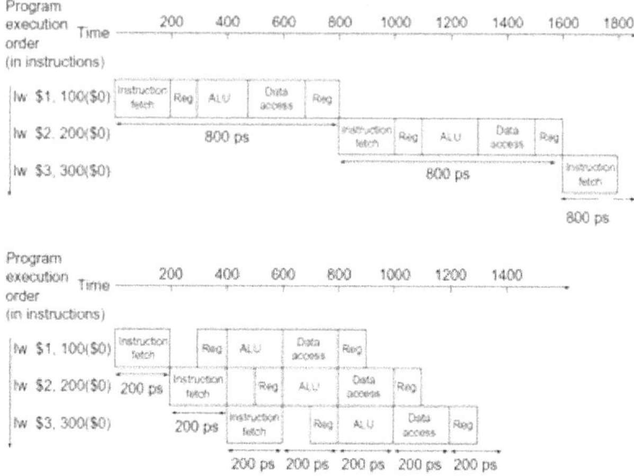

Single-cycle, nonpipelined execution in top versus pipelined execution in bottom. Both use the same hardware components, whose time is listed in Figure 4.26. In this case, we see a fourfold speed-up on average time between instructions, from 800 ps down to 200 ps. Compare this figure to Figure 4.25. For the laundry, we assumed all stages were equal. If the dryer were slowest, then the dryer stage would set the stage time. The pipeline stage times of a computer are also limited by the slowest resource, either the ALU operation or the memory access. We assume the write to the register file occurs in the first half of the clock cycle and the read from the register file occurs in the second half. We use this assumption throughout this chapter.

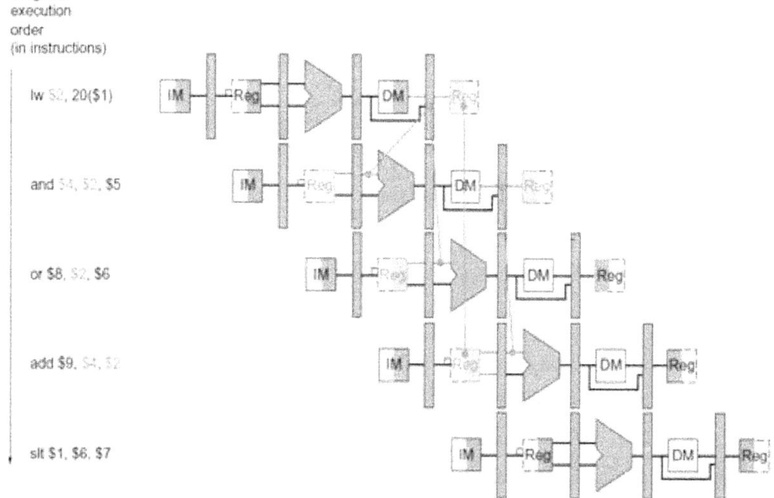

A pipelined sequence of instructions. Since the dependence between the load and the following instruction (and) goes backward in time, this hazard cannot be solved by forwarding. Hence, this combination must result in a stall by the hazard detection unit.

7. Explain in detail about pipelining hazards.

The types of hazards that can occur in the pipelining were,

1. Data hazards.

A data hazard is any condition in which either the source or the destination operands of an instruction are not available at the time expected in pipeline. As a result some operation has to be delayed, and the pipeline stalls.

2. Instruction hazards.

The pipeline may be stalled because of a delay in the availability of an instruction. For example, this may be a result of miss in cache, requiring the instruction to be fetched from the main memory. Such hazards are called as Instruction hazards or Control hazards.

3. Structural hazards.

The structural hazards is the situation when two instructions require the use of a given hardware resource at the same time. The most common case in which this hazard may arise is access to memory.

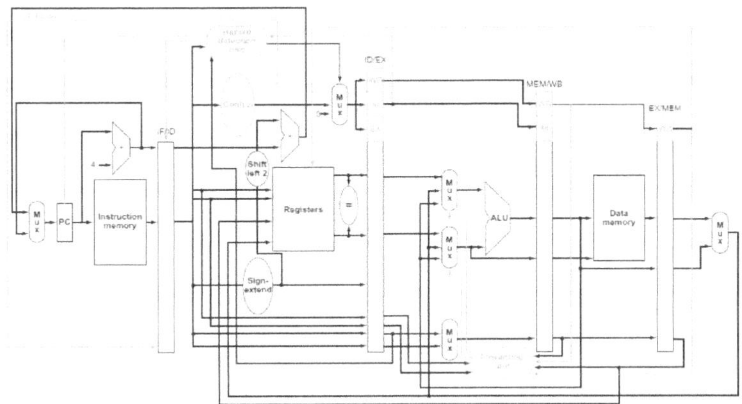

8. Explain in detail about Exceptions.

Type of Event	From where?	MIPS terminology
I/O device request	External	Interrupt
Invoke the operating system from user program	Internal	Exception
Arithmetic overflow	Internal	Exception
Using an undefined instruction	Internal	Exception
Hardware malfunctions	Either	Exception or Interrupt

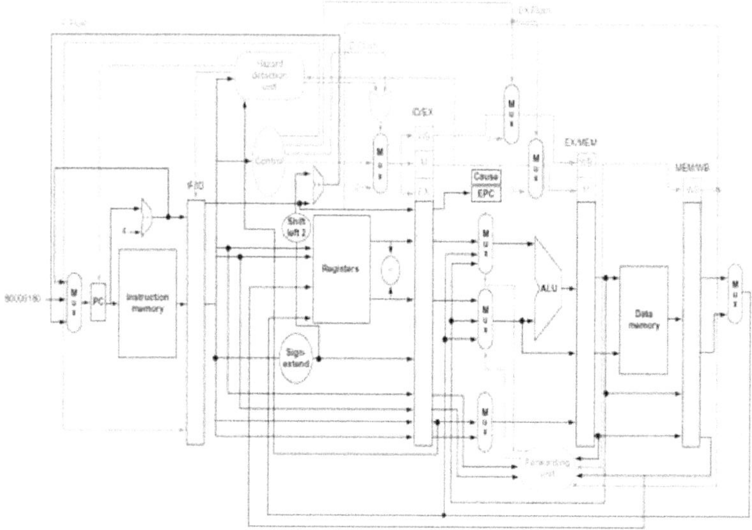

The datapath with controls to handle exceptions. The key additions include a new input with the value $8000\ 0180_{hex}$ in the multiplexor that supplies the new PC value; a Cause register to record the cause of the exception; and an Exception PC register to save the address of the instruction that caused the exception. The $8000\ 0180_{hex}$ input to the multiplexor is the initial address to begin fetching instructions in the event of an exception. Although not shown, the ALU overflow signal is an input to the control unit.

Unit IV

Parallelism

Part A

1. Define task-level parallelism or process-level parallelism.

   Utilizing multiple processors by running independent programs simultaneously.

2. Define parallel processing program.

   A single program that runs on multiple processors simultaneously.

3. Define cluster.

   A set of computers connected over a local area network that function as a single large multiprocessor.

4. Define multicore microprocessor.

   A microprocessor containing multiple processors ("cores") in a single integrated circuit. Virtually all microprocessors today in desktops and servers are multicore.

5. Define shared memory multiprocessor.

   (SMP) A parallel processor with a single physical address space.

6. Define strong scaling.

   Speedup achieved on a multiprocessor without increasing the size of the problem.

7. Define weak scaling.

   Speedup achieved on a multiprocessor while increasing the size of the problem proportionally to the increase in the number of processors.

8. Define SISD.

   Single Instruction stream, Single Data stream. A uniprocessor.

9. Define MIMD.

   Multiple Instruction streams, Multiple Data streams. A multiprocessor.

10. Define SPMD.

    Single Program, Multiple Data streams. The conventional MIMD programming model, where a single program runs across all processors.

11. Define SIMD.

    Single Instruction stream, Multiple Data streams. The same instruction is applied to many data streams, as in a vector processor.

12. Define data-level parallelism.

Parallelism achieved by performing the same operation on independent data.

13. Define vector lane.

One or more vector functional units and a portion of the vector register file. Inspired by lanes on highways that increase traffic speed, multiple lanes execute vector operations simultaneously.

14. Define hardware multithreading.

Increasing utilization of a processor by switching to another thread when one thread is stalled.

15. Define thread.

A thread includes the program counter, the register state, and the stack. It is a lightweight process; whereas threads commonly share a single address space, processes don't.

16. Define process.

A process includes one or more threads, the address space, and the operating system state. Hence, a process switch usually invokes the operating system, but not a thread switch.

17. Define fine-grained multithreading.

A version of hardware multithreading that implies switching between threads after every instruction.

18. Define coarse-grained multithreading.

A version of hardware multithreading that implies switching between threads only after significant events, such as a last-level cache miss.

19. Define simultaneous multithreading.

(SMT) A version of multithreading that lowers the cost of multithreading by utilizing the resources needed for multiple issue, dynamically scheduled micro architecture.

20. Define uniform memory access.

(UMA) A multiprocessor in which latency to any word in main memory is about the same no matter which processor requests the access.

21. Define non uniform memory access (NUMA).

A type of single address space multiprocessor in which some memory accesses are much faster than others depending on which processor asks for which word.

22. Define synchronization.

The process of coordinating the behavior of two or more processes, which may be running on different processors.

23. Define lock.

A synchronization device that allows access to data to only one processor at a time.

24. Define reduction.

A function that processes a data structure and returns a single value.

25. Define OpenMP.

OpenMP An API for shared memory multiprocessing in C, C++, or Fortran that runs on UNIX and Microsoft platforms. It includes compiler directives, a library, and runtime directives.

Part B

1.   Explain the basic concept of parallelism.

Parallel processing is a term used to denote a large class of techniques that are used to provide simultaneous data-processing tasks for the purpose of increasing the computational speed of a computer system. Instead of processing each instruction sequentially as in a conventional computer, a parallel processing system is able to perform concurrent data processing to achieve faster execution time.

- Task-level parallelism or process-level parallelism.
    - Utilizing multiple processors by running independent programs simultaneously.
- Parallel processing program.
    - A single program that runs on multiple processors simultaneously.
- Cluster.
    - A set of computers connected over a local area network that function as a single large multiprocessor.
- Multicore microprocessor.
    - A microprocessor containing multiple processors ("cores") in a single integrated circuit. Virtually all microprocessors today in desktops and servers are multicore.
- Shared memory multiprocessor.
    - (SMP) A parallel processor with a single physical address space.

2. Explain the difficulty of creating parallel processing programs.

Speed-up Challenge

Suppose you want to achieve a speed-up of 90 times faster with 100 processors. What percentage of the original computation can be sequential?

Amdahl's Law (Chapter 1) says

$$\text{Execution time after improvement} = \frac{\text{Execution time affected by improvement}}{\text{Amount of improvement}} + \text{Execution time unaffected}$$

We can reformulate Amdahl's Law in terms of speed-up versus the original execution time:

$$\text{Speed-up} = \frac{\text{Execution time before}}{(\text{Execution time before} - \text{Execution time affected}) + \dfrac{\text{Execution time affected}}{\text{Amount of improvement}}}$$

This formula is usually rewritten assuming that the execution time before is 1 for some unit of time, and the execution time affected by improvement is considered the fraction of the original execution time:

$$\text{Speed-up} = \frac{1}{(1 - \text{Fraction time affected}) + \dfrac{\text{Fraction time affected}}{\text{Amount of improvement}}}$$

Substituting 90 for speed-up and 100 for amount of improvement into the formula above:

$$90 = \frac{1}{(1 - \text{Fraction time affected}) + \dfrac{\text{Fraction time affected}}{100}}$$

Then simplifying the formula and solving for fraction time affected:

$$90 \times (1 - 0.99 \times \text{Fraction time affected}) = 1$$
$$90 - (90 \times 0.99 \times \text{Fraction time affected}) = 1$$
$$90 - 1 = 90 \times 0.99 \times \text{Fraction time affected}$$
$$\text{Fraction time affected} = 89/89.1 = 0.999$$

Thus, to achieve a speed-up of 90 from 100 processors, the sequential percentage can only be 0.1%.

3. Explain the various classifications of parallel structures.

- SISD (single instruction stream single data stream.
- SIMD(single instruction stream multiple data stream.
- MIMD(multiple instruction stream multiple data stream.
- MISD(multiple instruction stream single data stream.

4. Describe in detail about hardware multithreading.

- Hardware multithreading. Increasing utilization of a processor by switching to another thread when one thread is stalled.
- Thread A thread includes the program counter, the register state, and the stack. It is a lightweight process; whereas threads commonly share a single address space, processes don't.

- Process A process includes one or more threads, the address space, and the operating system state. Hence, a process switch usually invokes the operating system, but not a thread switch.
- Fine-grained multithreading A version of hardware multithreading that implies switching between threads after every instruction.
- Coarse-grained multithreading A version of hardware multithreading that implies switching between threads only after significant events, such as a last-level cache miss.
- (SMT) A version of multithreading that lowers the cost of multithreading by utilizing the resources needed for multiple issue, dynamically scheduled micro architecture.

5. Describe in detail about simultaneous multithreading.

Simultaneous multithreading (SMT) is a variation on hardware multithreading that uses the resources of a multiple-issue, dynamically scheduled pipelined processor to exploit thread-level parallelism at the same time it exploits instruction level parallelism (see Chapter 4). Th e key insight that motivates SMT is that multiple-issue processors oft en have more functional unit parallelism available than most single threads can effectively use. Furthermore, with register renaming and dynamic scheduling (see Chapter 4), multiple instructions from independent threads can be issued without regard to the dependences among them; the resolution of the dependences can be handled by the dynamic scheduling capability. Since SMT relies on the existing dynamic mechanisms, it does not switch resources every cycle. Instead, SMT is *always* executing instructions from multiple threads, leaving it up to the hardware to associate instruction slots and renamed registers with their proper threads.

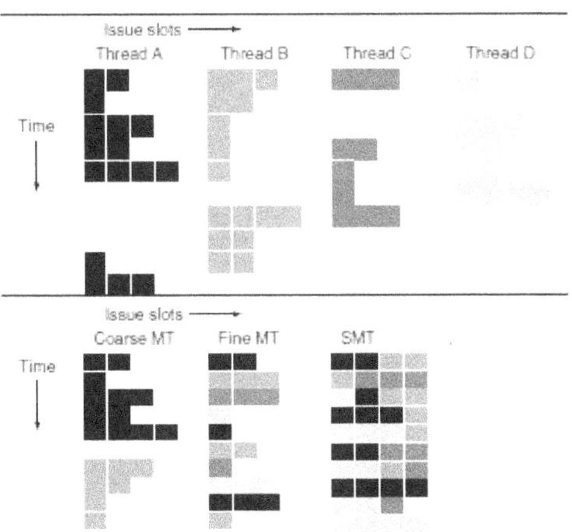

6. Give the organization of shared memory multiprocessor.

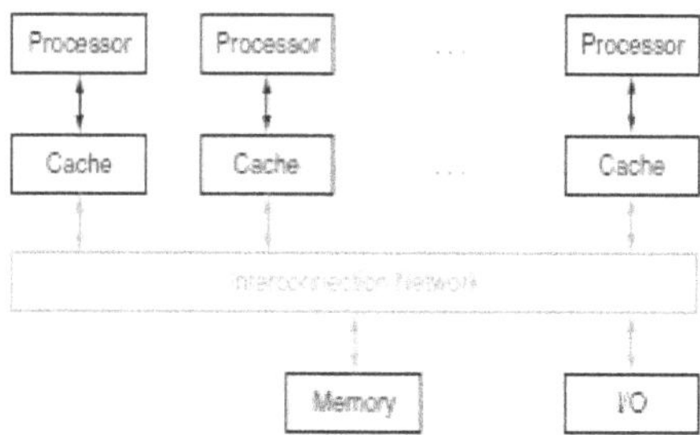

- (UMA) A multiprocessor in which latency to any word in main memory is about the same no matter which processor requests the access.
- Non uniform memory access (NUMA).
    - A type of single address space multiprocessor in which some memory accesses are much faster than others depending on which processor asks for which word.
- Synchronization.
    - The process of coordinating the behavior of two or more processes, which may be running on different processors.
- Lock.
    - A synchronization device that allows access to data to only one processor at a time.

7. Explain about multicore architecture.
- While hardware multithreading improved the efficiency of processors at modest cost, the big challenge of the last decade has been to deliver on the performance potential of Moore's Law by efficiently programming the increasing number of processors per chip.
- Given the difficulty of rewriting old programs to run well on parallel hardware, a natural question is: what can computer designers do to simplify the task? One answer was to provide a single physical address space that all processors can share, so that programs need not concern themselves with where their data is, merely that programs may be executed in parallel. In this approach, all variables of a program can be made available at any time to any processor.

- Single address space multiprocessors come in two styles. In the fi rst style, the latency to a word in memory does not depend on which processor asks for it.

- Such machines are called uniform memory access (UMA) multiprocessors. In the second style, some memory accesses are much faster than others, depending on which processor asks for which word, typically because main memory is divided and attached to different microprocessors or to different memory controllers on the same chip. Such machines are called nonuniform memory access (NUMA) multiprocessors. As you might expect, the programming challenges are harder for a NUMA multiprocessor than for a UMA multiprocessor, but NUMA machines can scale to larger sizes and NUMAs can have lower latency to nearby memory.

8. Explain simple parallel processing program for shared address space.

Suppose we want to sum 64,000 numbers on a shared memory multiprocessor computer with uniform memory access time. Let's assume we have 64 processors.

The first step is to ensure a balanced load per processor, so we split the set of numbers into subsets of the same size. We do not allocate the subsets to a different memory space, since there is a single memory space for this machine; we just give different starting addresses to each processor. Pn is the number that identifies the processor, between 0 and 63. All processors start the program by running a loop that sums their subset of numbers:

```
sum[Pn] = 0;
for (i = 1000*Pn; i < 1000*(Pn+1); i += 1)
    sum[Pn] += A[i]; /*sum the assigned areas*/
```

(Note the C code i += 1 is just a shorter way to say i = i + 1.)

The next step is to add these 64 partial sums. This step is called a reduction, where we divide to conquer. Half of the processors add pairs of partial sums, and then a quarter add pairs of the new partial sums, and so on until we have the single, final sum. Figure 6.8 illustrates the hierarchical nature of this reduction.

In this example, the two processors must synchronize before the "consumer" processor tries to read the result from the memory location written by the "producer" processor; otherwise, the consumer may read the old value of

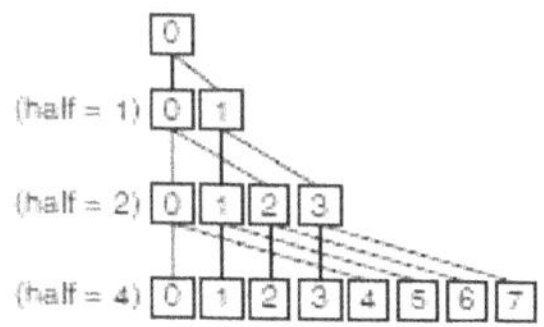

Unit V

Memory and I/O Systems

Part A

1. Define temporal locality.

   The principle stating that if a data location is referenced then it will tend to be referenced again soon.

2. Define spatial locality.

   The locality principle stating that if a data location is referenced, data locations with nearby addresses will tend to be referenced soon.

3. Define memory hierarchy.

   A structure that uses multiple levels of memories; as the distance from the processor increases, the size of the memories and the access time both increase.

4. What is block (or line)?

   The minimum unit of information that can be either present or not present in a cache.

5. Define hit rate.

   The fraction of memory accesses found in a level of the memory hierarchy.

6. Define miss rate.

   The fraction of memory accesses not found in a level of the memory hierarchy.

7. Define hit time.

   The time required to access a level of the memory hierarchy, including the time needed to determine whether the access is a hit or a miss.

8. Define miss penalty.

   The time required to fetch a block into a level of the memory hierarchy from the lower level, including the time to access the block, transmit it from one level to the other, insert it in the level that experienced the miss, and then pass the block to the requestor.

9. What is track?

   One of thousands of concentric circles that makes up the surface of a magnetic disk.

10. What is sector?

    One of the segments that make up a track on a magnetic disk; a sector is the smallest amount of information that is read or written on a disk.

11. What is seek?

The process of positioning a read/write head over the proper track on a disk.

12. Define rotational latency?

Also called rotational delay. The time required for the desired sector of a disk to rotate under the read/write head; usually assumed to be half the rotation time.

13. Define direct-mapped cache.

A cache structure in which each memory location is mapped to exactly one location in the cache.

14. What is tag?

A field in a table used for a memory hierarchy that contains the address information required to identify whether the associated block in the hierarchy corresponds to a requested word.

15. What is valid bit?

A field in the tables of a memory hierarchy that indicates that the associated block in the hierarchy contains valid data.

16. What is cache miss?

A request for data from the cache that cannot be filled because the data is not present in the cache.

17. Define write-through.

A scheme in which writes always update both the cache and the next lower level of the memory hierarchy, ensuring that data is always consistent between the two.

18. Define write buffer.

A queue that holds data while the data is waiting to be written to memory.

19. Define write-back.

A scheme that handles writes by updating values only to the block in the cache, then writing the modified block to the lower level of the hierarchy when the block is replaced.

20. Define split cache.

A scheme in which a level of the memory hierarchy is composed of two independent caches that operate in parallel with each other, with one handling instructions and one handling data.

21. What is fully associative cache and set associative.

A cache structure in which a block can be placed in any location in the cache. Set associative cache A cache that has a fixed number of locations (at least two) where each block can be placed.

22. Define global miss rate and local miss rate.

The fraction of references that miss in all levels of a multilevel cache. local miss rate The fraction of references to one level of a cache that miss; used in multilevel hierarchies.

23. State virtual memory and physical address.

A technique that uses main memory as a "cache" for secondary storage. physical address An address in main memory. Page fault An event that occurs when an accessed page is not present in main memory.

24. Define address translation and segmentation.

Also called address mapping. The process by which a virtual address is mapped to an address used to access memory. Segmentation A variable-size address mapping scheme in which an address consists of two parts: a segment number, which is mapped to a physical address, and a segment off set.

25. Define page table and TLB.

The table containing the virtual to physical address translations in a virtual memory system. The table, which is stored in memory, is typically indexed by the virtual page number; each entry in the table contains the physical page number for that virtual page if the page is currently in memory. translation-look aside buffer (TLB) A cache that keeps track of recently used address mappings to try to avoid an access to the page table.

Part B

1. What do you mean by memory hierarchy ? Briefly discuss.

   - Memory is technically any form of electronic storage. Personal computer system have a hierarchical memory structure consisting of auxiliary memory (disks), main memory (DRAM) and cache memory (SRAM). A design objective of computer system architects is to have the memory hierarchy work as through it were entirely comprised of the fastest memory type in the system. Explain the difficulty of creating parallel processing programs.

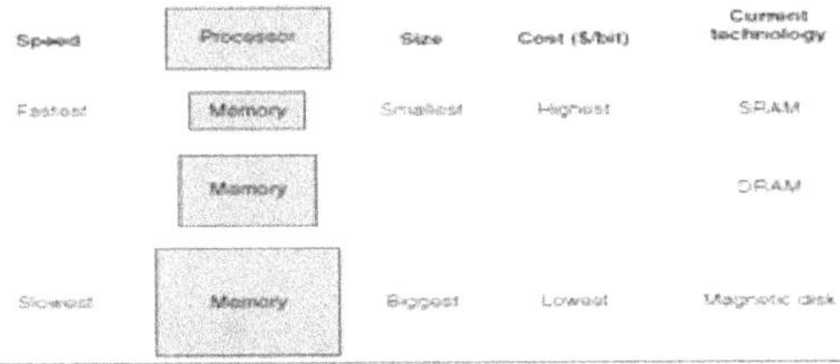

The basic structure of a memory hierarchy.

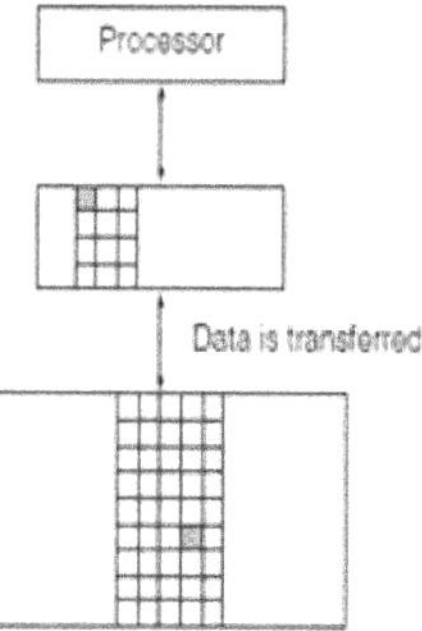

Every pair of levels in the memory hierarchy can be thought of as having an upper and lower level. Within each level, the unit of information that is present or not is called a block or a line. Usually we transfer an entire block when we copy something between levels.

2. Explain the cache memory.

Cache memory: Active portion of program and data are stored in a fast small memory, the average memory access time can be reduced, thus reducing the execution time of the program. Such a fast small memory is referred to as cache memory.

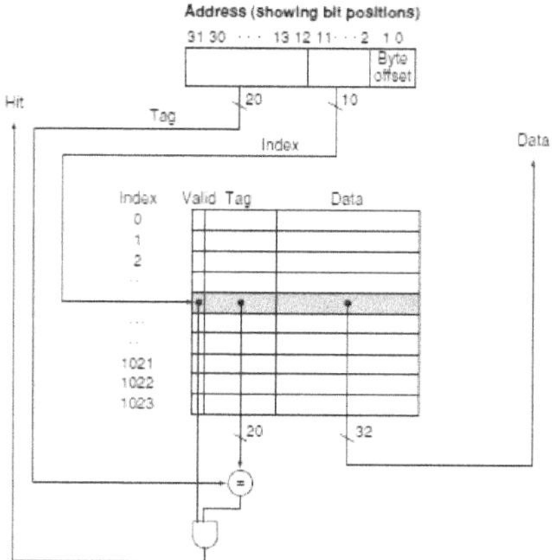

A cache structure in which each memory location is mapped to exactly one location in the cache.

Tag

A field in a table used for a memory hierarchy that contains the address information required to identify whether the associated block in the hierarchy corresponds to a requested word.

Valid Bit

A field in the tables of a memory hierarchy that indicates that the associated block in the hierarchy contains valid data.

Cache Miss

A request for data from the cache that cannot be filled because the data is not present in the cache.

Write-through

A scheme in which writes always update both the cache and the next lower level of the memory hierarchy, ensuring that data is always consistent between the two.

Write buffer

A queue that holds data while the data is waiting to be written to memory.

Write-back

A scheme that handles writes by updating values only to the block in the cache, then writing the modified block to the lower level of the hierarchy when the block is replaced.

Split cache.

A scheme in which a level of the memory hierarchy is composed of two independent caches that operate in parallel with each other, with one handling instructions and one **Handling data.**

Fully associative cache and set associative.

A cache structure in which a block can be placed in any location in the cache. Set associative cache A cache that has a fixed number of locations (at least two) where each block can be placed.

Global miss rate and local miss rate.

The fraction of references that miss in all levels of a multilevel cache. local miss rate The fraction of references to one level of a cache that miss; used in multilevel hierarchies.

3. Describe in detail about DMA.

The transfer of data between a fast storage device such as magnetic disk and memory is limited by speed of CPU. Removing the CPU from the path and letting the peripheral device manager the memory buses directly would improve speed of transfer. This transfer technique is called Direct my Access (DMA) During DMA transfer, the CPU is idle. A DMA controller takes over the buses to manage the transfer between I/O device and memory.

The DMA controller is among the other components in a computer system. The CPU communicates with the DMA through the address and data buses with any interface unit. The DMA has its own address, which activates with Data selection and One the DMA receives the start control command, it can start the transfer between the peripheral device and CPU.

4. Explain the concept of virtual memory.

Permit the user to construct program as though a large memory space were available, equal to totality auxiliary memory. Each address that is referenced by CPU goes through an address mapping from so called virtual address to physical address main memory.

There are following advantages we got with virtual memory:

Virtual memory helps in improving the processor utilization.

Memory allocation is also an important consideration in computer programming due to high cost of main memory.

The function of the memory management unit is therefore to translate virtual address to the physical address.

Virtual memory enables a program to execute on a computer with less main memory when it needs. Virtual memory is generally implemented by demand paging concept In demand paging, pages are only loaded to main memory when they are required. Virtual memory that gives illusion to user that they have main memory equal to capacity of secondary stages media.

The virtual memory is concept of implementation which is transferring the data from secondary stage media to main memory as and when necessary. The data replaced from main memory is written back to secondary storage according to predetermined replacement algorithm. If the data swajd is designated a fixed size. This concept is called paging. If the data is in the main viil1ze subroutines or matrices, it is called segmentation. Some operating systems combine segmentation and paging.

5. What is memory organization ? Explain various memories ?

The memory unit is an essential component in any digital computer since it is needed for storing programs and data A very small computer with a limited application may be able to fulfill its intended task without the need of additional storage capacity, Most general purpose computer is run more efficiently if it is equipped with additional storage beyond the capacity of main memory. There is just not enough in one memory unit to accommodate all the programs used in typical compui Most computei-users accumulate and continue to accumulate large amounts of data processing software.

There, it is more economical to use low cost storage devices to serve as a backup for storing. The information that is not currently used by CPU. The unit that communicates directly with CPU is called the main memory Devices that provide backup memory The most common auxiliary memory device used auxiliary system are magnetic disks and tapes. They are used for storing system programs, large data files, and other backup information. Only proposed data currently needed by the processor reside in main memory All other information is stored in auxiliary memory and transferred to main memory when needed.

There are following types of Memories:

Main memory

RAM (Random - Access Memory)

ROM (Read only Memory)

Auxiliary Memory

Magnetic Disks -

Magnetic tapes etc.

6. Explain about TLB architecture.

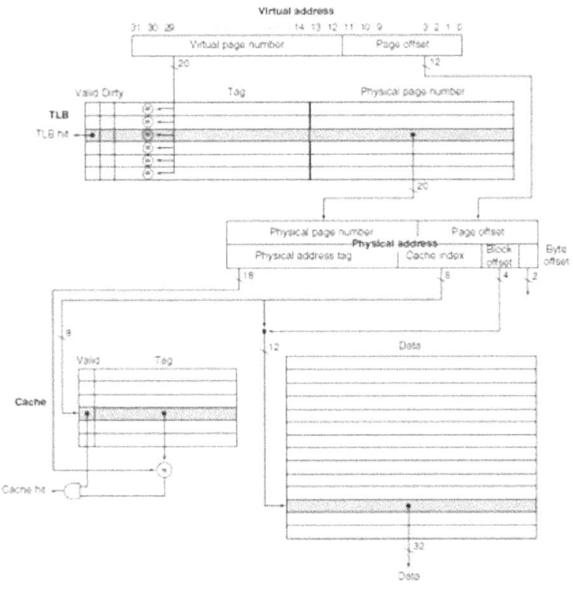

The TLB and cache implement the process of going from a virtual address to a data item in the Intrinsity FastMATH. This figure shows the organization of the TLB and the data cache, assuming a 4 KiB page size. This diagram focuses on a read; Figure describes how to handle writes. Note that unlike Figure, the tag and data RAMs are split. By addressing the long but narrow data RAM with the cache index concatenated with the block offset, we select the desired word in the block without a 16:1 multiplexor. While the cache is direct mapped, the TLB is fully associative. Implementing a fully associative TLB requires that every TLB tag be compared against the virtual page number, since the entry of interest can be anywhere in the TLB. (See content addressable memories in the Elaboration on page 408.) If the valid bit of the matching entry is on, the access is a TLB hit, and bits from the physical page number together with bits from the page offset form the index that is used to access the cache.

7. Explain various mapping methods.

Scheme name	Number of sets	Blocks per set
Direct mapped	Number of blocks in cache	1
Set associative	Number of blocks in the cache / Associativity	Associativity (typically 2–16)
Fully associative	1	Number of blocks in the cache

8. Give architecture for cache controller.

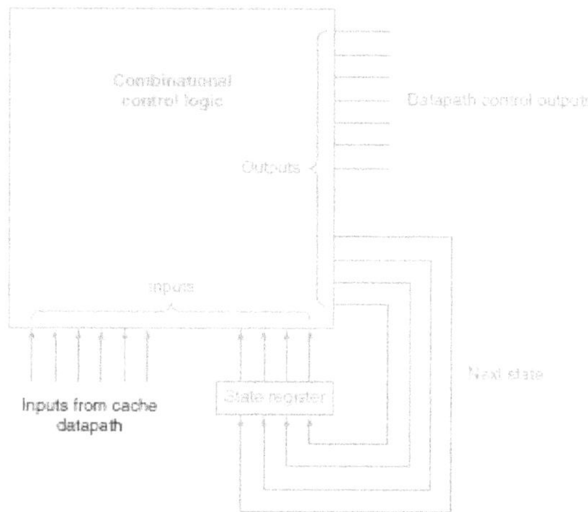